LARRY'S

P.

10 STATES

15 SCHOOLS

24 MOVES

CALIFORNIA

OKLAHOMA

BISHOP

LONE PINE

BAKERS field

RidgeCrest

INYOKERN

OIP '66 !

Sitgreaves '66

PASS!

DAY 4

TUCUMCARI

Amarillo

DAY 2

D.
Sr.

Hwy '66

KINGMAN DAY 5

Gallop

The El Rancho

DAY 3

$50000 !!

CARPENTERIA

NEW MEXICO,

ARIZONA

TEXA

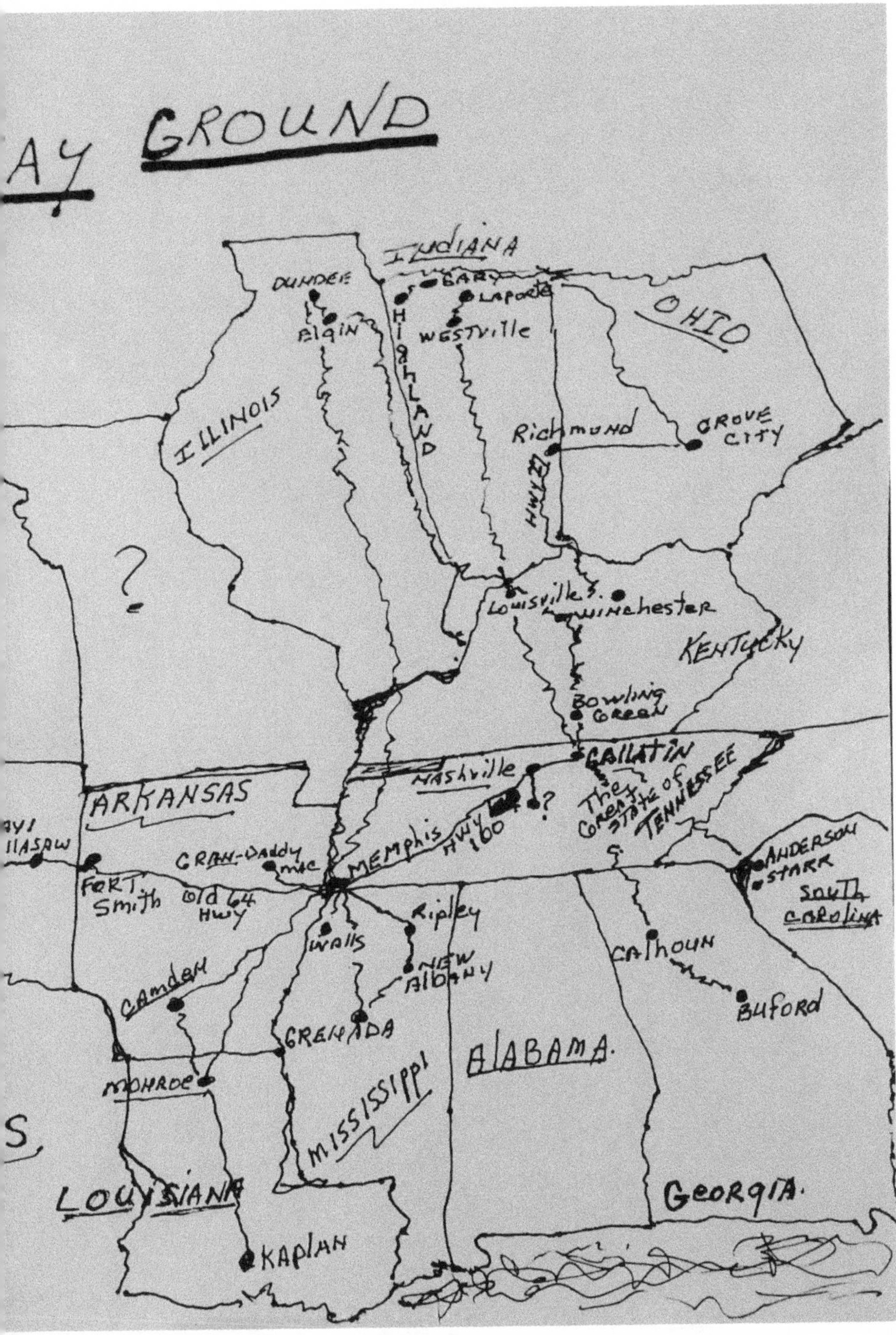

AY GROUND
INDIANA
DUNDEE
GARY
LAPORTE
ELGIN
WESTVILLE
HIGHLAND
OHIO
ILLINOIS
Richmond
GROVE CITY
HWY 27
?
Louisville
Winchester
KENTUCKY
Bowling Green
GALLATIN
Nashville
The Great State of TENNESSEE
ARKANSAS
GRAN-Daddy mac
Memphis
HWY 100
?
FORT Smith
Old 64 HWY
ANDERSON
STARR
SOUTH CAROLINA
Ripley
Walls
NEW Albany
CALHOUN
Buford
CAMDEN
GRENADA
ALABAMA.
MONROE
MISSISSIPPI
S,
LOUISIANA
GEORGIA.
KAPLAN

NO EXCUSES

The True Life Adventures of a
Little Trailer Boy

J. Larry Simpson I

Fulton Books, Inc.
Meadville, PA

Published by Fulton Books 2020

ISBN 978-1-64654-564-3 (paperback)
ISBN 978-1-64654-960-3 (hardcover)
ISBN 978-1-64654-565-0 (digital)

Printed in the United States of America

Dedications

To Sandy my courageous, sacrificial, loving support, without whom this work would have been impossible.

To my Father Walker Eddins Simpson. He taught me how to be a man and go my own way. To my Mother, Janice Victoria McCollum Simpson, who's loving and happy spirit gave me much of my internal and outgoing personality. She never knew a stranger.... and of course, never spoiled me.

To my God, Lord and Redeemer Jesus Christ.

Thanks

To Elizabeth my daughter, who typed the hand-written manuscript, then reviewed it with me and typed it again! There would be no book without her;

To Jeanie my sister, for being my cohort in many adventures;

To Marie (Langford) for rejoining our lives after sixty-one years and finding some irreplaceable photographs we had never seen, some used here;

To Alice, Barbara, Doc, James, Elaine and my wonderful grandparents;

To my old-best buddy Harry Warrens whose story is the largest in the book;

To David my good brother, much like Daddy;

And to all who have been a part of my adventures.

Story 1

Life on the Road

The fire was roaring on this cold November day as we gathered together to enjoy—yeah, even rejoice for our many God-given blessings as family.

Just getting back from taking clothes, canned goods, and such to a wonderful local Christian center, which help those less fortunate, we stoked the fire, added some oak logs, and talked, some softer and others louder.

"Pass it to me, boys," I barked as Caleb spun the old-faded football straight toward me. Snatching it out the cold air with my left hand, pulling it swiftly to my stomach and covering it with my right arm, I took a step or two as if to run.

"Here I come," I said loudly, scratchily crying and "hobbled" a few steps with a reminiscing dash for a touchdown.

"We'll block for you, Granddad!" Walker (named after my daddy) shouted, catching me as I fell to safety into his strong sixteen-year-old arms with Joe Mac standing close by.

As I managed my way back to my warm chair, in this thirty-nine-degree sweet afternoon with the sun beaming, the grandsons traveled, grinning with me.

"Fffuuaah," blew out of my mouth while I plopped down recklessly into my half broken-down faded green-and-yellow summer chair.

Micol Anne was looking way off through her daddy blue eyes all the way back to Mississippi, softly singing with Ricky, her husband, picking his old guitar to Jimmy Reed's "Baby What You Want Me to Do," playing on my well-used jam box.

"Boys, Granddad could do it!" Joe announced as Tony anxiously spoke up, "Dad, we've heard you tell some of your old-time stories. Tell us about traveling with the trailer and Granddaddy's green Ford truck, where you lived, the Mojave desert, the muscadine highway, Harry, Marie, Aunt Jeanie, Hoppy, and all the others."

"Son, son, it was 'Happy!' Sure, sure, tell us the stories."

And all began to gather in a little closer.

"Keep the fire hot, and I'll need some black—I said, black coffee."

"Come on, Granddad," Regan insisted as Tara, my youngest, and her three girls, along with Hannah snuggled in a little closer.

Piersen couldn't be here because he had to work on that heartfelt day, but my Sandy put her warm hand of love on my aging shoulder.

Lizzie, also so sensitive and caring, said, "Dad, it's black, double black and hot as fire, enjoy."

*****

First, Dad bought a big 1950 Buick and a thirty-two-foot trailer. Two adults and four children, ages six to five months, all riding in that car, and the gray house on wheels trailing us relentlessly and weaving just a little.

In the next ten years, we would live in nine states, and I would attend fourteen more schools.

Life on the road brought a world of good people—some hard times and an education all its own.

Trailer people are often considered less than "house" people. Some are. We weren't.

Both Dad and Mother were raised in God-fearing homes. Dad's people were landowners, farmers, the salt of the earth. He was raised by a progressive college-educated mother and a grandfather who read his Greek New Testament every night. Granddaddy Eddins died in 1930. A very stately gentleman taught Dad to be a little man, and Grandmother taught him proper decorum.

My father was a man of his word, a hard worker, and he loved my mother and his children.

Mother was raised by Mississippi farmers, some of whom were sharecroppers. They were fun-lovin' people and strong individualist.

Dad and Mom together were a good team. They taught us to be thankful, show respect, say "Yes, sir" or "No, ma'am," and to pray.

God blessed us with outgoing personalities, strong views of ourselves, honesty, and some athleticism.

We made friends wherever we went.

People seemed to "take to us," and we them.

We learned many things on the road.

The highway was our schoolmaster.

In Monroe, Louisiana, in a new trailer park, I was outside playing in the dirt. My eyes startled, blinked two or three times, and I said to Jeanie softly, "Look."

Jeanie looked. We looked back at each other and whispered, "A bald-headed girl?"

Yes, a bald-headed girl. We became fast friends. Shirley wanted to be accepted as normal. We accepted her. Sixty-six years later, I don't know what caused it, but I knew it wasn't good.

We learned people are different and that we should accept them that way.

Uncounted memories flood my mind.

Now living in Kaplan, Louisiana, in 1952, Dad took me out on the job with him. He was keeping the "Euks," as we called the Euclid earth movers that hauled dirt and kept road graders going.

"Son, do you want to ride?"

I beat him up on that huge earthmover, and away we went. Black diesel smoke rolling, the engine growling, and Walker (Dad) steering it and shifting gears like a race car driver.

I'll never forget it.

On the road meant good times.

Back when there was only two-lane roads and we weren't worried about danger like today, we would stop on the side of the road, set up a folding table, chairs, and eat on the "road." Baloney, lettuce, tomatoes, mayonnaise, and cheddar cheese with sweet tea on ice. We loved each other and the open road.

By 1952–1953, a long, long trailer, "The Liberty" was introduced. It was fifty feet long and eight feet wide. Dad bought one of the very first ones. There were three bedrooms.

Our car could not pull such a vehicle, so we bought a 1953 Ford F-350, and Dad made a dually out of it eventually. That green fifty-three ford Dad kept until 1972. Wonder what stories it has to tell?

Years later, 2007, I drove up in the driveway of my best high school buddy's drive in a 2006 Ford F-350 *dually*!

Harry later said, "Like father like son, now you've got a dually."

Thank you, my good friend!

Being Thankful

Our living had been meager. Six people but two beds, this must have been a little trying to me because I cannot remember how we slept—I guess, I wiped it out of my mind.

What I do know is that when Dad pulled that trailer into a trailer park, we were happy to tears. Three beds now and the envy of everybody.

Being thankful for what seems to be normal is a great life experience and builder. Thankful for a bed for two brothers, two sisters, Mom, and Dad.

Life on the road and its freedoms would now be better. There's no excuse.

> The greatest glory of a freeborn people is to transmit that Freedom to their children.
>
> —William Howard,
> *Regis a Tragedy*, act 4, scene 4

Story 2

The Inyokern Picnic
First Peter 5:5

Pulling out of Bakersfield early that Tuesday morning, we had already told my Uncle Travis and family goodbye. We headed up the Greenhorn Mountains on Highway 178 to what would be our next adventure. The terrain told us we were in rugged country, and the 1953 Ford F-350 pulled hard. Dad was pulling the trailer alone that day as I was sitting in the front seat of the fifty-three Buick Roadmaster with Mom. Jeanie, David, and Susan sat craning their necks in the back seat.

Trixie and Tony, our good dogs, stood on Dad's handmade tool-box just panting with excitement. As hard as the wind blew while driving, I never knew why their jaws didn't flop off onto the high-way or blind another car with the slobber flying fifty miles per hour backward.

After about two and a half or three hours of driving, we stopped and ate lunch. Mom fixed the best sandwiches from a baked ham on the bone with mayonnaise, tomatoes, and lettuce that a growing thirteen-year-old could ever taste. Homemade tea, which is cooked tea, with lots of sugar on ice was just right for the road.

Pulling a trailer was fun and challenging. Dad was a great driver and especially of big equipment being a diesel mechanic and having to drive Euclids, caterpillar, cranes, and the likes.

So we pulled off the side of the road at the top of the mountain and had a picnic.

My brother David would say one sweet day as we traveled, Sandy, myself, David, and his wife, Connie, that he thought that those stops were just a picnic and that's just what life was. David has lived life like a picnic, "Everything was all right."

So once having eaten, we pulled back out onto old, ragged 178.

In a little while, as we descended the eastern slope of that rug-ged mountain, we could start to see the desert, the Mojave Desert, brown, rolling on forever, vast. It stretched out endlessly before us.

Dad got to the stop sign first and pointed five or six times downward, turned left, and there we saw it, Inyokern, down below. Our new town.

Lying at the foot of the mountains with Ridgecrest in the distance, Mother started crying. "Surely, this is not where Walker brought us! Surely, we're not going to live here!" And she cried, almost broken. The sign with an arrow on it had thick black letters.

We four children kept quiet.

She turned left. We followed the fifty-foot-long turquoise-and-white trailer, a half mile behind.

Turning right down toward the little town, we came to a wel-come sign with the population on the bottom, 356 it read. It came to my tricky mind that we would be the largest growth spurt Inyokern would ever have.

"Now the population, Mom, will be 362!" "this will be the largest growth they've ever had"

Mom started laughing.

Now that was Mom, and we knew we were going to have an Inyokern picnic.

Dad had already been to Inyokern and found a trailer park for us to move into. We parked in the first spot directly behind the owners' house and dog lot.

After the weeks trip to California, two weeks in Bakersfield, here, it is August, and we are settling in once again.

Dad was miserable. Jobs were not as plentiful as he had been led to believe. He took a job in a rock quarry as the company mechanic. Crushed rock dust flew everywhere, covering up anything in its path for about two hundred feet, less pay, and Dad's skills were greater than the job.

Dad was miserable, less pay, and not full use of his skills. Disappointment was all over him. Living in the desert, so different from our green tree covered country in Tennessee and almost broke.

Dad was miserable. While passing through New Mexico to California, the state patrol stopped us on the outskirts of Tucumcari on Highway 66. Dad was ticketed for being two feet over the maximum length for trailers.

"That will cost you $500," the arrogant officer said.

The fine was $500! That was a lot of money to a man with four children, a wife, and two dogs. It took about half of what Dad had saved for the long move.

So now, in Inyokern, Dad was trying to recover his losses and almost instantly decided to move back east although he didn't let us in on it.

How could we get back? This rig was too long. Not enough money!

Here's what Dad did. He cut the truck in two! Yes, sir, he cut the truck in two. With torch and determination, he cut out two feet and four inches of the bed, drive shaft, and all other parts in the way, then welded it back together.

By March 1958, he was ready to go back home, anywhere east of the Mississippi! Besides, this was aggravated by the sad death of his father, Granddaddy Simpson.

In the meantime, life was a picnic.

The little Baptist Church—that is its people—was sweet. The smell of the desert, the sea of spring flowers, Betty Jo, an undefeated basketball team. The bully and tacos for the first time just freshly made by a good Mexican family (that's all we knew to call them) from our church, visits by LT and then Travis with their families, got us through.

Yeah, a picnic. Mom made it that way. It came from the McCollum's, "Just enjoy what you're doing every moment."

I learned a lot in Inyokern.

The bully was determined to make me afraid of him, so I told him I was going to the restroom and for him to come in—he didn't show up. From that day on, he changed his ways. It was said that "bully boy" came from poverty, a broken home, and no discipline. He was known for punching holes in the walls in his little home with his angry fists. To this day, I can still see his brown chiseled face, greasy long ducktail hair, and angry look. I know he sits in a prison cell or lies in a lonely grave today, sixty-one years later.

Basketball

It seems to me, as a lifelong experience, that everyone has to locate and define themselves.

Now I can see more clearly who I am, but I was content with myself even in those early days mostly. Sometimes I felt inferior, but that drove me to "be somebody." Dad and Mom taught us that but let us be a kid and ourselves. Somehow, they made us believe that we were just okay like we were, significant, could do anything, and gave us a rope. The rope we were attached to was pretty long, as long as we were respectful and obedient.

This carried over into mine, Jeanie, David, and Susan's lives to make us positive, ambitious, and workers.

God was good to me. He gave me victories in life that made me know I was okay, strong, and could achieve. I was locating and finding myself.

Basketball became a defining moment of personal strength and self-image in Inyokern.

There were only thirteen, or was it sixteen students in the sixth to eighth grades? But the administration wanted us to have a basketball team. There was only six or seven of us on the team, had only a few days to practice before we played our first and only game against Ridgecrest.

Ridgecrest was a big town and a big school compared to Inyokern.

They arrived to play in our little gym.

They beat us—badly.

But the Ridgecrest coach saw potential in me. He approached me, my parents, the school, and the Inyo County School Board about allowing me to play on their team.

The permission was granted, and I became the first student allowed to be in one school yet play ball on another team in Inyo County.

Not having trained skills and no coaching, yet I was blessed with speed, great jumping ability, a will to learn, and absolute determination. I became a starter.

We had a six-foot-four boy, but who do you think jumped center to start the game? A five-foot-nine boy from Inyokern.

Boys from military families filled the roster. Boys with skill, determination, and physically strong.

We went undefeated, winning two tournaments and beating much larger schools from Bakersfield and beyond.

What I look back and see is that I can have no excuses. Blessed in many ways—doors always opened in front of me. I walked through them. I seized them. I worked. I found myself by the grace of God.

Thank you, Lord, Dad, and Mom.

My Job

Work—a job has been part of me from age ten. By age twenty, I had had twenty jobs.

Inyokern gave me a great job.

The man who owned the trailer park must have seen some hope for me, so he offered me a job.

Mr. Carter barked out, "Son, would you like to have a job and make a little money?"

"Yes, sir," I said.

"Okay then, here's what you'll do. Can you drive?"

"Yes, sir, I can."

My new employer stretched his eyes.

Dad had let me drive his truck in 1956 in South Carolina at Granddaddy Simpsons. A four speed, I had ridden with Dad all these miles from move to move, so I picked it right up. Just a few days before Uncle LT had let me drive his '57 Ford Convertible! So I was ready.

My job? Drive from garbage can to garbage can, picking up trash. Milk cartons, wet paper, coffee grounds, green bean cans, and all the things in a garbage can was my objective. I did it—on time. Every piece of trash, even diapers!

Then he added this, "Now, Larry, clean up my backyard and get rid of all the dog do-do."

"What!"

So I did it. Twice weekly, I cleaned up his backyard for all eleven dogs he owned and got rid of it in a hole I had to dig. There must have been one hundred piles of "do-do" every third day.

Today I love the thoughts of that job. Thankful.

No excuses. Just do it.

Moving Away

Dad was headed back to our homeland just about as soon as we arrived in California.

March 1958 arrived, and Dad said, "I pulled up today. Let's pack up. We're going back to Tennessee."

I was stunned and very sad. Moving now at age thirteen was getting harder. A basketball success story, a job, friends, and a girlfriend made it hard to leave.

We told our church family goodbye, our school friends goodbye, and I told my girlfriend of two to three months goodbye. I cried as we passed through Ridgecrest in the dark of the early morning. Heading up Highway 395 with my face wet and against the left rear door window, staring out toward Betty Jo's, I thought, *This is getting harder*. Moving away was getting harder! I began to realize that strong attachments were now harder to let go of, as I grieved for two or three days. I hoped to see Betty Jo again, but we would be two thousand miles apart. Yes, it was getting harder.

But I had to do it. We were rollin'.

No excuses. A new adventure lay ahead.

Inyokern was a picnic.

> Our God is in the heavens, He had done whatsoever He hath pleased.

> —Psalms 115:3

Story 3

The Summer of '56

It was still cool outside as spring was blooming in Gallatin. In March 1956, Dad came home from his diesel mechanic job and said gently, "Vicky, we're moving to Northern Indiana to help build a new highway"—taking a deep calming breath—"close to Lake Michigan."

Mom, just like always, sighed and wiped off a tear because she really didn't want to move from Gallatin but said, "When do I have to be ready?"

She pulled me and my three little family members close to her stomach and hips and just held on. "It'll be all right, and we'll be ready."

Mom could always do it—get over it, and comfort us, even with tears.

Sure enough, we were ready, the dogs loaded, and lunch prepared as the sun still lay behind the black eastern sky. Mom drove the car, a 1954 black-and-white Buick with the other kids with her and Dad and I in the green '53 Ford truck. We pulled the fifty-foot home on wheels out onto North Water and North US Highway 31, we were rolling once again.

The farmland of Indiana, flat as a flitter, was okay with us. We liked the Tennessee hills better, but it was all right.

Forty-eight hours later, having slept at a truck stop in our moving home, we drove into La Porte. There weren't many trailer parks, but Dad found one, paid the first months' rent, and we set up camp!

Being on the west side of town on Highway 2, Jeanie and I entered the same school, a new school, and set about making friends.

The teacher I was assigned to couldn't get my name right—he called me Joe.

"No," I said. "My name is Larry."

But like most adults, he couldn't get it. To him, my first name had to be the name. I put up with it; besides, I knew we wouldn't be there long anyway. Not long after that, he was calling me "Larry Joe."

I had never skated before, but there was a really nice skating rink just a half mile from the trailer park. So being invited to go with some friends, especially one girl, I went, more than once. But somehow, I couldn't get it. Skating was hard for me even though I was a pretty good athlete.

Music playing, boys and girls skating close, boys flying, and girls swirling, I fell!

Ben, a rather "rotund" eighth grader rolled over my right hand. I never skated again. I knew what I liked. I never skated again.

Dad didn't like where we lived. I don't know why. But one of the great things about trailer living is you can move anytime you please. So Dad moved us to Westville, eleven miles away, and there began the saga I'm going to reveal.

*****

Westville

The town was known for its mental hospital. Jokes were always coming from others about any of us who lived there. Some or all of it was well placed.

One of the great things about Westville was that our great friends, the Rice's, moved there also. John and Wilma only had one son whom they named Happy.

"Happy?" I said when we first met in Granada, Mississippi, where Dad and Mr. Rice worked together. Happy and I became close friends.

So when I heard the Rice's were comin', I jumped up and hit the ground runnin'.

We were buddies and could play together for hours.

The summer of '56 started hot, and we had to make some friends. So we built a little "house" out of canvas, paper, lumber, logs, nails, wire, rocks, loose bricks, which we dug up out of the ground and plastic at the bottom of the railroad tracks. The railroad tracks were built upon a fifteen-foot-high bank, so it was exciting to have our "summer home" at the bottom with a few little trees and the train roaring above us flying.

After a few days in that hot June, Happy and I were talking about money. We needed some money. After all, we couldn't buy any airplanes or trains to put together without money!

I loved airplanes. Eventually, I had about fifteen I had put together, and Mom and Dad let me hang them from the ceiling in mine and David's bedroom. What a wonder. I could lay in bed early in the morning and fly anywhere and fight the Germans and Japanese! I always won those air battles. My mind flew in those planes.

So lying in the "railroad shack" one early morning, we talked about how we could make some money.

Mr. Rice recently had taken an old refrigerator down to the salvage yard, where they bought metal stuffs. So he suggested that we gather up any metal we could find, take it to the salvage store, and earn some money.

As divine providence has always been so good to me, we scouted the countryside and discovered that the west side of the land owned by the trailer park had been a railroad equipment storage facility, and guess what? Scattered over a half acre was metal of all kinds—some on top of the ground, and some covered up.

Getting the okay from the owner of the park, Happy and I started to work. Pulling all sorts of metal off the ground and out of the ground, we began our financial future. Rusty metal, a fender or two, metal strips, train car parts, engine parts, metal of all kinds lay like a buried treasure. With some cuts and bruises, we kept going.

From morning to night, we worked. Happy was a redhead and fair-complexioned while I was brown like a Navajo Indian. So the sun burnt him up, and I just got darker.

We were the talk of the trailer park. Ole Mrs. Jones fixed us lemonade. Mr. Jones loaned us a shovel. Mom and Wilma fixed plenty for lunch, and the other kids just made fun of us. But work we did.

By mid-July, we had a pile about six feet tall and thirty feet around.

Daddy said, "Son, it's time to load all this up and take it to the salvage company."

Dad drove his truck over to the "metal for sale" work pile, and we loaded it on the truck—six feet up and the bed filled full.

Arriving at the salvage yard, we were greeted by a very skinny tall man with a beard like Abe Lincoln and a black patch over his right eye. His hands were like saucers and all cracked up.

As Happy and I jumped out of the truck, he said, "Well, men, what have you got for us?"

I said, "You see all this metal? We brought it to you to sell," never being one to mince words.

Ole Abe said with a growly voice, "Where did you get all this?"

So we told him the story while Dad stood back with a grin on his face from ear to ear.

Ole Abe said, "Pull your truck over here by the scales, and we'll weigh it." Having weighted it, he said, "You've got 649 pounds."

Ole Abe was proud of we boys for doing all that work in six weeks as he pounded us on our backs. Dad was proud, still grinning his big smile. Our pay? It was to be .03 per pound!

Happy, speaking up like a man, said, "well, what's it worth?"

Calculating every ounce, ole Abe said, "You've got $19.47 coming to you. Here, I'll count it out."

Count he did, and happy we were. What a pay day for twelve- and fourteen-year-old boys! We split it up, and Happy gave me the extra penny!

Going home, rejoicing all the way, we cleaned up and went downtown one long block and one short one away. First to the Black Hawk Grill for a chocolate milkshake and then across the street to the Variety Store where they had models of all kinds. Happy bought a Cadillac car, but I bought a B-17 Bomber to put together and hang it on the ceiling. It flew in my bedroom for five years until we traded out home on wheels for the new home on Grace Street in '61.

Happy and I learned a lot that summer but especially that smart, hard work pays off.

Soon we would leave Westville and move back to Gallatin, but with the memory of the hot, moneymaking summer of '56 forever on our minds.

How I wish I knew where Happy is so we could talk about it— the summer of '56.

Even trailer boys have no excuses.

*****

The Black Hawk Grill

I wanted information for memories' sake on the hot place for kids in Westville, the Black Hawk Grill.

In March 2018, I called the city building in Westville to see if anyone remembered the old meeting place.

A young lady answered the phone. I told her that I was looking for information on the grill. She didn't seem very interested in helping me.

However, when I told her my story with the Black Hawk and this book, she instantly warmed up.

The nice young lady asked, an older lady in the office if she knew anything or someone to help. The younger ladies knew nothing of the famous spot. The gentle older lady said she knew someone who could help.

"Call Cheryl. She'll remember!"

Wow.

Very excited, I called Cheryl's number, got the answering machine, and told her what my interest was. Before the evening was over, Cheryl sent me an e-mail with a nice and knowledgeable response.

Being very excited, as I was also, she described the Black Hawk as the meeting place almost all the townspeople, but especially the young people.

But to top that, Cheryl said, "I worked in the grill from 1954 and into the summer of '56!"

Amazing! She worked there for two to three months that I went there with Jeanie and Happy weekly. I'm quite sure I knew this lovely lady, saw her, or was waited on by her. Or did I? I can have no doubt, but that in the mystery of the streams of life I surely met Cheryl in the summer of '56, or did I?

Sandy and I drove to Westville in early spring of 2018 to meet with Cheryl. She didn't make the proposed rendezvous, and I couldn't reach her by phone. I can only hope that life is good for a once upon a time Black Hawk Grill girl.

Story 4

The Road Will Push You

Having finished first grade at ole Bethel Grove in Memphis, I really only remember the third grade in Jeffersonville, Indiana.

I surely wasn't a faultless child. Besides, I wasn't going to be ignored. I would get a name for myself. A few of the boys started talking big, so I thought, *Just "spit" on the floor*! Dad and John "spit," so why not me? Besides, "this is a way I can get in with the guys." I was always having to always get in with all these new guys in all these new places.

So with a careful gathering of "spit" in my mouth and rolling it around, I let it fly down with a splatter on the floor. The boys laughed; the stern lady teacher didn't.

"Here she comes," Bobby said.

With fire flashing out of her ears, her teeth gritted, and those big brown eyes "smoking."

"What in the world do you mean—do you have no manners?" And other such questions.

I was caught. I was guilty. I was ashamed.

Of course, I knew better. But to get a place among the "boys," I did it. Mrs. tooth gritter paddled me.

I carried a note home, and as I expected, Mom and Dad would be hurt and upset. They disciplined me with some old-fashioned discipline.

I never did it again.

The road will push you. Oh, I forgot to tell you, Ms. Fire Eyes spanking was just an "ole-time whipping." I got one in almost every school. The difficult matter in going to so many different schools and more than once, two schools in a single grade is the education and learning gaps I have.

Often remarking about that to make fun of myself, someone will say, "That's not true." In 1958, after we left California, we landed in Dundee, Illinois, in March. They were studying Illinois history, and I was lost. They being more advanced in math; I was lost. Besides, their accents were strange. Two months of school were lost, and it was enough to open up some new gaps of loss of schoolin'.

Having gone to two different schools in the third, sixth, eighth, ninth, and tenth grades, I have learning gaps! Some of these moves kept us out of school a few days to a couple of weeks. Education gaps!

How have I made it? I'm not sure, but I've got no excuses.

We were happy moving. The good side of following the highway is the education we got in meeting people, learning how to handle ourselves, seeing America, and love of family. But the road will "push you."

Look, there's no excuses even for a trailer boy.

Story 5

Adventures 1

John Wayne to Kim Darby as Rooster Cogburn in *True Grit,* "Baby sister, I was born game, and I intend to go out that way!"

God put a natural explorer's heart in me. "I was born game!"

The road gave me the occasion constantly to stimulate my adventuresome nature. Traveling gave me a big world to view and enter into. It always stirred my imagination.

To this day, when driving, I have to see what is around the bend or over the hill. Hardly anything excites me more than a long highway stretched out in front of me. Often, I'll say to Sandy, "Look at that long highway laying in front of us."

The highway opens a visionary treat, going out there in my mind, dreaming and seeing things clearer. Being in so many different situations calls for a wandering treat. But you must be willing to fly out there in "your" mind.

The Muscadine Highway

Buford, Georgia, is built on small ridges. Houses up, houses down.

Arriving there on a cool, clear blue spring day in 1953, Dad stopped at a truck stop on the southside of town. Leaving the truck and trailer at the big truck stop, Dad said, "Son, let's get in the car, and we'll find a place to stay."

Seeing a local pickup pulling in to get fuel, Dad drove up next to him and said in his deep voice, "Sir, do you know where there is a place to park our trailer?"

"Sure do," the old-timer said.

The good gentleman gave us directions, and away we went.

He said, "It's next to Hughes old grocery store!"

Pulling up to this unusual treat, we beheld the oddest little parking area and spots for only two trailers. Here was an old-timey grocery store with a porch across the front, three or four chairs, a large weathered sign that read, "Hughe's Grocery—Since 1925" and an RC Cola ice chest with every flavor in the world. Super, super cold blue, white, and red and rusty all over the corners. The porch was covered with rusty tin—some twisted upward in the Georgia air.

The wonderful old store was built out from the edge of the road. The store and porch were four feet off the street, and then six to eight feet away was a twenty-foot drop-off under the marvelous store. The rest of the store was in space, built on large poles of brown cedar...I think.

Think of it, the store was built out beyond the drop-off and set on thick poles all around the bottom of the store. Large rough rocks lined the edge of the porch to the drop-off. I stayed close to Dad.

"What do you think, son? It won't fall," but I stayed really close to him for a few more minutes.

Down below was an small faded old white plank house. Moss grew on the roof and two big square rock smokestacks. Both the house and the store were covered with that old brown shingle from bottom to top with green shingle roofing, worn and faded some of the roof curled up heavenward.

Walking into the historical landmark, we were greeted by the comforting smell of bubblegum, popcorn, burnt wood and coal, candy jars filled full, a red and white Coca-Cola machine full of more "coke" on melting ice. It was wonderful.

"Dad, Dad"—as I tugged at his sleeve—"this is like the old store where Uncle Melvin," (Aunt' Louise's husband, Mom's sister), "took me, and we sat around the fire and got to hear all the men talk."

"I'm glad you remember that," Dad softly said as he bent over close to me.

In the center of the floor was the coal stove and woodstove where friends met to tell their stories. All this was set on oily dark brown and blackish oak planks that smelled like a sawmill.

"Y'all come in and what can I get fur ya?" The voice came from behind the counter with the cash machine hiding her face. "I'm Mrs. Hughes," a voice came forth as the dear lady emerged from behind the counter. Short, fleshed out, with gray hair under a red handkerchief do-rag, and a large smile.

Looking at her, I was amazed at the wart just below her nose with a couple of pretty long hairs and curly ones! That occupied my vision, along with the smell of it all.

"We need a place to park our trailer for a few months."

The gracious, inviting soul said, "Let me call my husband. Homer, Homer...," she cried from the small back porch, with twenty-five or so steps down to the ground.

I was terrified. "A store built out into the air!"

Dad just grinned at me as the wife of Homer held to the wooden rails tight enough for her short, fat fingers to turn white.

Here came Homer. I thought he was a hundred years old, yet he climbed the steps like a billy goat. Dad and I looked at each other in grinning shock. He wore faded blue overalls, with a starched, well-worn white shirt, starched stiff, cracked, with brown brogans on both feet, all with a well-used black country dress hat, all dusty and bent.

"Welcome to Buford."

We talked, laughed and listened to Mr. Homer tell us about Buford and World War I.

"I was with our Army in '17 as we crushed the Germans into 'bits' like red Georgia gravel."

With wide opened mouth, I pulled Dads sleeve, "Dad, I just read that story last week."

"You did? Good."

In spite of all that, we got the deal done, and Dad set on to get us parked and hooked up. I helped, but I couldn't get my eyes off the front of the store. On the left was a faded "Confederate" flag, and on the right, an almost new "Old Glory." Over the door was a saying I'll never forget, "In God we trust. All others must pay cash."

"Would you like to go to our Fourth of July gathering at our sons? He just built a new home, and we want to celebrate with him…," Mrs. Hughes said.

We did go.

The Hughes's hearts were big. We found out they didn't live by their sign, but they also gave lots of people credit, and some never to see again. But they were happy.

Dad backed the "home on wheels" into the narrow spot by the water, sewer, and electricity. The deal was done, and the first month's rent paid, and we set about living, but with the southside of the Liberty only five and a half feet from the ragged blacktop street.

Buford was an old town, quaint, and happy with the Hughes's store two blocks off main street. Next to the store was a muscadine patch that grew from the street over to the two or three hickory trees. *How did they grow twenty feet across?* I wondered.

I asked Dad, "How strong are these grapevines?"

Not thinking about the question, he half interestedly said, "Son, Georgia muscadines are strong enough to hold a bear."

Wow, a bear! my gleeful mind declared with the wheels turning.

I had never seen such a thing. Here was a "muscadine highway" stretched out over the high "gully" to the trees. "We had those in Walls, Mississippi, and I climbed, um, a whole bunch."

"Thanks, Dad," I responded. Being quite sure, I had not revealed my secret plan.

From day one, I began to study the situation, figuring out my travel route across my vine highway to those big trees. There I could climb to the sky. Not being impetuous, of course, for several weeks, I figured, calculated, and planned.

Having made several friends those last few weeks of school, I began to work on their poor little minds about the "vined highway." On Saturday, we'd hike around, walk downtown, or just sit and tell stories. With two nickels, we could buy an RC Cola and moon pie at Hughes's grocery. Mrs. Hughes was so kind to us, but I could not keep my eyes off those stiff long hairs, black as coal and curling up tight.

34

So upon one of those heavenly sun-filled days, I said, "Boys, let's go cross the 'muscadine highway.'"

"But nobody has ever done that before," said my good, plump friend, whose name I unfortunately do not remember.

He had just finished the fourth grade while the rest of us the third. His argument only challenged me and pushed me on. Nobody could discourage that enflamed and tickled mind...of a little trailer boy.

One cute girl hung out with us, redheaded, freckle-faced, and pretty. Jenny was a tomboy of the highest order.

"Let's go," she said with flames in her words as red as her hair.

Strangely, my first real girlfriend—that is as much as a fourth grader—in conservative times could have been was a look alike to Jenny.

Walking down the street like Wyatt Earp to face the gunfighters at the O.K. Corral, we headed for the universally first-time challenge. We walked deliberately, silently seeing ourselves as world shakin' conquerors. The competitive juices flowed.

There we were at the muscadine bridge strung out like a mountain gravel road with holes in it, daylight down below and open all the way to the earth.

I had to face up to my well laid out plan.

"I'll go first," I stutteringly squeezed out of my mouth. "I'll tell y'all what it's like."

Slowly inching up to the sight, I saw daylight below even though the green bridge looked solid. "A long way to the bottom," I whispered to myself.

"Hey, any of y'all want to go first? I don't want to hurt any feelings," I said, hoping to find a first-time victim, instead of sacrificing myself.

No one spoke. They just shook their heads side to side.

Off I went, placing my feet on the best clump of vines I could find. But the vines were swinging with me both directions as I bobbed up and down!

"Ohwee" came out of my mouth when my foot slipped off the vines with a great jar to my private area. Worst of all, I could see the ground twenty feet below, but I couldn't let my fear be known. After all, this was my gang and my "game"!

At least there was some bushes down on the ground below me, so I took some comfort that if I fell, at least I could land on them. Swinging as I crept along, it seemed as if I were on the Empire State Building with it swinging back and forth.

I looked back to my buddies. Their eyes were swelled up as big as coffee saucers, and even though they were gripped with fear, they yelled encouraging words, "Go, Larry, go!"

Lo and behold, when I got to the middle of the muscadine passage, the vines began to violently swing like a rockin' chair. Too far to go back, couldn't turn around, and "way" down…to certain death. Besides, once I got to the trees, I'd have to eventually come back, but my pride said, "Go on! You can't quit…"

On I went. Swinging, slipping, and grabbing vines, suddenly, violently, I swung *under* the vines! Hanging on for dear life, I swung under the "highway" but got my right leg over the top of the vines, grabbed a bundle of the green strands, and wiggled back up on top as I swung side to side. I was winning over this adventure but wet with sweat!

Making it to the trees, I climbed out on a big limb, blew out air with a big, "Sheeewww," as the four safe buddies clapped and yelled. I tried to act as if it were nothing.

I clung to the sweet, comforting big tree. I felt good while shaking from top to bottom, front to back.

"Who's next? There's room over here for all of us," I breathlessly said, still excited, as if I was the victorious gladiator. I was proud I had shown the way.

The other two boys followed, leaving Jenny and "Plumpy" behind. We didn't use that term for our heavy friend; it was just a name. He didn't care—well, I hope. Both had learned from watching me, and they traveled with great success and better than me. Now they were on the limb with me.

What a worldwide marvelous thing. Now Jenny was to come as our plump friend wanted to be last. She almost flittered across the green highway being little, lighter than us, or so we agreed. Jenny was a good tomboy! We liked her. She was the winner so far. I was humbled…by a girl.

However, our plump friend was the real story. "Is it really my turn? Don't some of you want to go again? My stomach hurts. Mom will call me soon...."

"No, you gotta come," we all cried out. "Come on!"

He began to navigate the vine passage very well, but being bragged on, he let go of the vines to clap for himself, and then it happened! He flipped helplessly under the vines!

The rest of us hollered, "Hang on! Hang on!" as our eyes almost popped out of our heads. Our mouths dropped wide open as we watched him fight for his life.

His right foot caught some vines that twisted around his leg and foot, so now he hung upside down.

Plumpy boy yelled, "Help me! Help me! I'm caught...!" he hollered until he whimpered with fear, almost to tears.

"Don't wiggle," I cried out. "Do not move!" I said, as he turned to grab vines and throw his left thick leg over some of the dangerous highway. "Stay still. We can't let you fall and land on your noggin!"

The poor boy was helpless, and so were we. "Get me off! Get me off...!"

And I said, "We'll save you."

We were in trouble. We couldn't reach the sad victim, so the only thing to do was for me to slide down the tree and go in the store and have Mrs. Hughey call somebody.

"What...," and I can't tell you the rest of what she said, but in about five minutes, the fire department and policeman were there, sirens blaring.

The fire truck had a "body bucket." Up the bucket went with a skinny small man in it, who loosened the poor boy's foot from the vines, caught him, turned him right side up as Plumpy cried. Both were lowered to the ground as I stood by the red and yellow truck.

Up went the bucket again. The other victorious four in the big oak tree were loaded into the ride, and happily down they came!

What a turn of events. The planner and leader of this forever story was left standing, lonesome on the ground! Plumpy was the attraction.

"Who is this boy...?" the policeman asked.

Mrs. Hughes's said, "The orchestrator of this fiasco!"

I'll never forget as the fireman, policeman, and then others walked away. Yes, I was the motivator; they were the winners.

We never tried that mighty highway vine passage again... except in our minds. I hope at this very minute, some place, Jenny or another is telling this story.

Buford is the first place I learned I could tell stories as I set with the kids on the block and told them of my exploits in World War II, on a tank, in the jungles, or in the air, saving America. And they listened.

Sandy and I recently went to Buford. The old store was gone, but not the glad memories.

The Runaway Tractor

My soul is very grateful for my life as a trailer boy, all the places we saw, and people we met. It gave constant occasions, for me, to explore the world and loving the outdoors.

Jeanie, my sister, two years younger, was all in for almost anything I wanted to do. As the McCollum's say, "She was set on go!" She was my good friend. We even double dated a couple of times as older teenagers. She was truly an innocent victim on the next caper.

The Rice's—John, Wilma, and Happy, good friends since Granada, Mississipi, in 1949-'50—moved close by us, in Dundee III. With John working with Dad. Mr. Rice was a great mechanic.

Rice had told Dad that "since there are so many Johns, just call me Rice," so Rice it was.

Happy, two years older, and I had become fast friends.

We lived in several towns and six states together, and here they were in a park close to us in Dundee. Illinois.

On this particular July day, it was a Saturday, the Rice's had come to visit. The sun and blue sky were brilliant. Arriving at about 9:00 a.m., Happy, Jeanie, and I got outside as quick as possible. We headed down the gravel road to visit the mink ranch (as told in "Jobs").

In about thirty seconds, we turned our heads from talking, and behold, a remarkable, frightening sight. A big round object moving with a goal in mind.

"A snapping turtle," Happy said, and Jeanie lightly screamed. He was crossing the road headed toward us and the trailers.

"What's he thinking?" I asked, and both shrugged their shoulders.

Huge, but we easily ran up to him as he slightly turned toward us, raised his body up about three inches, let out a loud hissing sound, as if blowing his nose. It was a fearsome sight, his eyes glared at us, all brown and wet-looking.

"Be careful," Happy said as if we needed that information.

Covered with moss, very green, with a head the size of Dad's fists, he kept up his journey. Jeanie screamed, and we chattered with excitement. Neighbors began looking out their doors and swiftly emerging from their homes on wheels. The "oohs" and "aahhhss" filled the air.

Robin—another trailer boy, but not an outdoor type—ran up, almost stumbling down on the beast.

"Get back, Robin," Dad said to the "light in the loafer" kid, "or he'll bite your foot off. He screeched like a little girl. *Stink?* The big boy on four legs stunk!

By the time, the owner of the park, who had lived in that country all his life, told us that this happened every once in a while. There was a large "swampy" area across the road that always looked very frightful. He said, "The swamp is full of them and *other creatures!*"

Jeanie, Happy, and I looked at each other with stretched out eyes.

The owner said to Rice and Dad, "Walker"—as he glanced over at Mr. Rice—"this is the best meat in the world. We'll kill him and have a cookout later."

So Dad and Rice went to Dad's green Ford and got a "pic" handle and held it down to the monsters pointed mouth that inevitably attacked the handle with severe violence. He then clamped his mighty jaws down on it. The two mechanics, with sleeves rolled up, picked up the turtle and carried him to the owner's home. The crowd still stood and chatted, all in a furious excitement.

Later, the men said, "He weighed at least 105 pounds and was two feet wide and long. Once he clamped on to the handle or if to a human, he wouldn't let go until the skies light up with lightning."

But he let go quicker than that as an ax took care of him. No doubt those things were true.

We talked breathlessly about seeing him killed, meeting his abrupt end, being dressed (prepared), cooked, and tasted. I loved his taste. It was the only time I've ever eaten a swamp creature. This excitement set our blood to flowing and set us up to do some exploring in the woods close by. Jeanie was ready to go, so we looked at each other, blinked our eyes in slight hesitation but said in strict determination, like Warren Oaks in *The Wild Bunch*, "Let's go," as if we were going into battle or some world-shaking adventure.

Heading northward, Happy led us through the woods, looking for anything we could find. The deep green moss and clear water seeping up through the moist Lake Michigan earth was fascinating. We turned in about twenty minutes eastward and came up on a beautiful large pasture and a fencerow. Cows and a donkey were fenced in. The farmer had told me a few days before, "There are a lot of coyotes, and the 'jackass' kept them away."

"Jackass!"

"Yes," he said.

And I felt awfully worldly to hear such a word.

The floor of the woods was covered with red, yellow, and all colored flowers.

Jeanie said, "I love this." The woods were very low lying, only twenty-eight miles from Lake Michigan.

Looking and walking down the rusty fencerow way out in front of us was a dark, vine-ribboned object. It was huge, brown, and covered with moss and old crinkling leaves and limbs.

"A tractor," Happy burst with glee, strangely smiling from ear to ear.

"Come on. Let's get on it and see if we can start it and drive it," Happy said as our pace quickened.

I thought we could silently, then said boldly, as if in charge, "Go on up. Help Jeanie up." Walking up to it, it was, all rust-covered, square-shaped, and huge. A homemade metal roof set over the two seats with two steps up to the seats. All three of us climbed upon the ole-timey machine.

"I figure it has a key start," start less crank. "Let's crank it and take off."

Happy, more thoughtful and cautious, said, "No, we can't."

I retorted, "Sure, we can!" while I wrinkled my eyes like "I think" with a very uncertain face on Jeanie and rightfully so.

We could find no key or way to start the monster, so climbing down, I began to look around the front to see what was what. Both Jeannie and Happy were perched up in the cab with Happy in the driver seat. They now felt more at ease.

"Here it is," I yelled, "an old crank!" with breathless words. That's where the saying "Crank your car" came from. Then I remembered seeing Dad start an old Euk dirt Grader by cranking it.

"No, no," Happy exclaimed, seeing what was about to happen while Jeanie silently, wild-eyed, waited for the event with the green and hazel flashing like a flashlight.

Grabbing the handle, I tried to twist it clockwise around in circles, but it was too tight and stuck. Breathlessly, turning it clockwise slowly then faster as it loosened up. Determined, with sweat now running down my face to my chest and middle of my back, I worked with all I had. Stopping to slap a mean bloodsucking giant mosquito, it came to me.

"Counterclockwise," I said out loud and twisting the "crank" one time, two times, three times, and out of breath, I gave it one last heave with all I had left in me.

"Now!"

"Listen, Jeanie, it's starting," Happy said as he hit her on her left shoulder. The engine sputtered, turned over, and finally set into a rough, missing run, then a steady stuttering purr.

But! But the big old square Allis Chalmers started to move forward!

"Oh no," Jeanie pleaded, as Happy said, "We got to stop this Simpson!"

"Yeah I know!"

"Larry!" Jeanie, chocking, cried, as I madly, with every muscle, scrambled from the front of the tractor and jumped straight up, poking my left foot into the square step.

41

"Move over!" I pantingly shouted as I tried to pull myself up. But like Happy, I was stupefied and rendered, almost malfunctional.

As the 1930s fifteen-thousand-pound tractor started rambling forward with increasing speed, Jeanie hollered "Larry!" again.

I shouted, "Move over! I'm coming up!"

My next step on my right foot with my dirty white tennis shoe slipped off the step! I was holding on frantically to the step handles now hanging out in the middle of the air. I knew if I fell, I'd be run over. I refused to let that happen.

"Come on, buddy," my great Granada pal encouraged.

The giant man killer was moving faster, and I thought, *What if it goes through the fence and all the cows get out? What if I never see Happy and Jeanie again? What if...? What if...?* As I fought gravity, hanging out in midair, and the shaking ole machine seemed to be trying to eat me up. As it jerked forward and shook me like a freezing man, my hands were wet from sweat and slipping dangerously.

A huge faded, cracked half-flat black tire was reaching for my right leg as it hung, swinging way too close to it. I saw the black, rubber monster with my right eye, looking over my shoulder, and pulled with all I had.

By God's dear mercy, with all I had left, I pulled myself up, my feet dangling under the monster, and I climbed the next two steps and set in the driver's seat! By now, we were mowing down saplings and bushes. If we tore open the fence, I just knew we'd have to work for the old farmer for the rest of our lives...after we got out of prison!

Looking fearsomely for a switch or key, I finally discovered it but looked up, and we were headed for the fence! "Oh no!"

As I twisted the crude key, the motor whimpered down with a loud as a cannonball of backfire and smoke.

Shaking with tears of relief and words of thanksgiving, the three of us hugged one another, and Happy prayed a very short prayer to God for delivering us. We set silently, breathlessly a few moments as Jeanie squeezed my right hand with tears. The path of the tractor was about twenty-five to thirty yards!

We humbly walked back through the woods breathing deeply as a conquering and relieved, maturing spirit of success came over us. We were both humbled and proud.

"We better learn from this," Jeanie softly said, and we agreed… as I was looking sideways with a "sure."

The tractor path had only taken a minute or so, but we had lived through a war!

Soon no words were spoken, and we "crossed our hearts and hoped to die" if we ever told anyone. I didn't for years, and I only revisit that scene every few years and then with reverence and wonderment. We told Mom and Dad just before I went to Memphis State in a moment of family reflection.

Dad just said, "Son, son," slowly shaking his head.

The years passed and the secret miracle was just ours.

In 1986, I went to Mr. Rice's funeral. Happy and I briefly mentioned the day of the secret tractor run-away.

After another thirty-four years, I've not seen my good old friend. I'd like to talk about this adventure with him and other great times, but I don't know where he is.

No excuses. Live life as an adventure.

Arkansas and Ready

"The earth would move beneath my feet," said in a good old western.

—J. L. S.

"Boy, you're ready," Granddaddy Mac said one day to me as I was hanging around his rocking chair, the one with a hole or two in the seat.

I looked up at him and said, "Yes, sir. I'm ready."

He grinned, just puffin' on his pipe and patted my head.

Ready Teddy was another of those sorts of sayings in the fifties, and I was "ready."

Prince Albert was Granddaddy's favorite pipe tobacco, which filled the air with its august aroma.

"Why do you smoke a pipe?" I asked one morning as I filled in my time before tearin' up the countryside.

"Your great-granddaddy McCollum smoked one, so I do too."

I just looked at him and said, "Okay," and went outside in the cooler morning air.

Jeanie and I were in Arkansas with Mom's mother and father. I do not remember the nearest town, but we were there because we were about to have a baby brother born in a few days. Dad brought Jeanie and I to stay with Grandma and Granddaddy Mac for safekeeping.

"Joy" and "fun" best describe our stay with them as we waited for what was to be born. Back in those times, we couldn't know what sort of human was to be born, nor did we need to.

Nevertheless, Troy David was born into this world, August 6, 1949.

Dad called the neighbors phone, one mile down the dirt road northward, so they could get the happy news to us. Since Granddaddy Mac and Grandma Mac didn't have a telephone, they needed good neighbors. They knocked on the door.

"You've got a boy, Troy David," the lady said in excitement.

I stared at her because she had an Indian-lookin' face, all brown with some long-twisted hairs hanging from her head.

"She's just got 'em. That's the way she likes it," Grandma Mac said softly as I looked bug-eyed at her and said, "Yes, ma'am," and ran out the door.

"I've got a baby brother. Jeanie, we've got a baby brother. Barbara, Alice we've got a baby brother!"

And around to the rest of the family, I announced this amazing news. Everybody clapped and said words of excitement.

This three-week stay in Arkansas was a time to be told even at this late date. James, my uncle, was thirteen years old; Alice and Barbara, four and two years older than me; and Carolyn was younger than me; all were there along with two skinny short-haired hound dogs. Their ears hung way down, and they "panted" a lot in the Arkansas furnace. I learned that word panted' from Uncle James.

Now as we whooped and hollered on the front panel porch, the hound dogs stood on the bottom step and joined our celebration howling, barking, and whining with their tails justa fly'n.

James and I became close friends forty years later when we could travel to see each other. He was a lanky, strapping, muscular, tough kid with whom I rode horses in the west many times before his passing in 2006. He treated me like a brother.

My sweet aunts Alice and Barbara thought of me as a baby brother, wagging me around on their hips. They spoiled me until I was seven or eight with my feet scratching the ground. I guess, eventually, I got too heavy, but they, thankfully, tell those stories today as delightful almost eighty-year-old women.

Carolyn and Jeanie were close to each other, and she still has the sweetest, brightest smile and soft voice this side of heaven.

This combination of little humans with me born "ready" was a catalyst for excitement.

"Are you ready?" Alice would say after breakfast, and away we'd go to the wonderland beyond the steps of this old plank sharecroppers' house.

Arkansas was hot in that summer of '49. Humidity was sweltering in the delta, hilly countryside, on top of the red dirt. Cotton was standing big and tall with the "white" beginning to fluff up.

The house was small and, of course, with only fans to circulate the ninety- to ninety-five-degree wet air. Four or five rotating fans with one big window fan, provided by the farm owner made the hot air fly. Flies, green, brown, and black ones flew through the house with Grandma Mac being the fly killer.

"How'd you get so good at killin' flies?" I asked as a little sweat ran down my left chin.

"Practice, son, practice" was all she said, but I remembered those words, "Practice, son, practice." And it stays with me to this cold day in March.

Rockin' chairs were necessary in those days, not just a pleasure.

Granddaddy said one hot day, "Who can stand to just sit in this weather if you don't have a rockin' chair and a hand fan?"

And there were on the old church bench and chairs, fans for the hand, mostly form funeral homes or banks. They got worn out pretty fast, but that didn't matter. They still got used.

"How come there's so many swatters in here?" I asked Grandma Mac.

"Well, son, they are for killin' flies!"

I got it. Direct, simple, and funny. Why else? Of course, to kill flies! Those were good, hot, fly-killin' days.

This setting was perfect for outside adventures as Alice said, "Let's go," and away, I, Alice, and Barbara would fly. Hogs in the shaded hogpen with lots of hard dry mud until it rained, a barn to climb up in, two hounds, and a small dirt road beyond the fence laying to the west called us.

The barn had a loft that I loved to sneak over to, to climb the ladder and look out, for which I got in trouble.

"Boy, get away from that loft," I heard many times, and "Do you want to break your neck?"

Well, of course, I didn't, but I did want to see the world below and out "yonder."

For the first day or two, I would stand and look down that long dirt road and wonder. The earth would move beneath my feet.

In adventure, questions, mystery, new things, my world…the earth moved beneath my feet. I did, and it does.

"Larry, you ready to go."

"Yep."

I'd gleefully go back to Alice. Always, she, Barbara, and I would say anything to be with one another.

"Let's travel the old dirt road," the sisters said.

"Ready, let's go."

It's been my motto for these years: "Ready, set, go." Did it come from those days? Yes, and more like 'em.

It seemed to this five-year-old that we walked a long way, especially as the time flew by, looking, climbing, and talking.

We came to our first barbed wire fence and carefully went through it. We then crossed another and another.

"How far have we come?" I asked.

"Oh, about a half mile."

"Will we be in Texas soon?"

"Texas?" Alice replied. "No, not yet."

I had a cowboy book about the Texas Rangers, so I thought, *It'd make me sound "big" to ask such a question.*

"Let's climb this tree," one of them said.

So up we went, as high as possible. We looked all around. Up high! Three kids. Warm breeze blowing at 9:00 a.m.

Coming to a place, as the sun got high in the sky, where some blackberry bushes were growing, we went over to see if any were ripe.

"No, they're still too green," Alice said, when suddenly, Barbara yelled out, "A SNAKE! A SNAKE!"

We swirled around, started to run, and what do you think?

"A BLUE RACER! A BLUE RACER!" Alice shouted. "RUN! RUN!"

Turning back down the little road that split the huge farm, we lit out.

"What's a 'blue racer'?" I yelled.

"A snake that chases you."

I pumped my arms all the harder, but they kept up with me.

The blue "killer" followed. As I looked over my shoulder to see the varmint, it seemed to be closer and closer, making a continuous "S" figure in sailed along. It wasn't afraid of us! Surely, it would swallow us up!

"Faster, or we're sure 'goners'!" Barbara barked at the top of her voice.

The prospect of a snake with huge teeth biting my rear end was scary indeed!

"Up this tree!" Alice cried out, and we scrambled up like monkeys. Now I don't want to belittle monkeys, but from the bottom, looking up it looked like that to me as we ascended to our safe spot.

Gasping for the Arkansas morning warm air, we swallowed in gulps. "Look, look at that! The thing is climbing the tree!" Barbara barked out.

It did raise up a little and looked up at us as if to say, "Now there, this is my country."

Then he swerved slowly back toward the blackberry patch as if he had another accomplished mission.

Alice, sweating profusely, said, "Let's get down and get on to the house."

We were happy to get home.

Granddaddy Mac was sitting on the front porch, reading his big worn black Bible. I blurted out what happened as I jumped upon the front porch, and he never lifted his eyes and said, "Yeah, son. They'll do it."

I went inside.

"That was close," Alice said, who had already gone inside while Barbara, usually second to speak, said, "I'm just glad to still be here."

"Listen," Alice said, "let's just keep this to ourselves," to which I nodded in agreement and never telling them I had already told my Bible-reading Granddaddy.

Grabbing some iced tea with the ice chipped off the big block of ice, we whispered a repeat of the story as Jeanie listened quietly. She didn't ask a question but tried to understand.

"Larry, you will keep this secret, won't you?" Barbara asked.

"Yes, I can. I will," I said, having learned that phrase from Dad.

Jeanie just looked wide-eyed with a slight frown. She was only three years old.

I only saw one other blue racer in all my journeys.

A Granddaddy Lesson

"Lessons come hard but make life easier," I read somewhere. It seems to be true.

Running around with Alice and Barbara, who were seven and nine, I was feeling pretty big. Besides, "cool" James, at his grown-up age, being born in 1936, taught me some "slick" behavior as I followed him around.

On the second Saturday of being in Arkansas, I came in from outdoors all full of myself, and Granddaddy Mac said, "Son, go over there and get me my pipe." He loved his pipe.

I replied quickly, precisely, and definitively, "In a minute," and I never looked up. I had lost my mind.

"Boy, what did you say?"

And I could hear some aggravation in his gruff voice. "In a minute," I confessed, and I knew I had transgressed the law! Like a sheep killing dog, I tried to handle it, saying, "But, I'll do it now."

Too late.

"No, you won't. Come here. Bend over this old knee!"

"Yes, sir," and he then and there taught me a lifelong lesson. "Don't cross the one with the power, especially Granddaddy!"

He bent me over his knee and spanked the hurting behind for what seemed like an hour. I was shedding some wet tears from shame and pain when he ceased. "Do you understand me now, son? Like Randolph Scott to his young companion in "Ride the High Country"."

"Yes, sir," as I fell into his arms, knowing I was wrong, and he was right while the tears rolled down my red cheeks. I could not stand to know I had disappointed Granddaddy and aggravated him. I was hugging him. He was hugging me. Correction with love.

"I'm sorry, Granddaddy!" "I'm sorry... I'm sorry."

To which he replied, "We'll be okay. I'm not mad."

I was comforted and corrected. With his hands on my shoulders, he explained respect, honor, and duty. He did right, and I learned a life lesson even now sixty-nine years and a million miles later. He's gone, and I thought I couldn't live anymore when he died too young in 1961. The earth moved beneath my feet.

The Bull

"Larry, Jeanie, hurry, you've got a baby brother!"

The reason we were there had happened. Not having a clue as to where the new brother came from, Grandma Mac said, "His name is Troy David, named after your Granddaddy Mac."

Jumping up and down, we celebrated, and then I asked, "When will we see him and Mom and Dad?"

Secretly, I had gotten very homesick.

"Four days. They'll be here."

Jeanie and I jumped up and down together, making a lot of celebration noise. Then we settled back in for the last few days of our Arkansas trip.

The next day was cloudy, and we'd had a little sprinkle. That ole dirt and clay was slick with the rain.

"Hey, let's go see the cows in the back pastures," Barbara suggested.

So away we went with a picnic lunch of bologna sandwiches and a jug of water in case we got too hungry.

So through the fences, past the blackberries, over stone by stone in the creek and through the fence to the red with some white cattle.

There were a few cows and calves that we could get close too. We rubbed a nice cow, massaged her ears, and scratched her back.

But we had to get back for lunch pretty quick. Through the fence, cross the creek and into the next parure, we went. We walked slowly, enjoying being together for one of the last times on this trip.

Suddenly we heard a thundering sound, limbs breaking, rocks flying, and as we turned back and here, he came. *What!* We thought he was put up. *What?* A huge rumbling and rolling *bull!* His horns had been cut but were still six to eight inches long. Weighing in at two thousand pounds, he looked like a mountain rolling at us. The dust was flying, and his snorting created a dust storm!

"Run! Run!"

We ran as hard as we could. The fence was getting closer, but so was the *bull*.

"Run!" Alice hollered.

I did keep up with my aunts, but the old bull wanted us. We had invaded his domain. Alice grabbed my hand and pulled me through the air, my feet hitting just every once in a while.

He was saying, "Leave my girls alone! Don't come back!"

We made the fence with the bull ready to spear us. Alice went through, held the next wire open as fast as she could, and I flew through, and then came Barbara, screaming, "Bloody murder!"

The bull stopped, snorted, pawed the ground with his right then left foot, and shook his head as if to say, "No, don't ever do it again" as "slobber" flew out of his flopping jaws.

We were safe. But when we went to the sharecroppers' house, Grandma Mac asked, "What is it? You're wet, dirty, and you look wild-eyed."

Alice told her, and all my wonderful grandmother said was "You knew better. Get cleaned up, and no one will ever know."

Thank goodness. Granddaddy didn't know until they moved back to Memphis. He was okay that a lesson was learned, and that's enough. That's the way my wonderful grandparents were—"always have a good time."

We did.

No excuses. Live life to its fullest.

Story 6

Adventures 2
The Runaway

We are free to face with our destiny and we must meet it with a high and resolute courage. For us is the life of action, of strenuous performance of duty; let us live in the harness, striving mightily; let us rather run the risk of wearing out than rusting out.

—Theodore Roosevelt,
"The Duties of a Great Nation,"
New York City, October 5, 1898,
Campaign and Controversies,

vol. 14 of "The Works of Theodore
Roosevelt, National" ed., chap. 45,
(New York City, 1926), 202.

Moving from town to town, school to school, and the traveling along
the old black highways left my mind in wonderment. Who are these
men standing at the gas station? How fast could that red plowing,
smoking tractor run in its day?

I was on the run from New Albany to Memphis to Blue Springs
or Wise Hollow. The Mississippi River following like a mighty del-
uge or the flat fields of corn in Indiana my mind was wandering,
strolling.

Astonishment was my world.

By the tenth grade, I had lived in ten states, gone to fifteen (15)
schools, and gotten a whipping in all but two of them because of my
roaming mind. I wasn't mean; I was excited, adventurous, and my
spirit wandering through many places, with many people, hugging
them all, all the time.

Coming into different schools so many times and places, I was
always reestablishing myself, getting my place. "I will not be ignored
or be unnoticed. I'll have my place," I told Betty Jo.

No wonder by the spring of '57 in Gallatin, Tennessee, I said to
Dickie, "Dickie, let's run away!"

"What? Run away? Where?"

"Away," I exerted. "We'll catch a train!"

"A train?" Dickie asked, both excited and terrified.

"Yes, a train. We'll take our school lunch money and get a job!"

"A job?"

"Sure, we'll work on a farm."

By now, Dickie was getting ready. Dickie asked, "What about Jay?"

"Yeah, I was going to say. Let's get Jay!"

We sure got him! Heading him off on the way to gym, we told
him. "When do we leave?" the red head asked, blinking his eyes in
nervous disbelief.

Dickie was a cool guy who lived on the corner of the two-lane
separated street across from Langford's Trailer Park. I thought his

family must be rich. He had a flat top, a little pudgy, a good athlete, and we were buddies.

Red-top Jay was a roustabout, a little raw, a "cat," and ready to ride the train to glory.

We met after school on that fateful day and made plans.

Dickie said reflectively, "We'll get in trouble," while I retorted in a careless, boyish mind, "What can they do?"

Now that's the mind of a twelve-year-old.

"What about our parents?"

We had no answer to that. We agreed we didn't want to get in trouble or hurt anyone, but the long road of adventure called us. Blinded by the thought of the "open road," we agreed that "we've got to do this. It's our destiny."

"All right. Let's get with it," Dickie said.

And Jay said, "I'm ready."

I just nodded with a "cattish" grin. "Here's what we'll do for money," I said, and proceeded like an executive. "We'll take our savings for food."

"What savings?" Jay said, but Dickie stepped up, saying, "I'll loan you $2.00, and that'll leave me $2.55."

"What you have, Larry?"

And with a humble, hesitating reply, "$1.90."

"When do we leave?" Jay asked.

Stuttering, I said, "This…this Friday! After school."

We were "antsy" all week, but Friday did come. We rushed out of school, dropped out books off at a specified bush close to our homes, and making sure no one saw us. Racing across town about a mile to the train station, we were breathless. Huffing and puffing, we arrived and hid behind the station. "Without a question, a train would be there, waiting for us," we planned.

No train. We waited for an hour, but no train.

"We'd better go on home, boys," I said.

"Okay, okay, but what about next week?" Dickie responded, and we came up with this astonishing plan.

The plan: Monday morning, we would head out to school because we walked to school in those days, dump our books in "the bush" when nobody was looking, and head out. After all, we'd have our savings and lunch money of $1.25! All weekend, I was lost in our plan, the fear, the thrill, long highways, new people, farms, mountains, the *Navajos*, freedom, and independence.

Monday did come. We were a tangled but determined mess. We knew that without a doubt, "our train" would be waiting.

We carefully drug along behind everybody the "walk to school," dumped our books to a specified round green bush, and lit out across town through the graveyard, past Randy's Record Shop, crossed Highway 31, and arrived breathlessly at the grand ole station.

No train. "Is there a train coming?" we asked the old conductor with that special stripped blue-and-gray cap on.

"No, not for two hours. Why?"

"Well, well," Dickie sputtered, but I jumped in being quick with a deceitful mind, "we're doing a project for history class, ugh, about train stations."

"Where's your notebook and paper?" the suspicious conductor asked.

We just looked at him with blank, stretched, dead, bulging eye-balls.

We knew we couldn't wait because the school would be contacting our parents, and we'd be caught.

I had to take control if we were going to pull this caper off. "We've got to get out of here. So let's walk down the tracks, get up on Highway 31, and hitch a ride."

Away we went, leaving the good ole train man behind.

Off we went. Scrambling over the tracks, in the gravel, then the ditch, passing the backside of the trailer park I had lived in for a year and a half, the fields I played in, and had found some baby rabbits. In about a mile, we came to the bridge over the tracks, climbed the steep bank, slipping on wet grass, walked across the highway to the west end of the bridge, and started our hitchhiking vigil. We knew we'd get a ride to Bowling Green, so we got our thumbs ready to go to work!

Standing for just enough time for us to get our wind back, Jay stuttered out, "A car…a car."

We stuck our twelve-year-old thumbs-up in the air to the front and side of ourselves, moving them back and forth. Feeling so worldly, the car stopped. The very first car! Our thumbs-up and wide-eyed faces had attracted a victim!

"Where you goin'?" the handsome, clean-cut young man asked. To this day, I can't figure out what in the world this man was thinking, picking us up and we so young.

Dickie, with a trembling voice, said, "Bowling Green."

"Bowling Green? That's a long way."

"Yes, Bowling Green," I said as Dickie was nodding anxiously up and down.

He drove off with three starey eyed, seventh graders, heading ninety miles north to Bowling Green, Kentucky.

"Where're you goin'?" Jay asked.

"Louisville." Such little talk lasted only a very few minutes.

Then we had to face up. Watching our Tennessee rollin' hills roll by, and reality smashing us up beside our head. The young man began to ask us questions about ourselves, our family, our moms and dads, school, and the Lord!

Our answers were twelve-year-old answers, trying to sound "grown-up." We drove on in silence, looking back and forth at each other, with a rare whisper or two.

"You're running away, aren't you?" Then he began to talk about life, it's responsibility, it's goodness, family, and such. He repeated, "You're running away, aren't you?"

"Yes, sir. We wanted to see the world."

(You see, the sights of the wide world had already stricken this twelve-year-old boy!)

"How you gonna live, eat, sleep…?" He drove the question and true meaning of life upon us. The miles rolled by as did our "boyish" plans.

The driver of our "getaway car" then began to talk to us about our moms and dads and how we'd hurt them. "What about your brothers and sisters and all your friends? How will they feel?"

Shame covered me, and so on Dickie and Jay. We were caught.

Then he began to talk about Jesus, how he died for us, loved us, and his plan for us. He asked each one of us if we are Christians yet, and I quickly said, "Yes, I am."

I began to cry with shame and sadness and guilt. *How could I hurt my good parents and family so?* I thought to myself. Mom was so sweet and tender toward us; Dad worked hard to provide; and I loved Jeanie, David, and Susan, and what would I do without Trixie, my three-legged dog? Christ was my Lord and Savior. "How could I do this?" How?

By the time we got close to Bowling Green, this compassionate young man's instruction had us ready to go home. Dickie just stared with his head hanging down while Jay "hummed" almost silently, and I wiped a tear away.

"I'll stop at the truck stop on this side of town and find someone going to Gallatin." As providence had it, the very first semidriver he asked was headed to Gallatin! The first car, the first truck!

"I'll take these youngsters back," the large tall man said.

We squeezed into the big red smoke-covered semi with its large, sticking-out overhead sun visor, and in two hours, we were in Gallatin. He dropped us off at the corner of Gallatin Pike and Main Street. He had barely said a word, but I remember this, "The Lord and family come first."

I knew he was right.

We knew we had to get to school so we could trick everybody as if we had been in class all day. Furiously, we ran through the cemetery without reverence then down Martin Street to Highway 109, grabbed our books, and got to school in world record time, wet and breathless.

The Trouble We Cause

It was two thirty. Our hands were full of lunch boxes. We were tired and wet, but we had to get to school.

We thought we could just mingle back in with the other students after picking up our hidden books, and nobody would know. Think of this: We actually believed we could pull this off as if we had been there all day! Twelve-year-olds! My, my, the thoughts of children!

When we arrived, school was being let out. A police car was there with lights twirling. Our classmates and teachers began to holler and shout, "Where've you been? Are you all right? Your parents are here. It's been on TV and radio. Everybody's been so worried!"

Within seconds, the principal walked out with our parents following close behind.

The three of us just looked at each other with red wet faces and went to our parents. Hugging and kissing mine, I told the truth.

What pain and fear we caused. What trouble we caused for everyone.

We didn't run away because we were mad at our parents, felt mistreated, or any such things. We were overwhelmed by the thrill to see the world, be grown-up, follow the open lonesome mystic miles of the tracks before us, seeing the country, and freedom.

We were wrong.

We were twelve.

We were children.

Mom was heartbroken from fear, but most of all, just because I hadn't thought more of her and Dad. Dad was hurt and mad.

"How could you do this? What did you think you'd do? What have we done wrong? How ungrateful are you?"

Such questions were right, natural, and bone-crushing.

Nashville TV stations had the story going on. "Where are the three missing boys? Are they lost? Dead? What?"

The radio stations were asking where are the three missing boys? Our town was torn up and in an uproar. The principal, schoolteachers, and kids were crazy with fear.

Our families just wanted us home and safe.

I thought Dad would spank me, but he didn't. Mom just silently shed tears slowly. Both told me how bad this hurt them and how scared they were. I cried. I saw the truth. I was sorry. I asked for forgiveness.

That evening, the trailer was dimly lit, no TV, nothing spoken by all six of us. It was like a funeral.

David, Jeanie, and Susan couldn't understand…and I knew my desires and motives must include the well-being of others, especially my loved ones. Strangely, we never discussed the runaway and didn't even mention it for almost twenty years then with quiet reference.

The marvel of God's goodness to direct my path...our driver to Bowling Green, one driver back! How I wish that I could thank those men and hug Mom and Dad.

I went back to school, apologized to the principal, teachers, and friends. A lesson learned. Forgiveness given.

Epilogue

Thirty years later, I visited Gallatin and looked up an old friend working as a secretary in an insurance office. After a few minutes, Brenda asked, "Larry, why did you and Dickie and Jay run away in the seventh grade?"

I tried to tell her. She listened. We had a sweet reunion, and then I left. That adventure left an indelible mark on many people.

Now another thirty-two years have passed. I visited Brenda at her office one more time. She asked the same question. I still feel the thrill of the "thrill" and the shame of a selfish act.

I'm still sailing down life's highway, but I'm not running away! Join me. Larry.

Best wishes to my good friends Dickie and Jay. How I wish I could see you.

No excuses, just the truth.

"Sneaking Out!"

"Where are you moving?" Mary and Bert asked as they saw us from the street, hooking up to the turquoise trailer.

"Back to Gallatin."

"Where's that?"

"In Tennessee next to Nashville. Don't you remember me talking about that at the grill yesterday?"

"Oh yeah, and, man, we hate to see you leave."

I shook hands with Bert but gladly hugged Mary, a beautiful small black-headed girl who kissed my cheek. I wish I'd had more time with Mary—one more of my lost dreams.

We arrived in Gallatin, in '56 in August, and I went the whole seventh grade there. This was the year in the spring of '57 that Dickie, Jay, and I had runaway...for a day. Adventure was my "middle name."

The Refrigerator

From the time I was two years old, the whole family tells the stories of some of my adventures. I've always liked the thrill of climbing, seeing above and about what was beyond my world. After all, it was all mine anyway—that was my adventure.

In fact, I was so good at climbing that some of the family questioned whether or not I had some monkey in me; of course, yes, I did.

Living in Memphis on the second-floor apartment just off South Parkway, close to a small park we had one of those white ice-boxes. Today it is still said, "Get the bottle out of the icebox please." Most don't know why. I went with Dad more than once down to the ice company to get a block of ice about twelve by twelve to put in the icebox. That's how we kept food cold and safe.

Eventually, as a four-year-old, I had sized up the icebox until I had it all figured out. I could climb it! I just had to see from "up there."

Mother went into another room, "Larry...Larry."

"Yes, ma'am."

"Just color in your new 'Hopalong Cassidy' coloring book or build me something with your building blocks."

"Yes, ma'am."

I wasn't as much of a builder as I was a cowboy, so I colored up old "Hoppy" on his giant white horse.

Then I whispered softly, "This is the time to make my move."

I pulled a chair over to the icebox, very silently creeping along, with visions of conquering the icebox rolling in my brain. I knew very few people had ever done this, especially here in Memphis. I was sure Granddaddy Mac never had or Mom. Barefooted, I climbed onto the chair with the back of it against the icebox.

Reaching up, I got my fingers—of both hands—on the top edge, stepped up on the back of the chair, swung my right leg over the edge of the "box," and pulled with all my might.

"I'm slipping off," I silently whispered. "I'm slipping off."

So I pulled and strained and grunted the harder.

Slowly, I ascended to the top, got my left knee next to my right knee, and then it happened. My left had slipped off the edge, and I hit my chest on the top of the "box," and my chin, my teeth bit my tongue, but I stayed quiet.

A little blood never hurt anybody, I thought, remembering what Daddy said. I came up on all fours. Victory! I was on the icebox. I really was the "king."

I had gasped for air banging the chair against the door, but Mother had paid no attention.

"Pshaw," I blew out of my mouth.

I was higher than everything! Looking right, then left, and back, I made it. Only the top of the house was higher.

I knew I would get in trouble, but I planned not to get caught, and if I did, I'd just think about the next tricky escapade!

Such is the heart of an adventurer.

I had climbed Mt. Everest. I was king. My "blue eyes" scanned the sights below and beyond. I had the advantage. Here I was. I had done it!

But it was too quiet.

"What's Larry doing?" Mom must have thought. "Larry… Larry," with that upward ascent to a high pitched, "LARRRY! LARRRY!"

I didn't answer. I lay flat on the back side of the "box" and glared with wide eyes, wanting to see if I could win this battle. But the bad big patrolman entered the room, looking sternly from corner to corner.

"Where are you? What are you doing now?"

I just lay as flat as a possum and silent.

She looked and looked—looked in all the rooms.

Then slowly scanning, looking around everywhere, she glanced her "blue eyes" upward and saw a flat, hiding boy.

"What are you doing?"

"I had to see from here, Mother!"

"Come down right now," she said, reaching for me as I slid off into her threatening arms.

"Son, don't ever do that again. You scared me. You know I'll have to tell your daddy."

Sure, I knew it, but I'll take the "talking to" to see from that mountain again, and if I can't get away with it, my little devious, adventurous mind confessed that I'll find something else!

After doing this several times and getting two spankings, Dad said, "I'll fix you, you little bugger!"

So he put a lock on the door, one he had made as a great welder with a rail around the top. When family came to see us, they'd always ask about the icebox rail.

I wouldn't get up there anymore, but a memory lay in my little mind. Looking from the top of the "box," I could see out the window down to the sidewalk and bushes. It had excited me. It was a long way down from the second floor.

The Radio

Just beside the window was a brown radio on the small table. Flowers set next to it and a white linen under it.

"Uh-huh, the radio." I couldn't resist. "A flying radio" raced through my mind.

If I could only get the window up. The next day, Mom did it for me! She opened the window for fresh air as the curtain blew in every direction from the warm breeze. Silently, with Mom ironing in the bedroom, I tiptoed over to the radio. I couldn't help myself. "But you'll get in trouble again," I whispered. I couldn't resist! I had to see that flying radio sailing through the air. I had to see what would happen when it hit the sidewalk.

My right eye stayed on the radio and my left eye on the open door, where Mother was, as I crept along tiptoeing.

I jerked the cord out of the plug-in, grabbed up the radio, and pushed open the freshly ironed curtain. Then I sent the music box as far as I could, "justa flyin'." It turned over in the air, and it became slow motion. Flying, sailing, it seemed to ride the air. But *crash, boom, crack, pop*, the flying machine hit the sidewalk...next to the feet of a man in dress pants and exploded. He jumped off the sidewalk onto the grass and headed up the steps. What? Up the steps!

Oops! I hadn't figured the exact logistics correctly.

Knock, knock, knock, the front door shook, and Mother came running. What is it?

"A man...a man?" And Mom opened the door. Such anger I had never heard and words I didn't know. Mom listened, apologized, and said "goodbye," then turned to me. Mom's eyes now looked red or at least pink as I wondered, *What happened to the blue?*

My eyes blinked only once as Mom walked briskly to me, took me to the bedroom, and you know what happened next.

"How did this happen?"

"It fell out the windows."

"How?"

And I just shrugged my shoulders in silence and pretend innocence. Mother said, "You did it, didn't you?"

Dropping my head in guilt, I said, "Yes, ma'am."

After my spanking, we went down to the crime scene, and Mother made me gather and pick up all the scattered parts and put them in a paper bag. I had to sit silently on the sofa for one hour, waiting for Dad to show up.

You know how he reacted to this crime. He wouldn't have been wrong to think, "I'm raising a little gangster."

What I learned was to be more discreet in my adventures since adventurism was in me...and not hurt others.

Sneaking Out at Midnight

After living in the wonderful little town of Gallatin all my seventh grade, Dad was convinced by Mom's brother, Uncle LT, that work was aplenty in California.

Dad's wandering spirit, since he lived in quiet Walls, Mississippi, which we have never understood that he just couldn't resist. At the end of June of '57, he, with all of us around the supper table, quietly announced, "We're moving to California." Mom had waited for Dad to tell us, "I know this is a shock to you."

Jeanie said, "Oh no!"

David and Susan just looked confused.

I was thinking, "Not now, Dad. We've got so many friends and love it here," but I wouldn't say it.

"Why?" I asked.

"Work is plentiful, and I've always wanted to see that country. I wanta see the orange trees, the ocean, and be close to your mother's brothers."

"We'll pull up stakes in two or three weeks."

I went by myself and cried a little. I loved my friends, the Langford's who owned the trailer park, and the Rice's who had moved back from Westville, where Happy and I worked most of the summer of '56 gathering metal for money.

We had been there a whole year, loved our friends, the Gallatin swimming pool, the movie house, and Friday night football.

But we had to go.

My friends and I tried to be together as much as possible. Besides, I had a really cute eighth-grader blond-headed girlfriend. The thought of leaving all I loved there was heartbreaking.

So as the day, a Friday, for pulling up stakes was just two days away, I sat under the tall maples next to our "fox hole" dug three years earlier. It came to me, "Get out of bed at midnight, the night before we leave, sneak out of the trailer, join our friends, and we'll all be together on last time," I whispered to Jeanie.

My friends loved the idea and were ready for the midnight venture. My sister Jeanie and I, our sweet friend Marie, daughter of the owners of the trailer park, Marsha, Myron, Betty Lou, and Will would slip out at midnight. We would meet at Marsha's and roam the neighborhood just for fun.

That lonesome last day came. I was sad. The darkness came; midnight was waiting. After going to bed, Jeanie and I were whispering from bedroom to bedroom.

Dad said, "Quit talking and go to sleep, daylight will come in a little bit."

We stopped, not wanting to upset our plans.

Time went slow. It was 11:00 p.m. Dad walked down the hallway, drank some milk for his stomach, as I peeked around the corner, and he went back to bed.

"Is he going to ruin this?" I whispered to myself.

Midnight came on the clock with its light glowing, and I got up. No one else was stirring.

"Jeanie, Jeanie," I whispered as my partner in crime had gone to sleep. "Let's go."

"Okay," she said almost silently.

Having gone to bed with our clothes on, we put our shoes on, our hands shaking from fear and excitement, trying hard to see our shoelaces. We were ready.

"Shhh, shhh," we whispered with our fingers over our lips.

Tiptoeing to the front door, we opened it like true thieves. I pushed the lever down. We crept out the open door, softly closed it silently, and stepped to the ground.

Jeanie said, "Well, I guess we pulled that off."

"Sh…sh," I whispered, blowing the least amount of air out of my dry mouth, holding my right finger to my lips.

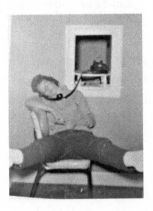

We crept around the front of the trailer to Marie's window, just thirty feet away and tapped it with "click, click, click" of our fingernails. Marie's face appeared as she pulled her curtains aside, with a look of fear, raised her window, swung her leg outside, and we helped her down. Three of us were now in the outside. She was a very obedient and compliant child, so this escapade was way out of her mind-set.

Having made it to the ground with my help, we hugged and moved through the moonlit night like panthers passing the sleepy trailers and locked cars.

We crossed Maple Street, crept through yards, picked apples off a neighbor's tree, crossed ditches, and talked in loud whispers incessantly. In three blocks, we arrived at Marsha's just as Myron came around the corner. Marsha's window was already open, so she slid out and dropped to the ground just like an acrobat!

Betty Lou and Will had been up since 11:30 p.m. and were waiting at Oak Street, by the sign, hunkered down. They appeared to be part of the shrubs and the sign!

All seven were together!

Our plan was seventh-grade simple. Just walk around, talk over the last few months, and years with old-time stories and remembrances. This was a last time together. It seemed to us that this could never happen again. What a time in the night air, privacy of darkness, and no one else around. Friends. Loving friendship and mystery.

But we had a problem. This time, we got too loud. We were having too much fun, and lights began to come on, and doors began to open as we ran to hide.

We couldn't be quiet enough now. An older lady, whom we called Mrs. Bad, who always fussed at we, kids, said with screechy voice, "I see you, little devils. I'll take care of you. I'm calling the police!"

We had been had! All of us ran toward Marsha's.

"We'll get there and say 'so long'," Myron said, as we flew in the night. A car turned the corner with a big light on the side of the door and was making circles, up and down, to try to find us!

"The cops!" I said. "Hit the dirt behind these bushes."

And we lay as flat as we could, holding our chuckling to a low tone, covering our mouths with wet hands from the wet grass.

"We'll be in jail tomorrow for life," poor Will said.

The copper's light skimmed over us, across our quivering backs, through the bushes.

"Thank God for the hedges," Will proclaimed in a loud whisper as the cops slowly crept by us. We knew all the policemen but still didn't want to get caught.

We lit out across the street, running through yards, and here comes the black-and-white police car and lights a-searching.

"Down," I cried, as all seven of us hit the wet grass.

Slowly, he drove by, and his big light missed us again. Up, we night crawlers took off.

"Just one more block," one of the girls said as Will gasped. Swinging through the air, he hadn't got low enough and got "hung" by a clothesline!

"My voice is messed up," Will squeaked out of his mouth. "I'm hoarse." And he was.

The poor boy was hurt. "We've got no time for this. Get up! Let's go!" Myron said, always a bit cynical, speaking through his teeth.

Gasping and choking, Will ran on, trying to keep up.

Marie, the good girl (really), whispered to me as we traveled in the dark. "We're going to spend the rest of our lives in jail!"

"No, we won't. It'll be okay," I faintly but tenderly said, as if I understood her dread. I did want to be good to mine and Jeanie's special friend.

Myron, the little dynamo, proclaimed, "We'll get a whipp'n' for this if we get caught, so I don't intend to get caught!"

"We're gonna make it. Now let's go!"

The cop came, one last time, surveying everything, in trees, over and through the hedgerows, the houses, the air, up and down shined his frantic light.

"The policeman must be mad," one of the boys voice from the back of us proclaimed.

We had learned to flatten ourselves like a lizard.

"Don't breathe," I told everybody, but we had to after running, jumping, and dodging clotheslines.

We crossed the last street, ran through the last yard, and came in a whirl to Marsha's open window.

All of us turned in silence to each other, seven wayfaring kids. "This is it, y'all. We'll write you from California."

"Let's call ourselves the Midnight Riders," Myron said, and we all said, "Yeah, yeah."

And, we were, yes, we were the "Midnight Riders!" I remember.

We hugged one another, said goodbyes, wiped a tear, pushed Marsha into her bedroom, looked at one another again, turned, and ran our separate ways. I only saw this adventuresome "clan" of friends one more time in the fall of '58. But you see, the love and thrill still abide.

Jeanie, Marie, and I swept home. We hugged Marie. We agreed one more time that we would be together again. She climbed through her raised window. I looked back at Marie's window one more time as Jeanie and I crept into our home on wheels. It was 2:18 a.m. We went to bed exhausted and fell asleep.

"Rise and shine! Breakfast is now being served in the diner," Dad said loudly and with glee.

It was 6:00 a.m. We ate scrambled eggs, hooked up our home to the green Ford truck, and I looked one last time at Marie's window. We headed to Memphis, Tennessee, ten hours away.

We looked longingly back at Gallatin with thoughts of our last night together with the "Midnight Riders."

We mentioned it a very few times to one another in whispered tones. It was still thrilling. It still is. Jeanie and I never told Mom and Dad until we were grown.

"We'll see each other soon," we seven had said.

"The Train Ride"

After leaving Betty Jo in California, we moved back to Memphis and into the famous Leahy's Tourist Court and Trailer Park on Summer Avenue. Dad was looking for a job and just thankful to be out of the desert and back to green country with trees. It was the spring of 1958 and staying for two weeks in this beautiful Tourist Court.

It seems, in fact, that the great author James Jones (1921–1972) wrote at least one of his classic novels *From Here to Eternity* while living at Leahy's in the early fifties. Did I see him? Did he pass through there while I was there? Did I see him? I'll guess I did.

Back in the early 1980s, I spent a night in Leahy's Court. The earlier times swept over me, wonderful.

We had a schoolless ball at Leahy's, clean, well-kept, and gorgeous.

The 1880s house, a swimming pool, and tourist cabins were a delight. The streets were laid out straight as an arrow and smooth. Each mobile home had its own lawn.

When we arrived at Leahy's, I went to the door of the old home with Dad as Mr. Leahy came to the door.

He graciously invited us to come in. The antiques, classic furniture, with historic pictures lining the walls, was amazing to a little trailer boy. It all looked expensive to me, and I guess it was. We got a spot, moved in, and Dad set about finding work.

We three older siblings walked the park daily, played ball, or whatever in the streets and waited for Dad to come home.

That's the way Dad was, a rolling stone, a great husband and father, a man of his word, a hard, faithful worker, and honest.

We didn't settle down just yet. That wouldn't happen until May of 1961 but settle down we did, and Mom would be expecting child number 5! Janice Marie came along with Mom's new home.

Mom had said, "This is enough."

Dad traded the Liberty for a brand-new home in Highland, Indiana, and we did settle down, but this didn't happen until another three good years passed.

But for now, we moved to Dundee, Illinois, into the trailer park where the giant snapping turtle was and the runaway tractor. Later my job at the mink ranch would happen.

Happy, our great traveling buddy was just up the road. Amazing to me that such good friends could travel part of the way with us, all the way or none at all but end up together. The world was so big yet so small.

While in Memphis at Leahy's, Dad had called Mr. Langford in Gallatin, and then the two women got on the phone.

"Mom, can I go see Jeanie and Larry?" Marie jumped in and inquired.

After a few minutes, they talked it through, and plans were made.

"Oh, Mom, good, good," Jeanie yelled out, and I said, "Good!" Marie left Nashville's great train station on a Saturday and arrived about 8:00 p.m. in Chicago. After almost a year of separation, the three of us had an exciting, loving reunion. Jeanie and Marie could talk up a storm endlessly then I would get a word or two in sideways every once in a while.

At breakfast on Sunday morning, before church, I said, "Dad, it's really important that we have some friends we can see. Do you understand?"

He looked at me with those searching brown eyes for a minute and replied, "Sure, it's like me and Rice."

"Thanks. I'll get the girls up."

We had a fantastic week. Marie was pretty, tall, and thin, very calm with a kind personality to match. Two years older than me and four older than Jeanie, we could set and chatter a long time, then go out and just fool around. We showed her the swamp where the turtle lived, the runaway tractor, and the mink ranch.

Jeanie was more mature than other twelve-year-olds, so she and Marie got along famously.

We danced to Fats Domino, Elvis, Little Richard, Jerry Lee Lewis, Jimmy Reed, and Doo-wop. Sitting out in the dark, we had a full moon and stars brilliant like fireballs in the sky.

"Let's dance."

And Marie said, "I wondered when you'd ask."

"How can we—?"

"We're so far apart!"

"Yeah, let's just let it be," my voice cracking.

That's the way God made me. "Let it be."

We did the "bop" and "two step" and laughed over everything.

"I love it here, and times going too fast," Marie said.

And it came to we three saying, "Go home with her!"

All the plans were made. Time flew.

"Mrs. Simpson, thank you for this time and allowing Larry and Jeanie to go home with me."

"Let's go. The train's waiting."

And away we went. Very little talking on the way.

"How are y'all going to make it away from home?" Mom asked.

"It won't be long."

I knew we'd miss home, but the week that lay ahead was too exciting to be sad.

David and Susan couldn't grasp the meaning of our being gone a week.

Dad just shrugged his shoulders, saying, "We'll see you next Saturday."

Mom wiped a tear.

The old Union Train Station was large, open, and noisy. People talking, saying goodbyes, and trains running in and out. The first announcement over the speaker made me jump as it made my ears ring.

"Look at that," I said as I pointed to a handsome older black gentleman shining shoes. The booth was dark wood but shiny with a dark maroon leather seat and a man in a suit relaxing while he "popped" the tattered, shining rag. He jerked and whipped the old multicolored rag right then left. I walked up close with my eyes wide open, and the gracious man said, "Son, do you want your shoes shined?"

"No, sir, I've got tennis shoes on, but thanks," I said as I continued focused on this special art.

When he spit on the rag, I jumped with amazement, turned to Dad, who said, "What about that?"

I just nodded several times.

Marvelously, he sang the blues, "At the Crossroad', "Ole Mattie," and "Baby Please Don't Go," jerking my mind to Randy's and John R. in Nashville.

Mom and Dad didn't want me to listen to WLAC at night, but I couldn't help it. With the radio in the bed, under the covers, David learned the blues, and I danced with my feet as I sang softly to my own soul.

"Let's go to Randy's," I said to Marie once in Gallatin.

"Why? Let's go."

Randy's Record shop was the world's largest mail-order record "shop" in the world. Randy had a couple of new rock and roll groups with a flavor of doo-wop mixed in come to the small shop and then play in the theater to a full house every time!

We were young, rowdy, and in love. Life was mystical.

In 1985, traveling through Gallatin, I visited Randy's, but it was fading away. I now have in my "stuff" the newspaper announcement that Randy was closing the next Saturday. As kids, we could never have imagined that Randy's, the world's largest mail-order store, could ever be closed.

Even as an adult, traveling at night, within two hundred to three hundred miles of Nashville, I could pick up John R. at night. John R. and the blues program finally ended in the 1970s. Randy's Record Shop closed its doors after forty-five years on August 15, 1991, after mailing out as many as two hundred thousand records world-wide in 1949 and five hundred thousand by 1950. Randy Wood, the owner of Randy's, started Dot Records in 1950 and, within six years, became competitive with the biggest names in music, Decca, Capital, RCA Victor, and Columbia. He sold "Dot" to Paramount Pictures in 1967.

Here we were, 1958, in Chicago, leaving on a train! We were headed for a week in rhythm and blues country, old friends, Gallatin's wonderful swimming pool and happiness! After emotional goodbyes, we loaded up.

The train ride was magic. We must have been traveling one hundred miles per hour. The telephone poles looked like toothpicks, the sky bluer, the clicking and clanking of the railroad tracks and a song far away, life in another time and dreams. I was still singing the blues, the story of the real basics of raw life, looking ahead to my midnight dreams, the people, the places of my dreams, and memories relived.

Jeanie was ecstatic, Marie just smiled, and I was about to twist my head off my shoulder, looking and twisting in every direction at the sights inside and outside the train.

The conductor came with an order pad for eats and drinks. People everywhere, all walks of life, rich ones, foreigners, and old ladies. A pretty blond-haired girl sat just across the aisle with a pink top, white shorts, flats, and a look at me that cut to my soul. "What if...?"

Behind us was a blind man I helped down the aisle and, of course, some crying babies!

I was rich! A world traveler! And awkward.

I drifted away to California, our undefeated basketball team, Betty Jo, Uncle LT, the spring flowers from just that spring in Inyokern, the mesas and plateaus in New Mexico, road signs to Tucumcari, and just swooning romantic bathing of people, places, and "what-ifs!"

But I was on "this" train, a little trailer boy.

"You're here. You love it. Life's a miracle. Thank you, Lord Jesus!" echoed in my emotional soul.

The Indiana farmlands, flat, green, and beautiful. We were flying away. Marie and Jeanie hadn't stopped their perpetual whispers and giggling.

What a sense of freedom, power, independence, and magic. It came all over me like very warm melting caramel. It was like driving in the truck with Dad, pulling our home behind us through Tennessee or Arizona or Oklahoma with a free spirit both lonesome and loving.

"Don't you feel like it's just a wonder, a dream, that we could be doing this, together?" I said.

To which Marie replied simply, "Yes," and just looked at me.

The girls dozed off. Marie awoke and softly asked, "Where are we?"

To which I replied, "In the world, flying."

She was swooning also.

Jeanie aroused. "I'm hungry."

So we ordered chicken salad with grapes, milk, and apple pie. Oh, we were so independent, so grown-up.

"Let's talk about this week and what we can do next week," Jeanie said, so we started in, always interrupting each other, not with rudeness but happy excitement. It was all right.

Arriving at the Nashville "Union Station," we were bursting with anticipation. There stood Billy and Mrs. Langford. She was waving like trying to get a nest of bees off herself with a grin as big as a yawning cat, one as big as she could give away. Being a very refined and true Southern lady, she was kind and warm, waiting for our hugs.

"See you next time," the conductor said as we shook his hand, and I told the blond girl with whom I had exchanged boy and girl looks that I hoped I would see her again.... But, we lived worlds apart, just people passing by in the mystic of time and space, ready for the next adventure.

We had a great time that week living in Marie's home, going swimming, seeing old friends, listening to music and dancing, having friends to their home. Marie's mother cooked wonderful Southern meals, and she even took us to the movies in Nashville and saw the hilarious comedy *No Time for Sergeants* at the Grand Ole Tennessee Theater, doing everything she could to give us a special story.

She did. Here it is, sixty-one years later, and I'm celebrating this all over again.

Saturday came. "Going home day" came as we rode to the great old station in silence, just a word or two now and then.

"There it is, your train," Mrs. Langford said.

Marie said, "We see it," with a sense of finality.

We hugged and kissed, as Jeanie and I said, "Y'all were wonderful. We love you. We'll never forget. Let's do it again."

We never did.

Mrs. Langford and Marie stood outside our window with faint smiles, wet eyes, and memories as they watched us roll away.

"We'll do it soon." But it never happened, nor ever again.

Thankfully, I did go back to visit Mr. and Mrs. Langford's several times just for a few hours. After Mr. Bill deceased and Mrs. Langford moved, I visited with her three or four times. My last trip to just drop in on her the house was vacant and empty. A neighbor told me, "Mrs. Langford died a few months ago. What a wonderful lady."

Time won't let us stand still. We've gotta roll with it. Tears must be turned into joy, and that's why I tell this story with haunting joy!

The years are gone, haven't seen Marie for sixty-two years, but my soul yet fills with joy.

A trailer boy gets it—joy.

"UP Date, UP Date!"

Jeanie and I have finally located Marie and visited with her in mine and Sandy's home twice. Another gathering is planned. The story, the magic is not over. Marie told us her mother had found out about our midnight escapade, saying, "It was the only thing I ever did wrong." I believe her. She was always a "good girl." Marie brought a few pictures to our home from that trip. Four are used in "No Excuses." We had never seen them before. (thanks, Marie, how wonderful)

"The Corn Shucks, a Shotgun, and Dad"

"Walker…Walker."

"Yes, ma'am."

"I'm so thankful to be back in Gallatin."

Dad looked over his reading glasses to digest what Mom had said. Having just gotten home, his mind yet preoccupied. He was still lost in "what had been" versus "what is now."

In a soft, half-quiet voice, Dad replied, "Well, Vicky, I need to talk to you about what I've decided."

Knowing that the short stay in Nashville of three to four weeks, while school had started, and now about three weeks in Gallatin, this would be a shocker! After the summer of '58, train ride from Dundee to Nashville with Marie, we would return for this short stay.

"Well," he said again, "well, sweetheart…" (Dad liked to call the love of his life "sweetheart."), "this job is going to run out soon, and a 'company man' had told me they could use me in Indiana."

"Indiana? Walker, that means our fifth move this year. I don't know how long me and the kids can take this." Mom had begun to wonder this very deeply.

Taking her in his arms, as I snuggled down as deep in the mixed-colored sofa as I could to not be noticed, I knew this was a time to remember. "I'm sorry. You know I don't want to do this, but I've got to make more money, and you knew this would be a short one."

They hugged as he held her up tight, and she said in her usual stoic manner, "We'll make the best of it."

"When do we leave?"

That was Mother working with Dad, the situation, love for him, and honor.

"A week from this Friday."

"Okay!"

At supper with all of us around the table, Mom said, "Oh, Walker, where're we movin?"

"Indiana, Richmond."

"Okay, the cornfields should be in full color with the cool air, and, kids, we'll start packing next week!"

We moved from Gallatin for the third and last time, leaving Marie, her family, and the Rice's. Never living by Marie or Happy again, they remained loving memories for a lifetime!

Richmond was a very eventful stay, which I will gladly speak of on a better and later day.

Arriving in late October, we kids settled into new classmates, church, and a girl I could never forget.

We moved from Richmond in July of 1959 after nine memorable months and a life changer.

"Are we moving *again*?" eight-year-old Susan asked, and David ever "Mr. Picnic" said, "We'll have a new picnic," and it was so.

Arriving, after a brisk three hours, in hot air, 111 miles away, we drove down the classic main street in Grove City, Ohio. "Home of the Greyhounds," it read on a big billboard. The old clock on the courthouse was changing twelve sharp tones, and it was noon.

"Look for Howard street," and Mom gleefully said, "There it is. Right there between those two big flowering maples."

Those giant, wide maples covered the street.

Dad turned the sixty-six-foot rig, taking a wide, wide turn, drove one and a half or two miles, turning to the right, then left in front of and beside an old white 1890s two-story home with a long vegetable/fruit stand. The green Ford pulled us down to the trailer park on the right.

This park of about twelve trailers would be our home for the next few months; after all, how could we know?

Football

Fall came late that year with above-average heat. School was to start the first of September, so I went to get registered, meet the football coach, and see if I could join the team already in practice.

"Sir, can I come in and talk about practice?"

"Sure, but first, you need to find out if I'll let you join the team!"

"Yes, sir."

I just looked at him, wordless.

Coach Martin was a former Ohio State defensive tackle under the renowned Woody Hayes, known for his style of football "three yards and a cloud of dust." Run and run some more until you beat the opponent down and win. True power football.

This young coach, in his first season as a head coach, was six feet tall, about three feet wide, weighing in at 285 pounds. He was a load! And he coached like he looked. It was three yards and a cloud of dust! I reported to the team, got my gear the next day, and joined the forty to fifty boys.

Football practice continued in the hot heat at ninety degrees, getting ready for game one. I gave blocking and tackling dummies all I had. The coaches knew nothing about me, and at five feet nine and 145 pounds, I didn't draw much attention.

But I gave everything my all and finished second or third in our twenty- and forty-yard sprints daily. The coaches saw I could run.

But I got serious attention when practicing blocking coming out of the backfield on the right side. My technique was good from Gallatin days, and I was willing to lay my body out, both flying forward or a side body block. Meeting the first defender, keeping a full head of steam, I went low and hit the defender with all my might.

Down the defender went and our left, halfback ran past us, flying. The defensive backfield coach hollered, "That's the way to do it! Did you see that?"

The offensive coach took me aside after practice, saying, "You can play football. Blocking is where it all begins."

In the coaches and players meeting after practice, the defensive backfield coach told the team about my block and said, "That's playing football."

After that, I was on the coaches' radar screen. Oh yes, and he even said, "He's the best blocker on this team right now because of technique and willpower."

I knew I had to show them, to get to play.

On Thursday night, we had our first junior varsity game with a strong school from Columbus. They were big and bad.

I intended to keep impressing the coaches.

"Are you ready?" the coach asked.

"Yes, sir."

The opportunity came in the second quarter. Our quarterback called out the play, "Swing pass to the right. Larry, it's coming to you!"

"Get it to me!" I grunted as if it wasn't anything to me.

I was to run right straight toward the sideline, in five or six strides turn to the quarterback.

"The ball will be in the air before you turn your head," our quarterback said.

I did it. I turned to head downfield then looked at the quarterback, and the ball was already in the air!

"Jimmy, you're a great quarterback," I told him later in the locker room with "juices" running high.

"Yeah, I know," the confident boy said. "You get open. I'll get it to you!"

As I turned, I thought, *Yeah, we'll see*, and sure enough, the ball was one second from my "sure" hands.

Jimmy said, "I've got fire on the ball!"

He did!

A little behind me, I turned back on the dead run 'cause I didn't care about the defensive back and snagged the spinning new football with my left-hand fingers and pulled the ball in, tucked it away, and saw only two of their players in front of me—boys from Columbus! I turned the speed on and was in full blast in three steps.

"Run over this guy," my brain reported to me as I headed toward the first guy, hit him straight on, and he rolled over himself.

"Number one," I whispered.

Cranking back up to full speed, I faked the next defensive back to the right. He fell down as I swung and danced back left. I ran past the "faked" guy. Turning on the afterburner, I crossed the finish line eighty yards later! Six points, players all over me, and the coach hollering, "That's what I'm taking about...," then settled back down to a stern, "Good job."

After a break for both teams, we took the field, warmed up for ten minutes, then we kicked off and played defense. The Columbus team was pumped up, took the ball in nine or ten plays into the end zone, and now really fired up.

Two series later, we had held them on defense, and they had to punt the ball from about their forty-yard line.

"Simpson, remember, concentrate first on catching the ball, tuckin' it in, then run."

"Yes, sir."

The ball was high, the sun fading in the west with a glare in my eyes, but I received the punt, did what the coach said, looked up, and my blockers were knockin' players out of the way and a couple down. I took off with the ball tucked away, swerved to my right, cut back to the left, faked another guy, looked up, and saw an open field.

"Nobody's gonna catch me now!" I said out loud to myself.

Because of my good "blockers," I flew into the end zone after a seventy-five-yard run!

Being flogged by my teammates as we walked to the sideline, the head coach asked, "Why didn't you tell me you could run?"

"You didn't ask," I ecstatically replied.

I was earning my way to varsity playing time.

"How did the rest of your season go?" David, my good brother, asked the other day.

"Well, by seasons end, I had started every junior varsity game, offense and defense, and even started two varsity games."

The Challenge

Our new head coach was tough and meant to make us tough. He installed a "challenge" whereby a player on, say, the third string could challenge a player in the same position on second team. It was called the "blocking and hitting challenge."

Both players would get in the down position, two feet apart, then hit and block each other. When one of the players made the other one "give up," they were the winner.

Our third team, "halfback" (running back), a junior at five feet eleven and 169 pounds, challenged me.

"I'm not doing this against you, but I want to be the second string tailback. Don't hold it against me, but I am going to beat you."

"Okay, it's all right."

I did like Gary. I didn't want to do this "against" him, but I did like a challenge and had to win.

That Tuesday after practice, the coaches gathered players around as Gary and I got in the "down" position, one set of fingers were on the wet grass. "I don't mean to lose. I was not going to get beat. I would not quit, and I would hit as hard as I could, every time," I was telling myself all that day. I visualized myself hitting him hard enough and quick enough to wear him out.

I knew I was quicker, but he was twenty-four pounds heavier. I thought if I could hit him first, I was going to win.

The whistle blew. We hit. We hit again. Every thirty seconds, we hit each other. The coaches and players urging us on.

"Come on, Larry. Come on, Gary," and we hit and hit again and hit again.

Both of us were tired, out of breath, determined, and gave it our all. The Lord, using my dad and others, taught me to never give up. He had put in me a never-say-die spirit.

I was not going to quit. Neither was Gary.

I hit as hard as I could time after time. Sweat was blinding our eyes. Muscles were cramping. Blood ran from my elbows, fingers, and an eyebrow. His nose and lip was covered with wet and dried blood. *Would he never quit?* I thought.

"The silver metal whistle was becoming more shrill, loud, menacing, and a cruel enemy, as it blew us into battle, time after time," I told my good brother.

He just wagged slowly his head east to west with one hand on his hip.

After fifty-one or two whistle blows, I knew I still had more than old Gary. I could smell the win, the kill. I got a second or third wind. My confidence swelled as we both gasped for air.

I was able to stay more aggressive, firing off the line first. I knocked him down and drilled him into the ground. My determination was to get set up first, fire off the line first, and to get up first. It worked on Gary's weary brain.

Maybe just one more time! We both stood gasping for air. *Just another time or two*, I thought. He was almost whipped. I was going to "whip" him one more time. I was not going to let him whip me.

We got down, arms quivering, breath steaming heavenward, and through my helmet over my face guard as I looked upward. I needed some help.

The whistle, the coaches, our buddies, Gary, myself seemed to slow down into a rhythmic, bloody dreamlike collision. I flew with one last gasp of hot air, coiled like a mighty mountain lion, and struck my good opponent.

Gary grunted. He lay motionless, except for the urgent gasps of fall air as I landed on him.

With courage, my teammate said with gushing air from his lungs, a desperate sound, "You win."

After almost thirty minutes of violent, one man on one man, conflict, the challenge was over. I helped Gary get up. We put our red, wet hands on each other's shoulders and shook hands.

I don't know what Gary learned, but I renewed my inner knowledge that "a man has to do what a man has to do…all the time." That's life. "Keep on keeping on," "never say die," and know what you can't walk around.

Randolph Scott, the great Western actor and my favorite, in two of his 1950s Westerns, said, "There's some things a man can't walk around." John Wayne called him "Randy." Thanks, Randy.

Thankfully, I started two varsity games and gained almost a hundred yards per game on the junior varsity squad. I loved those guys, those tough times, the thrill of the game, and they took me in, just a little trailer boy.

"Now the Corn Shocks and a Shotgun"

In early November, on a frosty Saturday morning, after our last football game, I got up early, about 6:00 a.m., before the family and sneaked outdoors.

Jeanie roused and said, yawning, "Where are you going?"

"Out to see the world. You wanna go?"

Breathlessly from loss of air and energy from raising up in the bed, she said, "No…no…I'll stay here," as she fell, full weight back into the covers.

The air was cool. Tony, my dog, crawled out of her house. The sun was just rising, the sky becoming blue, a slight breeze and a heart full of wonder. We had won the second game of a 2–7, (two–seven!) season. Football was over. Now a new life.

Tony looked at me as she yawned and seemed to say with her head slightly tilted to the left, "What's next?" Wandering through the trailer park, up the small bank at the end of the park, I strolled with Tony into the woods, inhaling the crisp fall air. She sniffed every hole in the ground or tree and me feeling tired from the night before. Yet like Robin Hood with his Merry Men of old, I was free.

After a short while, being about half conscious, I came to a cornfield, and behold, a wonderment! Yes, I had seen this before, but as can happen sometimes, the sight gave me a new sense of amazement. Amazement of nature, farmers, crops, designs, and wisdom all seen through the barbed wire fence.

Corn stalks! Corn stalks tied together, looking like Navajo Teepees I'd seen in New Mexico. What a sight. "How many?" I breathed out. Fifty, a hundred, two hundred? I counted half the field, and there were seventy-five! Farmers art, knowledge, and "play" objects!

I saw them as football players to be tackled, blocked, and sidestepped. I galloped back home.

The family was up, and breakfast cooking.

"Son, where have you been?"

"Dad, I've walked through the woods and found a beautiful farm."

"How do ya feel after last night?"

"Awe, I've got a couple of bruises. A big lineman knocked me for a loop!"

"You play a man's game. You're gonna get roughed up."

"Yes, sir."

We had ham, eggs, and biscuits with grits. It smelled so good, tasted better, but I could hardly wait to get outside.

"Jeanie, let's go for a walk."

"Sure, is it cold?"

"Cool," I said. "I'm wearin' a sweatshirt. Just wear enough to stay warm."

"We'll be back in a little while. Is that okay?"

"Have you got your beds made?"

"Sure, Mom. We both had done some of it but left the rest for David and Susan."

Dad said, "Duty first."

Away we flew, trying to get away from the trailer so Mom and Dad couldn't call us back! We strolled through the park then into the woods. I led her to the farm and its decorated cornfield. Decorated with football players or old brown Indian's or German's standing so erect.

"Let's go under the barbwire. Looks like everybody is still in," I said, not considering how early farmers got up.

"What you gonna do?" Jeanie asked me with that "I caught you" look and voice.

"Play football!"

"What!"

"These corn shocks are players, and I'm gonna take 'em down!"

"No, no, you'll, uh, we'll get caught and have to go to jail."

"It'll be okay," I hoped but said it earnestly.

Although stiff from the game last night, I was going to wipe this team out.

I flew toward the first and ran through it. I blocked the next. I was winning. I tackled the next, yelling as I flew. I smashed another and another.

"Larry, are you sure this is okay?"

"Yeah, it'll be all right."

I was in my glory. These players couldn't stop me. Besides, I didn't think it would matter, or I didn't care.

I took my invisible football in my right arm and ran around one with the best fake I'd ever made. I destroyed the cornstalk quarterback and ran over their big defensive linemen.

"Go get 'em," Jeanie cried out as I got her all "glossed" up in my fantasy.

Players lined the field, laying beaten, destroyed by the best football player in Ohio! Jeanie was laughing at the destructive sight as I blasted another. Fifteen lay smashed, and then...a bold big voice rang out across the cornfield.

"What'a you doin'? Your destroying my corn shocks!" Then he disappeared into the barn.

Jeanie and I stood looking at each other, stunned, caught! Destroying property! It dawned on me...I had surely done wrong. Yes, after the fact, it dawned on me.

The barn door flew open, and here came the crusty ole farmer. I walked toward him, realizing my crude, selfish deed and wanting to apologize, but he had something in his hand.

"A shotgun!"

I bellowed out to Jeanie, "Let's go! A double-barreled shotgun!"

It looked just like Granddaddy Eddins Parker's brother's double-barreled twelve-gauge shotgun, dated 3-26-1875.

"I'll teach you a lesson." His face as red as an apple.

I grabbed Jeanie by the hand, running as fast as I could, jumping over the slain players and mounds of plowed earth with another human attached to me.

The good ole farmer was running as fast as he could, but we were stretching the lead. Getting to the rusty barbed wire fence, we slipped under it, both of us tearing a hole in our sweatshirts. The farmer got closer with the double-barreled shot gun in hand. He wanted us bad.

Sliding under the fence, we ran through the woods, dodging trees, bushes, logs, holes, and everything in our way.

Jeanie was crying out, "Let's go! Let's go!" until she had no breath.

We gained a little ground when he had to negotiate the fence.

Jeanie describes it like this: "Larry was running so fast with me attached to his hand that I was only landing on every other foot every few feet, flying through the air!"

She was right, but the farmer in his bib overalls wouldn't quit. The anger had lit his face on fire besides the running. Breathlessly, he tried to catch us, "I'll get you," and we understood him!

The shotgun looked like it was ten feet long with three or four barrels. It was well used, so I knew he could use it. He yelled (probably to scare us), "I'm gonna shoot you. Yeah, I'll do it," and we ran the faster still.

We flew past my favorite big maple tree, down the bank, and past the first five trailers headed to ours. Jeanie was holding on for life with one foot then the other striking the earth every few feet. Basically, she was mostly flying through midair.

Arriving at our home, I yelled, "Dad, a man is chasing us with a shotgun!"

Already being outside at his green Ford truck, he turned and looked toward the coming "shootist."

Jeanie and I ran indoors, gasping for air, and looking out a window. Dad saw the absurd spectacle.

"Dad, do you see him?" I shouted.

"I'll take care of this!" my faithful father thundered with his deep Mississippi brown eyes, flashing fire underneath his furrowed brow, which I had seen before. It was very menacing.

Dad said loud and furious, "Stop! I'll take care of my kids, and you put the gun down. If you don't, I'll take it away from you and whip you with it."

Dad meant it and could do it. The good ole farmer stopped and panting, trying to get out of his mouth what he had seen and how destructive it was. Dad calmed him down and assured him it was wrong, and he would handle it.

Speaking to us through the screen door, Dad said, "Larry! Jeanie! Come out here and get this right!"

Feeling more safe now, we came out, apologized to him, and said we didn't realize how bad it was. Still, a little aggravated, he told us how he used that for the cows, calves, and his bull, as well as fertilizer.

I explained that it was not Jeanie's fault that I had led her to do this. I was ashamed even as Jeanie was and said we'd come back and stand the "football players" back up on their feet.

He graciously allowed us to do that.

From then on, when we saw him, we just waved. Dad felt that running from an armed gunman was lesson enough, and he lectured us on the matter. Thank you, Dad.

I learned that you cannot have a good time at someone else's expense and to think through things before you do them.

That night at the supper table, Mother prayed for me and Jeanie that we would be kinder and more thoughtful. I think the Lord heard her prayer.

Well, I mostly learned to be more thoughtful...mostly.

We had had another exciting adventure.

Little trailer boys do that.

No excuses. Just do it, do it right, but do it.

Story 7

Jobs

A Trailer Boy Needs to Work

One of the great blessings of the life God gave me was being taught to work.

The trailer life gave me the occasions to get jobs. Even though I was involved in sports, I still wanted to work. So I got jobs…with a little help from Mom. She was always looking for work for me. What could I do? I worked!

Yards to Cut

At the beginning of summer on North Water Street in Gallatin in 1955, while I was approaching eleven, Dad said, "Son, would you like to make some money?"

"Sure!"

"Okay, then I'm going to buy you a lawn mower, and you can go door to door to get your yards."

"Okay, Dad." I exclaimed with both excitement and fear, a little. *Talk to people at their door? I'm only almost eleven! Talk to adults? Cut grass? My own lawn mower?* Nervously, I got my mind ready. *Money? Yeah, that too!*

In a few days, Dad pulled the green '53 Ford up behind our trailer. I saw something tied in the bed.

"Son, come see what I've got."

Over to the back of the truck, I trotted and saw it. There it was—my own lawn mower! A push-blade mower with five or six blades. Yes, I had to push it and keep the blades sharpened with a file! I was to get a good schooling on work! We were partners in business. Dad was beaming.

My own lawn mower and shiny in most places! The tires did look worn. Some of the blades were brown.

"Let's get it off, son," Dad, with a slight grin, said. So we untied it. "I'll get on this side."

"Well then, I'll get on this side," Dad said, and we lifted the slightly yellow and mostly "brown" machine off to the ground.

"It's yours, son," Dad proudly said as I looked at it as if it was a mysterious space machine.

Dad went inside, smiling.

"All mine," I breathed to myself. Looking at it a long while, I studied all its shapes.

I sat down in the grass on a little bald off "skint" piece of earth. My eyes slowly went from top to bottom then side to side. I was quiet and still in reverence of my new machine.

From bottom to top, handlebars to blades, I beheld this marvelous yellow masterpiece.

Sparkling light, in yellow beams, seemed to reach toward me. I pulled my legs, crossed into Navajo-style, bringing my feet up close to my bottom. I seemed lost in this cloud of wonder.

I slowly sailed off to a blissful moment of a vision of cutting a very high stand of grass at the doctor's house. How easy my new mower took the thick very green grass down, slinging it many feet away. None of the grass seemed to hit me. My mower was so strong.

A humming tune rolled out from the blades as they happily, so easily rolled along, making the giant lawn like a soft, perfect blanket.

Soft clouds surrounded me in the sparkle and comforting music, my mower.

"Larry, Larry, lunch is ready," this loud disturbing voice invaded my sweet, mysterious travel.

I jerked to awareness, quickened by my ordinary life, felt the drooling in the corners of my lips, and the disappointment in my plain, ordinary life.

My mower was still there. I patted the green rubber handles as I walked by and said, "Your name will forever be 'Sky-rider.'" "Sky-rider" it was.

After lunch, I stood close to my own mower. I turned it over, studying all the workings, and pushed it around for a few minutes.

But I had no yards to cut! How could I be in business with no yards to cut?

"Son, go up and down the street, knock on doors, and tell the neighbors about your lawn mower service," Dad said in an instructive voice to get me to earn their business.

But, alas, house after house, no one wanted my skills. Finally, across the street from the trailer park, Mr. Jones, about one hundred years old, said, "Yes, sir, you can cut my yard."

Running back across the street to home, I told Mom of the good news while Dad found out that evening.

The next day, I was to start.

"When you come tomorrow, I will go over the yard with you."

"Yes, sir!" I waited a little too late. It was about ninety-five degrees in a southern summer, and "I started late!" Pushing the lawn mower with one hand across North Water Street with a jug of ice water in the other. I proudly, almost boastfully, got there and began to push what I would later call the "blasted contraption!"

The yard was rough, with several bushes to mow around and besides it hadn't been cut in three weeks.

Of course, the grass was thin, tall, and dried out but still with a little dew on it. I had to make double trips in most spots. By now the sweat was dropping from my head, face, chin, armpits, and points below. I pushed, backed up, and pushed again. My arms got tired, my back hurt, my feet felt sore, but push, I did.

By the time I quit, two and a half hours had passed, my water was gone, and I was worn out. But it was bred into me to never quit. At age seventy-five, I guess it won't ever leave me.

"Son, I'm glad you did your job, Dad will be proud."

Dad had started to teach me to work. I guess I'll never stop, and by the way, after summer was over, I had $32, enough to by my own school clothes. Thanks, Dad.

The Mink Ranch

After working for my good friend Loris, who asked me to help him with his paper route in Gallatin and then the great job cleaning the trailer park in 1957 and 1958 in Inyokern, I was a worker. We moved for a few months to Dundee, Illinois. We lived on a gravel road. As it was given to me to do, I would be out adventuring around and seeing the countryside. Topping the hill to the west, I came to a strange-looking farm covered with cages standing on four posts about four feet off the ground.

While approaching the cages, I saw some dark movements in the cage. A little scared, I slowly walked up to the first cage. What was in there? A rat, a cat, a muskrat?

"It launched at me, and I jumped three feet high," I later told Mother.

As I was standing there, feeling a little strange with extreme inquisitiveness, a voice boomed out, "Hey, what are you doing?"

Startled, with a slight shake, I looked around and saw a tall man and said, "Looking!"

The big man walked up to me and said gruffly, "Do you know what that is?"

With a squeaky voice, "No, sir."

The man almost immediately took a liking to me. I think because I said, "No, sir." He softened up. Yankees weren't used to people saying "sir," I guess.

After telling me his name and that he owned "this place," he said, "These are mink. This is a mink ranch."

"Minks?" I asked. "What do you do with them?"

"Why, I send them off and have mink coats made."

"Wow" was all I could say, but he (I think his last name was Massey) said, "You want a job?"

"Yes, sir. I do. What would I be doing?"

With a very brisk reply, he said, "Cleaning the cages, putting out fresh water, giving the mink food, and whatever else there is to do."

We shook hands as I said, "Thanks," ready to return tomorrow at 8:00 a.m.

"By the way, what did you say your name is?"

"Larry."

"Good, you don't call the mink 'minks.' You just say mink.' Got it?"

"Yes, sir!" I turned briskly. "See you in the morning."

But he was already gone.

When I went home, Mom and Dad were very pleased.

"Son, you'll make a man of yourself yet," while Mother said, "Be careful."

By eight o'clock the next morning, I left with a packed lunch and a small water jug filled with ice water. Mom fixed a big breakfast because she wouldn't think of letting us go without a hot home-cooked meal. That was my home. Mom hugged me tight as I left. That was my mother.

That day was spent with Mr. Massey teaching me how to manage the mink with big, thick gloves that went up to the elbows. When he opened a cage to put his hand in, the mink immediately attacked his glove as if it was a mortal enemy. Such sounds I'd never heard with angry teeth justa chomping and clicking away. But they couldn't bite through the glove. The mink seemed very angry and unthankful to get fresh food and water. You *talk about bite the hand that feeds you*, literally.

"By the way, payday is every two weeks."

Shivers went up my spine as I thought about doing it. Within an hour, I was doing it under Mr. Massey's dark eyes, but I jumped every time my hand was attacked. I wondered if any moment they might chomp my arm off!

Mr. Massey asked, "Are you afraid?" I said.

"Sure am."

"You'll get used to it," he replied as he turned to walk away, seeming to like my honesty.

Within a couple of days, I knew where everything was: feed, soap, water, gloves, shovels, rakes, picks, and everything else necessary. I was adapting quickly.

I worked three and a half hours per day at 0.95 cents per hour. Learning all the ropes, helping in every way I could, I was excited to get my first paycheck after two weeks.

Figuring out that I would get paid $33.25, I was excited and loved the job. I even learned to like my boss! Besides, I knew it wouldn't be long before I had my own mink ranch!

Playing center field on an American Legion Baseball team, I made the all-star team, but I was more enthused about my paycheck. Even the adventure of the runaway tractor with Jeanie and Happy didn't daunt my paycheck excitement.

Two weeks passed, and I was early for all my mink friends. Figuring that Mr. Massey would pay me early, I kept peeking around every corner. No Mr. Massey. Eleven thirty came, and here came my boss in his old 1940 Chevrolet pickup with the fenders flopping in the wind, the dust flying, he squealed to a stop.

"Larry, here's your first paycheck."

He seemed happy. I trotted over to the window. He handed me a white envelope, and I could tell it had a couple of sheets of paper in it.

He said, "I'll see you Monday. Hit a home run for me. You're doing great."

I took off flying up the gravel road for that half mile that seemed longer than before. I didn't open the envelope because I wanted Mama to open it with me.

Mom was breathless too, knowing how excited I was, and she was proud. As my three siblings stood close by, the envelope came flying apart as Mom tore off the end. She reached inside, pulled out the check. Her hazel eyes bulged, and then she showed it to me.

"$30.27," I exclaimed.

Mom said with her teeth gritted, "He stole some of your money," as I sank down on the sofa.

She said, "He'll not get away with this, son. You can't work for a man that will cheat you."

I did shed a tear, a brief little one.

When Daddy came home, he tried to reason with Mom, but it didn't work. She was too aggravated, feeling I was betrayed.

Monday morning, I went to my wonderful mink ranch and told Mr. Massey goodbye.

"Why?" he asked.

"Because you didn't pay me my whole money."

Mr. Massey said with hurt, "Son, I had to take out taxes."

After a few more words of explanation, I said, "I'm sorry, I'm pullin' up stakes," as I thought "that's what Daddy would say."

He expressed regret, disappointment, and hurt. "I sure am sorry." It's all he could get out of his forlorn face.

We shook hands as I said, "Thanks," and we said goodbye.

Yes, neither Dad nor Mom nor I knew taxes had to be taken out for a kid.

But it didn't matter. We were "pulling up stakes" and moving to Nashville anyway.

I've always been sorry. Neither Mom nor I knew about taxes. I am thankful for Mom's strength and Mr. Massey's trust in me. I've always felt I mistrusted my good boss, but I learned some lessons.

Richmond, Indiana, and Mr. Tuggle's Furniture Store

Pulling out of Dundee with the sun barely peeking through the sky and over the earth, I was both sad and thankful for the mink ranch. What a job!

Mom and Dad were stand-up people for what they believed was right. I knew that. But I wished I had worked a little longer. A $30.27 every two weeks paycheck is a lot of money for a thirteen-year-old boy!

Arriving, after the two-day trip because we could only travel about fifty to fifty-five miles per hour with the fifty-foot-long turquoise-and-white home on wheels, we were happy. You see we were always home, and Mom made it feel that way. A ham sandwich with lettuce, tomatoes, and mayonnaise was wonderful on the side of those two-lane highways—with iced tea, of course!

Once in Nashville, Dad found a parking space at Hendersonville Trailer Park on Hendersonville Pike. The trailer park was new and the nicest trailer park we had every stayed at with almost two hundred parking spaces.

There was a famous Grand Ole Opry star, Little Jimmy Dickens, living a few spots down from us, and we got a glimpse of him every once in a while. He always grinned and said, "Good day."

One Friday in early September, the park put on a dance. The building was full. Playing all those great "doo-wop" and "rock and roll" songs, the night was magic. I was the new kid, but I didn't care. I went to dance, and dance I did. As the night flew by, I kept noticing a beautiful blond girl, and she seemed to notice me. As she chattered with another sweet Southern girl, she would glance and look at me, but I was already staring at her.

I could wait no longer. I had to ask her to dance. She agreed, and we danced and danced until 10:00 p.m. In the restroom, Ron, my neighbor, asked, "Do you know who that is?"

"No."

"That's the daughter of either Lester Flats or Earl Scrugs of the Grand Ole Opry!"

"What?"

It scared me a little, but I liked her. We talked over everything. We took to each other quickly, badly. With our hearts "feelin' it" like a dream, the dance came to a close.

She and I had to say goodbye, promising to see each other again, soon. But we never did—to this day.

We lived there two more weeks and didn't even start school while waiting on Dad's work and a place to live.

I waited at home until the boys came home from school, and we played football. Nobody could catch me. No one could tackle me. *I was "boss,"* I thought.

"We're going to Gallatin. There's a place for us in Langfords," Dad said.

All of us yelped and jumped.

Within a few days, we once again and, for the last time, moved to Gallatin. Old friendships were renewed, one last time—yes, one last time.

Marie, Jeanie, and I reviewed our midnight sneak out, our marvelous train trip, dancing in her living room, the Gallatin pool, and all such things. These precious things would not be revisited together again until March 2019.

Feeling quite confident in my football skills, I walked into the head coach's office, and he said, "Can I help you?"

I said, "Yes, sir, would you like to have a good halfback?"

The coach replied, "Who is he?"

"Me!"

He looked me up and down, kind of chuckling. Coach Smith said, "Be in the locker room at 3:00 p.m., and I'll have your equipment ready."

"Thanks" came out of my mouth with sincerity. He didn't get it.

For several days in full pads, I did the drills as heartily as I could, paid attention in meetings, and hoping for a chance to show this great speed of which I had so boldly spoken of. I still remember the aggravation on his face.

I felt very assured that the coach would be impressed with my jitterbug fakes and have me ready pretty quick to start at halfback.

But apparently, the coach had not gotten over my brashful self-introduction. Why should he? Rude, disrespectful behavior digs deep.

"Simpson."

"Yes, sir."

"Here's your chance to be an all-star."

"Okay, thanks, I'm ready."

"Really, ready?" the coach asked with a twinkle in his.

"Yes, sir!"

"Go in at defensive right cornerback and show me…SHOW ME!" he said, pumping his fist!

I didn't notice until it came to me after the impending violent event a few moments away, but all the players had gathered up close and tight. The coaches were standing shoulder to shoulder with a stare of glee.

The practice field was small, so the sight would be clear to all.

On the first fateful play, I lined up at "right corner." I set up for the play as sweat began to roll, and my knees got weak. The lineman came trotting out of the huddle, blowing air like a mad bear. The quarterback got under center. The three running backs were lined up in the "T" formation.

The defensive lineman were digging their cleats into the earth; the linebackers were moving right to left and back again.

"Hut-Hut…Hut!" the quarterback barked.

I heard the ball slap the quarterbacks hands. He turned to his right and stuck the ball into the right halfback's belly. His arms went around and under the ball, and he turned on "his" speed.

I took a step forward in case I had to help tackle Billy Joe, and suddenly, shockingly, the defensive linemen separated, and here came the six-foot, 195-pound, all-state halfback. He streamed and steamed through the gigantic hole the retreating lineman had made.

Oh no! He headed straight for me. I was in mortal shock. I gathered myself, got ready to make the tackle, and "boom," he hit me dead straight head-on as my helmet flew off my poor head. He was too fast and too powerful. I never even got my hands up to his body, let alone tackle him. Billy Joe grunted as he hit me. I could feel and hear and see his new cleats coming down on me as I blacked out from a "real" football players lick. I learned my lesson.

As I struggled to get up and made it to all fours, then twos, the coach running out, asked, "You okay?"

"Shhhuuurrreee...," I squeezed out of my crushed and "deflated" body. My confidence so unfounded had mislead me. I had tricked myself!

"Son, I had to learn you a lesson!"

Breathlessly, I murmured, "Thanks, Coach. I'll never forget, and I'm moving next week to Richmond, Indiana!"

I learned a lesson in over self-confidence, respect, proper decorum, and know your opponent. Thanks, Coach.

After only four weeks in our beloved Gallatin, I left my old friends for the last time.

We loaded up and headed for our new destination. My mind filled with the lesson the all-state halfback, the head coach, and humility had taught me.

We told the Langford's goodbye, for the last time with tears and pulled out just at daybreak the next morning and headed for Richmond, Indiana, and Dad's new job.

It's what we knew. Such is the life of a little trailer boy, and he can have no excuses.

But he must learn his lessons!

Maybe, my newfound humility would create a new story.

Tuggles

Novelty happens sailing the highways. Many places and many people evolve into many unique encounters.

As Mom drove into Richmond with all four kids, Dad having gone ahead, a most unique site appeared. Heading east on Old Highway 40, better known as "The Old National Road," we passed Glen Miller Park. At this point, a site appeared that we had never seen before.

Just past "Madonna of the Trail," in honor of the national trail, the old highway called the "Mainstreet of America," once stretched from coast to coast. Now with a length of 2,285.74, it traverses twelve states. It was the first highway to cross the whole United States. In 1968, Sandy's mother was Downtown Richmond when a deadly gas leak explosion occurred, blowing away a section of the Ole Trail.

"Look," I shouted from the left back seat, "a lion! It's sticking its head out of that black car!" I pointed to it and, well, hollered with passionate joy. "A lion!"

Yes, a lion was riding, not driving, but riding in the back seat with its head hanging out! His mane just flyin' as his jaws were flopping in the wind. Strings of "spittle" was flying in the wind.

"Mom, turn around so you can see it better!"

"No, son, we've got to join Walker—I mean, your dad. This was sort of a symbol of our Richmond visit."

"Visit" is what we seemed to be doing. No matter where we were, we knew there was another town down the road we were just visiting! We were just visiting.

For the first time, I saw "peggers" jeans on guys that had been made to fit tight from the hip down. "One boy with long ducktail hair passed me in the hall. I exclaimed to Lewis that "those jeans looked 'oily,' like they had been on a long time."

"Yeah," Lewis retorted. "Since he has such a hard time getting them off, he just leaves those darn things on until they stink!"

"Peggers!"

As we headed up the road to the newly built school out in the country, Jeanie, my sister two years younger, said, "Looks like a new school. We're gonna have a good time." Her observation was right.

Mom took us into the New Pleasant View Junior High, and we met the principal. He assigned us each to our classes by alphabetical order. My sister in seventh grade and I in the ninth grade.

"Meet our new student," the principal said to the coach who promptly asked, "Do you play sports?"

To which I cautiously answered, "Yes, sir, football and basketball."

He then began to introduce me to a bunch of guys who had gathered around to see the new kid.

"Are you going to be afraid?" I asked myself, saying, "No," silently. I was not intimidated because I had done it already a dozen times.

Looking down the hall a few feet eastward, I saw two girls look-ing at the sight of a new kid in school. After all, it was late October. Where would a new kid come from? To our country school?

One was wearing glasses, and they both were tall. I thought, *I like the one with glasses. Her face is really pretty and sweet.* She was laughing and having a good time and looking or glancing at me. I noticed, but I had to talk to the coach and these guys!

Later, I learned her name was Sandy.

Joining the Southern Baptist Church, we immediately made friends and met Mr. Tuggles. He was tall, thin aged, and rugged.

"Son," he said, "are you willing to work?"

"Sure, yes, sir!"

"I own a used furniture store just off Third Street downtown, and I'd like for you to work on Saturdays."

So we made our plans, and I told Dad, "Dad, I'll ride my bike to work if it's all right with you? It's only one and half mile."

So every Saturday morning, I got up, Mom cooked breakfast, and I flew to work. On bad winter days, of course, she or Daddy took me.

At first, my job consisted of cleaning every item in the store, the floors, the lights, the counter, the big glass door, the windows, furniture, and small items for sale, like lamps or bowls.

On a Saturday in November, my boss asked, "Larry, do you think you can help me move a chest, a bed, rugs, and lamps up to a second floor into an apartment?"

"Sure, I can do it."

Thankfully, I was raised that way and was able to help.

The entrance into the staircase was small. Right then and there, I learned how to get furniture into a tight spot. The two of us, carry-ing the chest, Mr. Tuggle at the top, I on the bottom, my boss said, "Keep the chest pushed to me."

So with a great heave, I raised the chest up and pushed it into his chest.

"That's it," he said. "Keep it coming."

So I learned to move furniture.

In a few weeks, Mr. Tuggle asked, "Do you think you can han-dle the front, sell, and make change?"

"Yes, sir."

He liked that direct response and respect coming from a fourteen-year-old boy. Afterward, he reviewed with me the prices, how to help people make choices, tell the benefits and cost, and "close" the sell.

"Be totally committed to this, to your customer."

Reviewing how to make change, I realized that I could almost know in a few seconds that I could figure the change in my head. He taught me how to count change the correct way, now the forgotten way, to count change from the amount of the sell to the amount tendered. In other words, for you who still don't know, if the sell is $12.75 but a $20.00 dollar bill is tendered to you to cover the cost, you count up from $12.75 to the $20.00 dollars. Making change this way eliminates making a mistake versus counting out the change from the top and sticking it out as if it doesn't matter and saying, "Here's your change." (I count the change back today at any counter after a purchase.)

I like the old way better.

How different from today.

Mr. Tuggle's taught me this.

We used to be more concerned about others.

So I began to make sells, handle the money, and still do everything else.

I worked all day Saturdays, even after a basketball game the night before and am very thankful today for ole Mr. Tuggle's, owner of Tuggle's Used Furniture.

I had to give him my goodbyes, July 1959. It was sad to leave this good man who made an indelible mark on my life.

Little did I know how this would help me for my next job. I was taught to be thankful and know the Lord will always take care of his own.

Many more life-changing events happened in Richmond that I will speak of down the road, maybe in another book of stories.

The journey continued. Dad's highway building job ended. We pulled up stakes and headed to Grove City, Ohio. Richmond would be in my heart the rest of my life.

The Vegetable Stand

Grove City was only one hundred miles from Richmond, so we arrived at the site of our new life in about three hours.

Winding on a back road to Dad's newfound trailer park, we made a turn southward where the road wrapped around a beautiful farm. The house was white, old, and historic. Cornfields snuggled up to a fence, all white and old.

Mom spoke excitedly, "A vegetable stand."

Sure enough, a parking area, all gravel, lay between the house and a long building with wooden windows hanging from the roof. The chains that held them up were also white as the "vegetable" stand. Everything white, a little faded and "chipped."

Mom was good at this. "Son"—looking with glee and grinning from ear to ear—"you can get a job here."

Following close behind Dad, we turned left (back east) and, in a half mile, came to our new "picnic" park! A large green cornfield lay to the back and western corner of the "park."

Setting up only took about thirty minutes on the flat site. Dad had made from sheets of iron four balance jacks for the four corners of our "house on wheels" home. I set up the jacks, screwed them in with a lug wrench, and tight until the trailer looked and felt balanced. Mom would walk through our house and report "good" or "raise the right corner" until we got it to be balanced! She had an uncanny sense of such things. Besides, the "level" helped!

Later that afternoon, after grocery shopping with Mom, she said, "Son, let's stop by the farm and get you a job."

Grimacing, I silently thought, *Not yet!*

I was happy with the idea after a few moments, but Mom more so. She delighted in her ability to find me work, and I have thankful thoughts of it this day. As we pulled into the parking area, we saw an attractive, but not pretty, forty-ish-year-old woman sorting tomatoes. Mom and I got out, commented on the beautiful property, and introduced ourselves. Then Mom used that magical smile and sincerely sweet Southern voice, saying, "I bet you need some help here!"

With humor in her voice and a half laugh, Mother had a way of making you feel like you were the only person in the world and her friend. Her smile and interest in "you" instantly won the day. She could get the store clerk, milkman, or bank teller to bend over backward for her.

Mrs. Mitchel, her first name was Mattie, said, "You're right."

"My son would love to work for you," Mom said as I weakly smiled.

So we made the arrangements. I was to work from 10:00 a.m. to 4:00 p.m. at $1.25 per hour, including Saturdays with lunch provided. After school started, on Saturdays, I would work for six hours because business would be less. Besides, growing season would be over in October.

The deal was done with great enthusiasm on Ms. Mattie's face as she stepped out from behind the tomatoes. We shook hands as Ms. Mattie asked, "You really can count change and sell?"

"Yes, ma'am. I've been working at a furniture store in Richmond. See you tomorrow."

I had about six weeks to work before school started and up into October with apple, peaches, gourds, melons, etc. Football practice was in August with morning and early evening sessions interfering some, but Ms. Mattie said, "It's okay." Generally, I got there by 10:00 a.m. and left at 5:30 p.m.

Driving the half mile to our home, there was silence and a little uncertainty. I couldn't wait any longer.

"Mom, did you see how short her shorts were?"

"Yes, son, and the low-chest-showing T-shirt!"

I told Mom it made me a little uncomfortable, to which she said, "Just do your job and don't look!"

That I did….not looking too closely. Ms. Mitchel had said she would provide lunch for the two of us, and the first meal was great.

"Stuffed bell peppers," she announced as they set steaming at 12:05 p.m. They, with tea, were delicious. But filled to the brim, it took a couple of hours to recover. The apple pie didn't help.

"Larry, how do you like the vegetable stand?"

"Well," I paused, figuring out what I wanted to say, then continued, "I love being outdoors. The smell of the vegetables, meeting and helping people, the quietness, the lunch, and you."

It was true, but I had learned from the best mother.

The next day rolled by to noon, and Ms. Mattie said, "Let's eat."

As I walked into the kitchen, it smelled wonderful but familiar.

"Stuffed bell peppers," my boss lady announced, so I ate them up.

The next day, stuffed bell peppers, and the next and the next until I ran out of a job in October. She was a great stuffed bell pepper cook, but her culinary skills stopped there! Eight weeks of bell peppers...but apple pie!

As the days rolled by, I sold lots of vegetables, gained many new customers, and increased her business about $100 per week. She was elated, very kind, and willing to give me my due. God blessed me to be able to speak up, smile, help people, and count change!

She paid me in cash, so we had no more income tax (mink ranch!) problems!

Thankfully, I was able to save almost all my earnings and buy most of my school clothes.

I learned that I would always be provided for, be challenged to do right (remember the short shorts, etc.?), and that it paid to work hard. Ms. Mattie and her kindness will always be with me, even the "bell peppers"!

Many Jobs!

Thankfully, I had the blessing of many more jobs before age twenty—in fact, including a drug store, age sixteen; dairy queen, age sixteen; Pittsburg Plate Glass, age seventeen to eighteen; song leader in church, age fifteen to nineteen; truck stop, age nineteen; interim pastor, age nineteen; crane oiler, twice, age eighteen and nineteen; and tried to sell Kirby Vacuum Cleaners but wasn't very good!

Grove City was a wonderful place with wonderful people, sort of like Gallatin and the town in *Back to the Future*. I was voted in as class president of the sophomore class and started two varsity team games as a running back. I was blessed. Our church life there was a blessing also, making many friends that would be in our future. I'm just thankful.

There's no excuse, for a little trailer boy, just get it on and do it right.

Story 8

Great Mercies Even to a Trailer Boy

Ralph Waldo Emerson said, "A person can only account for themselves."

—"Heroism," Essay: First Series, in *The Complete Works of Ralph Waldo Emerson* 2 (1903), 259–60

It has been hard enough for me to manage myself, live up to my teachings, excel and yet enjoy the life I've been given. Truly there is no way for me to account for someone else.

This I know, I have been shown 'great mercy'. The sheer fact that it is Mercy and not of myself, is comfort indeed. Even a trailer boy has great mercies.

Great Mercies I

God told Moses, "I will have mercy on whom I will have mercy" (Rom. 9:15). So it is no wonder that Moses led God's people on dry land through the Red Sea (Exod. 14). We do not know on whom, as individuals, but we know God will show mercy on whom He will.

With absolutely no credit to myself, I have been shown great mercy.

Leading Up to the Storm

In the spring and summer of 1953, we moved in our fifty-foot-long trailer to Calhoun, Georgia. I was eight years old, turning nine that July.

Being only one block off Main Street and three blocks from the center of town, we enjoyed the little southern village.

The trailer park was situated on a level-square block of grassy land. Distances were about thirty feet to the other trailers and families. We enjoyed our privacy, and because Mom and Dad traveled with four active children, they didn't want to disturb anyone.

Interestingly enough, Sandy and I live only about thirty miles from Calhoun now and travel back roads there fairly often. The lot is owned by the First Methodist Church, and it is kept beautifully.

There are no signs of a former life there. Such is the passage of time and memories. But there is one single old, decaying tree trunk on the west side by the sidewalk that must have been there in '53. I took a chunk off the ancient landmark that rests in my study, telling its long-ago stories of my escapades and life there.

I did remember on my first trip back that at the entrance into Calhoun, there was a statue of a confederate soldier and a mighty Cherokee Indian "Sequoyah." They both stand tall and straight now, still recounting another day and time.

Some of the Civil War was fought right there as the "March to the Sea" was carried out.

Just up the street, I had made some friends. Their house set up on the bank with a rock wall holding up the earth. There were seven children in this one family and several other kids lived in the next two or three blocks.

The grass had been killed and trampled off the short front yard. The house only sat about fifteen feet from the rock wall with its four-foot drop to the sidewalk, and there was a porch. The yard was "plum" scrapped off into the look of a bald-headed man. The porch had four rusty metal chairs setting proudly upon it.

On this "bald" yard, we played "washers." I never had seen the game, but here is how it was played: two holes, about three to four inches in diameter, were dug in the "bald-headed" yard. The holes were dug fifteen feet apart. Washers, two inches in diameter with a hole in the middle, were pitched by each player. The object was to pitch the washer, so it went into the hole. Each player had four washers.

At first, I was lost and last. Henry Bob, who owned the holes since they were in his yard, was the best. Even very few adults could beat him. HB, I called him, needed a bath. I felt sorry for him because he smelled like a dead possum, and I noticed when I first met this rough bunch of kids, not many went close to him. His family must have been poor. Sadly, his clothes were not clean but also tattered with holes in them. I felt a sadness toward him.

He tried at first to intimidate me, but having had too many such encounters in our travels, I simply said immediately while looking deep into his eyes with my baby blues, "Stop it." I continued to look at him until he stopped."

The second best player was the only girl in the bunch and a true tomboy. Clara usually beat the other boys.

"Do you see HB trying to cheat?"

"Yes, Clara, I do!"

HB did try to cheat. "The washer has to go into the hole," I told him, "so don't think you can cheat anymore."

But he couldn't help himself. You see, the "washer" had to go into the hole, down to the bottom for three points, and lay flat. There was only one point for a "leaner."

If Henry Bob pitched a leaner, he'd lie and call out, "It's a three-pointer!"

I wasn't about to play with a cheater who sadly reminded me of a possum. As I began to get better, I passed Clara for second best.

"How do you pitch the washer so flat?" Clara asked, and thinking hard, I said, "It's all in the wrist," looking around to see the faces of astonishment. After several weeks, HB and I usually ended up with a two-man playoff.

"What about a final playoff?" HB said as schooltime was getting close, and we all said, "Sure…that's good…okay."

August rolled around, and I announced a little sadly, "I'm moving."

"So soon. You just got here," Clara exclaimed.

HB said, "Yeah, well, we gotta get this championship settled, and I'm the best, and I'll beat you in the finals," acting like a "smarty britches" staring at me. I just walked away like Daddy would.

The summer finals had been set for Monday, two days away.

"Dad, I've got the championship tomorrow," I said, hoping to get his attention.

"Aah, son, you'll knock 'em dead."

I grinned as I walked off to bed and fell asleep, seeing my "hole" in the earth stacked high with round washers.

Monday came, and one by one, my summer friends started to gather. HB stared at me as I laughed and teased with my friends with just a glance at the poor boy. Having beat him a few times but increasingly as the heat of summer burned us brown, I built my determination by talking to myself and crossing my fingers.

"You ready?" HB blurted out.

"No, I want to practice up a little more," I said, not going to be pushed around.

I was nervous but tried not to show it. All the "marbles" were on the line. The name "champion" was in the balance.

"A bully, the winner?" Clara asked, and I said, "No," shaking my head in defiance.

Clara was a year older than most of us but acted like a full-grown woman. She retorted, "You're going to beat his rear!" Her growling "voice" was a shock, but I believed her.

"I'm ready… Are you ready?" I asked, looking deeply into his shifty eyes.

"Yeah, yeah," he stuttered out. "Remember, I'm the best."

"We'll see," I said, with a warrior's glance back over my shoulder at the bully and back at Clara.

The toss of the washer was made, and HB won as his washer came closest to the hole in the hard, burnt, bald, yard.

"You can't beat me…," HB repeated, laughing, and I just looked at him and said, "We'll see. We'll see."

I had to pitch first. Missing each toss, I was a little unsure. Henry Bob was on. On his first four tosses, he got two "ringers" and six points. I missed again with all four being close but still a miss. HB, 6; Larry, 0.

HB got another three-pointer for nine points to my zero!

"See, you see!" my nemesis blurted out, and I was just determined but a little doubtful. Score: HB, 9; Larry, 0.

The next round, I took aim, focused on just the hole, and hit my second and fourth tries. I was getting more confident. Henry Bob got a little nervous and hit one of four. Score: HB, 12; Larry, 6.

More and more kids gathered so that a tight ring of brown human flesh filled the bald yard. Shoulder to shoulder, they seemed to be for me.

"Be tough, Larry," "You'll get him," "Aim clear…," and other such encouragements filled my sweaty ears.

The fourth round began as I slid one into the hole and one leaner, hugging the wall of the dark hole for four points. HB had two leaners. Score: HB, 14; Larry, 10.

Henry Bob was a little jittery and watching me out of the corner of his left eye. I stepped to the line and slid three into the bottom of the hole for nine points. My mortal enemy had finally quit talking but pitched one in the hole and two leaners. Score: HB, 19; Larry, 19! Tied with one more round.

"You're lucky, trailer boy. You can't beat me!" HB's aggravating voice declared bitterly as a "boo" or two came from behind us.

I feel sorry for you, my brain thought. I had to wipe the streaming wetness from my forehead and eyes. It was hot, hot, hot!

Everybody gathered up tight all the way around the "washer" field.

"Come on, Larry," I heard several times with only one such cry for poor ole HB. The poor boy's reputation of lying, stealing, cheating, and ugly language closed in on him. His raisin' was bad.

I knew I was going to win. HB knew he was going to win. I took my time carefully for the last four pitches. Toeing the line, which had almost disappeared, I pitched, but no score. My second pitch bounced the washer through the air into the hole. Sliding the third one straight for the hole, it stopped just on the edge for one point. *Your last shot stay calm*, raced through my nine-year-old mind. I stepped forward, left leg first, then right and back to the left as smooth as possible, spinning my washer into midair, looking yearningly, earnestly, the washer spun round and round in slow, tantalizing motion. Like the B-29 Bomber hanging in flight from the ceiling of my bedroom it seemed to know exactly where it was going.

A mythical haze surrounded me. *Boob*, it hit the bald earth, sliding slowly…into the fresh dug hole and hit the back wall with a thud. Then it gently settled to the deep bottom. There it laid. The massive crowd screamed, jumped, and hollered. Score: HB, 19; Larry 26!

Now comes HB. Very uptight glaring with hatefulness all over himself at me. I just looked away and, sorry to say, arrogantly chuckled. HB hit a homer, three points, and missed the second with the third washer coming up. He hesitated, rubbed his eyes, dried his hands, and slid the round washer into the hole. Score: HB, 25; Larry, 26.

HB sidestepped over to his only buddy for a little chat then returned to the line. The twenty or was it one-hundred or so kids openly began to yell negatively and a few naughty words against the poor boy.

Taking a deadly aim, he sent the washer sailing through the air as an old pro will do, and it lay teetering on the edge of the magic hole, rocking in the red dirt but stayed put. A leaner! Score: 26 to 26.

But as a cheater will do as he had gotten away with it for a long time, he ran over to the washer and pushed it with his bare toe into the hole to the bottom and declared, "See, see, I won."

We all debated the issue. He challenged me to a fight as I walked away, saying, "You know the truth," and I think I said, "Live with it."

I winked at Clara with my right eye and shook my head side to side, saying, "My, my," as Daddy would say.

Score: HB, 28; Larry, 26.

All my friends and I left for our trailer court to have some ice water, peanut butter sandwiches, and review the world championship of washers! It was all right. I recalled this powerful event in the summer of '55 when I filled my burgundy purse—a big purse with marbles.

Lesson: Once a cheater, always a cheater... Always stay true to your teaching. It was all right. We moved away in two weeks. Excuses? None.

Great Mercies

> O Friend never strike sail to fear! Come into port
> greatly, or sail with God the seas.
>
> —Ralph Waldo Emerson

"How do you feel about moving to so many places, meeting so many and different people?" my girlfriend's mother asked at the dinner table.

My reply in the warm Richmond, Indiana, home was simple, "The things we saw, the people we met, all the experiences of the road is exciting and eye-opening."

Truly, my life experience set me up to have adventure. I gained a whole "other" view of life than most kids. Imagination and anticipation of and from life filled my very being.

Adventures lay everywhere. It caught me, and I embraced it. "O friend never strike to a fear...."

It is true that living without enough respect of what is may well get you in trouble. But looking at the world as an "adventurist" opens the door to great surprises and great mercies.

Great deliverances are necessary for "venturing" souls.

Seeing the world through the eyes as a "trailer boy" opened up knowledge and daring adventures.

I seemed to have the spirit of imagination from my earliest beginnings. As my climbing the refrigerator, throwing the radio out the window, jumping the sewer ditch, standing on the arm of a chair and on the horses, I was "embraced" with adventure. Great mercy was a great gift...and necessity.

While I was yet under five years old, Mom and Dad took me to the Memphis Zoo while Jeanie stayed with "Little Grandmother."

All the animals, people, music, and snow cones put me into a state of amazement. I couldn't see everything fast enough. Even today at my advanced age, I will often ask Sandy, "Wonder where that road goes?" Or "Let's go over this one last hill...," Or "Did you see that sparrow dive down and peck that hawk?"

The world is amazing, an adventure, especially at the zoo. I had to see it all.

So seeing an opening between the legs of such tall people and around them, I dashed away to see what was behind all of them to see more!

Mom frantically asked Dad, "Where's Larry?"

"What will that boy do next?" Dad exclaimed.

I must have been staying just out of sight on the other side of such a mass of people, looking at the monkeys, lions, giraffes, and birds of all colors.

Finding a policeman after a few minutes together, they found me all safe and sound, totally delighted and unaware of the scare I put my parents into. I walked along hand in hand with the policeman dressed in blue. Just think at age four, I was a friend to the big man in blue packing a huge gun.

Would this excitement be my lifelong destiny?

Later, I heard how scared Dad and Mom were and hurt. They sat me down later, explained their hurt and fear and the danger of such disobediences. I tried to understand and hugged both of them.

But adventures lay ahead.

Besides, adventure is in the eye of the beholder. Some have it, some don't. From my beginning, I was in "wonder."

Seeing life from the window of the green '53 Ford, out the door of our Liberty trailer, in so many new places always set my soul on fire. I could see the marvel in the new, the different, the beautiful, the big, and the small of things. Beyond this, Mom, especially, and my extended family taught me to see the best, the enjoyment of every moment, and make "fun" or good out of everything! "It's all around us. Have a good time," Granddaddy Mac would say.

This wonderment of life was always exploding as we moved twenty-four times, going to fifteen schools and while living in ten different states. All this looking from the window of Dad's truck, through the doors of our home parked now in Tennessee then Indiana next Ohio. "Life is what it is. Get the most out of it," Little Grandmother said. I tried to.

Recently, a friend of mind and his wife took a trip "out west" to see that country. When I saw him at church, he said, "I didn't see anything out there for me!"

What! The plains, the mesas, desert, giant rocks, snow in July on Mt. McKinley, the Navajo, Indian rugs, cowboys on horseback runnin' cattle in Oklahoma, Old US 66, or Taos, New Mexico? You got to see it. The sight is in you. "Oh, run your race with 'soul,'" I said one time to Harry.

Venture into it all. Feel it all. Really see it, then comes that adventure. Get on into it with your very soul. Let it change you. Change yourself.

Think on the mystery, the marvel, and you!

The Pig

My great-uncle Virgil (Wise), Grandma Mac's brother, lived in the same house through his whole married life. Very quiet, so much, that someone else had to carry the conversation.

In my later years, living four hundred miles away, for about twenty-five years and before he died, I along with Uncle Elaine and others, would go to see him. We would sit on the old front porch and ask him questions about his father, Grandpa Wise, and others. This delighted him, and he would smile that wrinkled face and grin about halfway. We were in heaven.

His family, Uncle Elmer included, were taught to fear and give strict respect to storms. Uncle Virgil had a storm "house," as they called it, down in the bank of the old red dirt road. I was not sure why they were built this way, but he and most others did the same. The bank along the road was about four feet high.

Jeanie, my sister, and I spent the night with them one summer in 1954. The house was a "dogtrot." That is a house built with two living portions of the house each one being built on either side of a large open area running from the front of the house to the back. That open area was the "dogtrot."

The "dogtrot" let air blow through the house, keeping it cooler besides the dogs could "trot" through it.

We were put to bed in the north side of the house. Lamar and one or two of my other cousins were with him.

I admit I got scared. *Too far apart,* I thought. But tiredness and sleep go hold of me as I went to dream. Jeanie didn't.

"Larry, Larry," she whispered. "What's that noise?"

I half listened and told her it was the wind blowing limbs against the house. We went back to sleep.

In an hour or two, Uncle Virgil raced into our room and loud for him said, "Get up, Larry! Get up!"

"What? What?" I stammered.

"There's a storm a comin', and we gotta get in the storm house." I never saw him move or talk so fast.

Aunt Mamie Lee put an old red, green, white patch work quilt on us to hinder the rain, and out the door we flew with five or six of my cousins. Uncle Virgil had an old oil-burning lamp lit as he opened the door down into this hole in the black. Rocks and bricks were cemented together for the sides with a tin roof. The floor was deep red-mud packed in hard.

Down into the hole we went. Eight of us, cobwebs and spiders hung everywhere. Dust clung to everything. I just knew that water moccasins or alligators were down in there too!

Scared, we went in. Jeanie cried a little, but she was a trooper and stopped with a little urge from me.

It started to rain just a little and then as if the oceans had been poured upon us. The tin roof rattled as my uncle and Lamar held buckets under the steady-leaking holes. Every once in a while, they would open the door and dash the water out with a loud grunt like "whua" and close the door before the red sea poured in!

The deafening roar of the buckets of rain pouring down sounded like machine guns. The wind howled, making the loose tin edges of the roof sound like a paddle on our bottoms, except faster. Then suddenly, loud, sharp sounds pounded the roof and made us jump.

"Hail!" my great-uncle said.

Uncle Virgil said, "Pray...Lord God, save us from this storm like you saved us from the storm of sin. Have mercy on us as your children through the Red Sea. Have mercy if you please like the blood of Jesus cleansed us from sin. Thank you, Lord. In Jesus name."

It reminded me of Dad's prayer in the storm of North Georgia.

All of us were calmer now because we all believed that God had heard his and our prayers.

The process continued. Some of the other children a little older than me fell asleep in Aunt Mamie Lee's arms and lap. A huge limb cracked off the oak tree and landed partly on the shelter like to fall of a giant airplane.

Finally, the storm decreased and ceased. We got up and headed out and realized how dangerous it had gotten. An old rotten chair had blown off the porch about twenty-three to thirty feet. The house was safe; the water cool as we wiped ourselves off with wet rags.

We said good night and fell asleep in peace and gratitude.

The smell of country ham and fat back, biscuits, and gravy seemed like a happy feelin' dream. I jumped up, pulled my pants on, running across the "dogtrot" into the kitchen, and there was my aunt and uncle Virgil. He was reading his Bible as Aunt Mamie Lee cooked. A plate loaded with red, red tomatoes sat on the table.

Uncle Virgil looked up and said, "How're you?"

We all ate until we were full, helped with the kitchen, getting the table cleared. The daughters washed and dried the dishes, of course, by hand.

On a little country farm, even on Saturdays after chores to just keep things going, like milking cows, chopping a few weeds out of the garden, then we'd get ready to go to town.

Going to town in New Albany was pure joy because of the other farmers and their families being there. Dressed in colorful cotton dresses, of course, below the knees, fresh-pressed blue overalls, boots shined, a pressed white starched and tattered shirt, some men twirling a big round pocket watch and, naturally, their best hat on. Some used homemade chains for their watches. Even though I was only eleven years old, the brown country girls were too cute, but I just looked. Sometimes they would look back and smile. The men swirled their canes, made from different "wood," and you better stay ready to jump out of the way and dodge disaster. Some were carved on and a few with different paint colors.

This Saturday, after the storm, Lamar said he didn't want to go to town but that he and his little brother would stay home. Of course, I wanted to stay with my big cousins whom I thought were "mighty" near grown. That was okay with Uncle Virgil, first, because he was good with not to have to fool with more children. Lamar was like a little man at age thirteen. He said he would "take care" of the younger ones.

The girls went with them, just a giggling all the way to the old 1945 Ford and proud of their washed, gingham dresses. I especially liked the red and white ones.

We played in the barn, climbing up the stacks of hay, swinging on a rope tied, mighty tight to a big oak tree. The rope didn't have a seat but a big ball of rope about the size of a man's fist to sit on. We had to hold tight, twisting our legs together and raising them so as not to hit the ground.

After going down to the pond to see if we could catch a bullfrog or turtle, we headed back to the house.

Walking by the large pigpen, Lamar said, "Larry no one has ever ridden that hog."

I said, "Ride a hog?" with a slight grin.

There was silence as I put my chin on the top of my two hands on the fence post and thought about how big the pig was, with big long stiff hairs sticking out around his mouth, snout, and head. Besides, the pink, white hog was long and big all over with a curled tail like wire.

The dirt was mud.

Furiously thinking about the historical fact that no one had ever ridden the pig, I was rolling that notion around in my head... *No one. I'll be the first one!*

There was deafening silence as all of us stared at the animal.

"What's that coming out of his mouth?" I asked Lamar.

He told me what they were. They were almost white, scary, long, and pointed, "Tusks," so I imagined what they were for.

"Those tusks are mean," Lamar said, trying to strike up some fear.

Lamar, in good humor, asked, "Do you want to ride him?"

Thinking, of course, that I wouldn't.

My mind got made up. Without a word, I climbed the wood fence, walked around to the side of the beast, slowly, and said, "I will."

Strangely, the hog stood still, just barely turning his head toward me. Being used to people coming into the muddy pen for different reasons, no doubt he felt safe; besides, the warm sun had him relaxed. He was boss! I crept closer, ever closer to his back end. My older cousin whispering just loud enough for me to hear, "Larry, come back. He might spear you. Come back!"

When I got up close, Lamar spoke more forcefully, "No, Larry, don't."

I said nothing, but with a determined swing of my left leg, I lit onto his back. Realizing that there was nothing to hold onto, I got hold of his right ear and braced myself with the left hand against his neck on the top of it.

He snorted with orange liquid coming out of his nose and a big chunk; swirling, he came out of his snoozy state, with a walk, a jump of three inches, and a twirl to his left. Somehow I stayed on, being blessed with a great deal of balances that I would use later in sports, road racing, and riding horses. I gripped tight the right dirty ear. Switching his quick twirl to the left, I felt a little slip to the right. I squeezed his ear with all I had.

The pig got into a full realization of something on his back. He hunkered up, began to run with my cousins yelling for me, around and around in the sloppy, muddy pen he and his rider went. Mud and water flew all over the pen.

Suddenly he headed to the side of the pen straight for the wall of hand-cut logs. The animal instantly put the brakes on, and I lost grip, flying over his head into the mud. "Get out, Larry! Get out!"

Having successfully accomplished my feat with my crowd yelling, I scrambled to my feet slipping and sliding, almost doing the splits.

"Hurry! Hurry!"

I jumped to the second log, grabbed the top one, and furiously flung my left leg over the top like Roy Rogers on the right side of his horse.

(that's why) a good horseman teaches mounting from both sides.

Snorting in anger, the four-hundred-pound monster stood up on his hind feet, aimed his long tusks at my legs, caught my jeans, causing a four-inch tear and barely missing my skin. Away, I sailed and landed on both feet as Lamar grabbed me.

The big hog, still mad, flew around the pen, looking for his victim. Arriving at my getting[off place, he snorted a few times as if to say, "Now what about that?"

I was still shaking when Lamar put his arm around me as the hog snorted all around the muddy pen.

Here's what it's about: gaining more confidence, getting recognition, helping all have a good time, be more careful, and never ride a hog!

Uncle Virgil quipped, "That pig will always remember this day."

As the years have flown by, sixty-four of them, never do I see Lamar but that he brings that story to light. Uncle Virgil is gone, so is Aunt Mamie Lee, but the love and memories remain. I love them all.

Another adventure of a little trailer boy. No excuses and great mercies.

> To him whose elastic and vigorous thought keeps pace with the sun, the day is a perpetual morning. (Henry David Thoreau, *Walden*, 1854, chap. 2, [1966], 116–117)

The Storm

Living in Calhoun, Georgia, that hot summer of '53 left an indelible mark on our lives. My first vacation Bible school and the "world championship of washers" marked that time and place as a special adventure in my life.

But there was another marvel of natural and spiritual forces intertwined that lingers even yet sixty-six years later. We were only there three months but our lives, and yes, my life was imprinted with the power of God's world and his divine providence of mercy.

That summer was especially hot 95 degrees to 105 degrees. It made summer long. Yet we made the best of it as Mother was always an encouraging sweetheart. "Son, it'll be all right" forever!

Of course, we had no air-conditioning besides a hand fan or two that we got from the downtown mortuary and the Baptist Church. Besides those two hand fans, we had two rotating electric fans. We were very thankful for the huge oak trees, along with three or four big maples that surrounded the trailer park. Shade was given to us all day no matter where the sun was because of the towering, wide trees. Also, we had a colorful green-and-white awning.

It was attached to the trailer that you manually rolled out about seven feet. The Liberty, having been on the road now for one year, the awning, had begun to fade a little. We didn't care. We were just thankful for the shade.

Mother would turn the fans on in the morning and the ceiling vent in the center of the living room rolled up by the little handle. A good circulation felt just right. But I was in our home on wheels very little. There were always trees to climb, ball games to play, stories to tell, and washers to throw.

In fact, I found that I could tell stories (not lies!) very early in life. While in Buford, Georgia, upon a summer day, I sat some of my friends down and told them about "my adventures in the Second World War." Billy and Marie Langford bought me the wonderful little book *Boys Book of Famous Soldiers*, which I have laying on my desk even at this very moment.

My favorite soldier was Private Rodger Young of Sandusky County, Ohio. He gave his life for the other members of his platoon and saved them to safety. It moves me now as it moved me then. The great value of America's survival is now even greater.

Having written my name beside Private Young's picture in 1954, it still remains there in that secret place.

That's how I saw myself. The author J. Walker McSpadden wrote in such a way as to bring me into the experience of Young's death, the cause and the purpose of the Great War. In essence, Corporal Young threw himself on a grenade so his fellow army buddies could live. Running toward the enemy, he was hit more than once by enemy fire but continued his run to glory. A grenade was thrown in the midst of several buddies. He fell on the deadly blast. His buddies went to safety after paying the enemy back for killing their hero.

I still have my original copy and recently found and bought a new copy on the internet. I always thought of myself in that way, by that true story. After sixty-six years, I reread that wonderful story.

General Robert E. Lee was my second favorite soldier.

The friends in Buford, who heard me tell of my adventure in the great war for America's freedom, believed me, some any way. Happily, they never questioned me.

When we moved to Gallatin in the fall of '53, there was a huge open field behind Dicky Wagner's home. In the center of the field was a huge haystack. Within a few days, I was exploring that field, climbed upon the haystack, sinking very deeply, and had to save myself.

On a cool Saturday morning, I gathered a few kids together and asked them if they knew that there was a hole under the big haystack where the army was deployed. So as they looked wild-eyed at me, I told them how I had been in WWII and that I had gone down into the entrance to the Army under the haystack.

There were soldiers, tanks, machine guns, trucks, and a large number of soldiers. They sat dazed and bewildered.

They believed me. I think I was a war hero like Private Young.

Two days later, mysteriously, a single engine small plane actually landed in the field close to the military covered by the haystack. I ran to the trailer and close homes to tell my friends. Here they came just a runnin'. With huge eyes and open mouth, they could only stare. No words were said.

After a few moments, I said, "I'm going over there," and took off running.

I went alone. No one followed. There it was a plane most certainly commissioned by the Army under the haystack!

Being in Calhoun in that scorching summer of '53, I got to use my storytelling some although Henry Bob tried to ignore them. Sitting on the outside of my audience circle, he would pretend to be doing something else. I knew better.

Dad came home early on a Wednesday; I think it was. He was in a bit of a tither. While Jeanie, David, and I played outside climbing trees, Dad hurried to the trailer.

I heard Dad call, "Vickie...Vickie."

"Be right there, honey," she responded quickly. Mom said, "Walker! Why are you home?"

They lowered their voices to a whisper. We hung upside down, swinging on a rope Dad put up and talked with neighbor kids.

Sweating away, Dad said through the grey screen door, "Come in, children."

That's all he said, so it seemed like something was up like "we were moving again," but it wasn't.

Going into Mom's haven, we sat down, me on the floor. Susan was standing on a chair so she could be seen, so Mom sat her down. She was two and a half.

Dad, looking a little concerned with his forehead wrinkled and mouth pursed uptight, just sat at the table a few seconds. We were silent. Mom stood in the kitchen and was slightly, barely singing, "Amazing grace...how sweet the sound.../ that saved a wretch like me" very softly. Dad began to speak, and Mom fell silent.

"I'm home early because the foreman got a call from his brother in Alabama. There's a huge storm over there with strong winds and damage." Dad continued, "The foreman said that the sirens had been going off violently, and they say its headed to North Georgia." Speaking calmly but determined, he said that we had to get ready.

So Dad and I checked the trailer tie-downs and Dad's home-made jacks to make sure they were uptight. Everything, all the toys, chairs, table had to be put away. We knew we had to be ready to close the windows, pick up the small mat in front of the door, and tighten down the propane tanks. Of course, the awning had to be pulled in and locked.

The sky was already darkening and getting darker. It had an ominous orange and yellow cast. By 4:30 p.m., a slight sprinkle or two came on down. We stayed outside just a lookin' and throwing a baseball. Around 6:00 p.m., the winds started traveling faster. Leaves were sailing through the air like little jets from outer space and slapped our faces.

Besides all this, the air became cooler. It was so cool we had to put our jackets on. Darker and darker it got. The winds now, about 7:30pm, were rushing and pushing small loose things through the air.

The winds got heavier until we could hardly walk, so Mom called us in, and we were okay with that.

Normally, the sun didn't set until 9:30 p.m. or so, but by 7:45 p.m., the skies were mostly black with thick bellowing giant clouds filling the sky, flying. Every once in a while, the sun in the west would stick its yellow light through, but what hope it gave was soon gone.

Dad said the winds were now about forty-five to fifty miles an hour. At 8:15 p.m., the rain poured down like giant pitchers of iced water, sailing sideways.

"Dad, what's that!"

"Son, that's ice."

"What?"

"Ice!"

"Yes, Larry, ice…hail!"

After a very few minutes, Dad opened the door slightly, saying, "Y'all come here. Look!"

All six of us crowded at the door to see the mysterious balls of ice!

It was 8:50 p.m., and the trailer was moving all the time, some-times more than others. The rain was now like a river. The winds were howling like coyotes.

I was afraid. Jeanie cried a little. David sat watching us. Susan was clinging to Mother. Dad got his old Bible out and read Psalms 100 and 23 to us.

Mom sweetly kept saying, "We'll be all right. The Lord will help us."

By 9:30 p.m., Dad said, "It's time to get in the car," which was a black Buick he had pulled close to the trailer. His thinking was since the storm was coming from the southwest, the wind would be blocked a little by the trailer, and especially if a tree fell on us, we'd have the best protection.

We obeyed, grabbed our jackets, and climbed into the car through the rain. Susan, crying, was in the front with Mom and Dad, and the rest of us sat in the back seat, close together.

Black darkness was blown upon us. The rain was deafening, the wind sounded like a vacuum cleaner, and we could hear the wind blowing through the trees and a loud crack and smash every few minutes.

The next moments have stuck with me all my life since that fateful hour.

Dad said, "Let's pray and trust the Lord to take care of us."

So we bowed our hearts as Dad prayed like this, "Precious Jesus, we know you control all things. Save us, protect us, and give us faith to trust you. We praise you for your grace and mercy. We give ourselves to you. Have mercy upon us. In your precious name, amen." This was the first prayer Dad had ever prayed with us, which made a lifelong indelible mark upon my conscience.

That's the way I remember it.

Daddy's prayer in that dangerous moment has stayed with me all these years. By that fall, late in the year, Dad started going to church, taking we children with him. The four of us to this day seek to worship God almighty. Two other daughters came along, and they worship Christ also. Mom followed Dad to church, and forty-six years later, I baptized her.

We had heard limbs breaking off and loud "thuds" of a tree falling. The dawning of the next morning, we all got up early, so happy to be safe with our home, truck, and car undamaged.

But when we went outside, leaves and branches were everywhere, and five or six great trees were blown down, twisted off their trunks like celery stalks. This was divine mercy, the great mercy, and Dad's prayer.

Post note: Living now just thirty miles from Calhoun, I visit that site often. It is now owned and occupied by the First Methodist Church.

Walking around that historic place, as I try to visualize that dramatic time and moment, I discovered a decaying ancient tree trunk, decaying into soft dust. I pulled a chunk of it off and have it in my study today.

It was one of those wind-blown oaks that survived along with us. A God-ordained event of divine mercy, a prayer, and memories of love remain to this very day. It was a moment of life making character and a mother and father who trusted God for mercy.

I have no excuses. I am a "little trailer boy" with great mercies.

Story 9

Hard Times
But It's All Right

"Gratitude is the sign of noble souls," Aesop said in the sixth century before Christ (Joseph Jacobs, *Fables* [1894]), and certainly, it enables one to live more joyfully in a world of constant change.

Hard times are not bad times. "It is the way we learn how to stand up to the bullies of life," Little Grandmother said.

In 1956, we moved back to Gallatin, Tennessee, a second time. "Son, let's go knock on Langford's door and see if there is any room."

"Okay," I replied as I jumped from the green Ford with a burst of twelve-year-old energy while Mom and the other three children swung left onto Maple St. and parked.

All four of them quickly got out of the car looking with happy expectancy.

Frances appeared at the door, broke into a happy face, hugged me and Dad, and declared, "You're back!"

We sure were and parked in the one spot left.

This is how it happened.

Dad had taken a mechanics job with TVA, working on the nearest dam. An old-time buddy and job foreman had called John (Rice) about the work and said, "Where's Walker?"

With the Rice's living in the same park in Westville, John came immediately over, and the plans were made.

"Well, Vickie, we're pulling up stakes and moving back to Gallatin."

Jeanie jumped up and yelled, "Oh, okay!"

And all of us felt that way. "Oh, okay!"

Mom just said as a hardened warrior, "When do we leave?"

By this time, I was bursting with joy and cried out, "Going back to Gallatin! Whoopee!"

After only being in Westville, Indiana, for three months, I had made several friends who accompanied me on my adventures...and theirs. I was sad to leave them.

The job Happy and I created for the summer, collecting the metal in the open area by the trailer park for recycling took a lot of our time. But we did find time to join our buddies, play ball, chew the fat, or walk all over town, just being *cool!*

Elvis was just getting big with Jerry Lee Lewis and all the other great ones.

Mackie, one of our buddies, asked, "Don't you want to look like Elvis?"

I had let my hair grow out a little until Mom said, "Son, you'd better clear this with your dad."

"Dad, can I let my hair grow out long enough to comb it into a *ducktail?*"

He just stared at me for a minute or two as I squirmed around in my Levi's and said, "Yeah, go ahead, but not too long."

I knew what he meant. So out it grew long enough to comb it back in a shorter Elvis look with a part down the left side of my head...from front to back. The front had a big "puff" with a curve, and I greased it down with some salve out of a little round can.

"Happy, are you going to leave the flattop behind and go with me?"

"No, I'm gonna keep it red!"

And he did. He was still cool.

Downtown was two blocks long, heading southward. There was a dime store, "The Mart," where I bought two of my airplanes and an army tank that I put together.

"Larry, how many models are you going to put together?" Mom asked over the supper table.

"A bunch," I replied as I looked out from under my eyebrows. But mainly, there was a wonderful hamburger joint, "The Black Hawk Grill."

The Black Hawk Grill was great for kids with fountain cokes, handmade milkshakes, thick, very juicy hamburgers and hot dogs, homemade cookies, and a jukebox all lit up in bright colors. We could eat for 0.25 cents and play the music machine for a nickel. Now nickels and dimes and quarters were hard to come by for a twelve-year-old boy, but remember, Happy and I had made some money just a few weeks before. Besides, with a bunch of us contributing, we could play about twenty songs an hour.

On our last day there, our friends had gathered at the Black Hawk Grill about 11:30 a.m. We celebrated our good times together, ate the best hamburger in America, and danced to Fats Domino and others.

My little girlfriend, Diane, of the last few weeks was crying softly as we danced close to "Love Me Tender." I, at least, felt it at the time, so I told her I'd be back soon to see her and take her away. Even though I was an American-wide traveler, my passionate young mind couldn't see how far five hundred miles was. We left about 5:00 a.m., and by daylight, we were 145 miles south. The Westville gang, if they went downtown, could only ask, "Where is Larry?" or so I dreamed.

I never went back, except as a fifty-year-old adult and again in 2011 and in 2018.

The hamburger joint is closed, but another restaurant fills the building. There are no kids on the streets downtown. The dime store is gone. No dimes there! No ducktails, no rock and roll.

But the memory is still there. A hard time, a good time.

So down to Gallatin, we drove, a day-and-a-half trip.

Arriving at Langford's Trailer Park, we were greeted by the Langfords and the Rices. Hugs and kisses all around. We were "back home."

A few days at the swimming pool and walks downtown, me, Marie, Jeanie, and Happy started school.

Greeting my old buddies, school went good into the winter. We played lots of football in Jay's backyard, took hikes into the farm south of Gallatin, and walked downtown.

Alvin had some buddies on the north side of town, who said they could whip any and all of us on the south side in a real football game. Snorting and chattering, Alvin told all of us the challenge. We wanted them!

We began to practice. Alvin was a great quarterback and an out-standing athlete, naturally strong. His family owned Ford's Furniture Store just off the square on North Water and volunteered to help us with some equipment. They bought the shoulder pads, shirts, and padded pants. We bought our own white helmets that I paid for with the last of my "metal" money from Westville, and Dad gave me $7.50.

Most of us wore tennis shoes although a few had cleats.

We practiced in the back of our school, Guild Elementary, on the playground. Alvin made up most of the plays, about seven. I was a "halfback" and ran the football most of the time because I was the fastest boy. On defense, I was a linebacker and whatever else.

A big challenge faced us. The boys on the north side had played two or three games and were a little bigger than us, and half of them were a grade older. They also had matching uniforms; ours were var-ious colors. Ragtag would describe the Southside Tigers.

We were a little scared but determined. Besides, the north side had sent word to us that they would kill us and beat us fifty to nothing.

"Yeah, fifty to nothing."

At the last practice, being a fighter by nature, I bellowed out, "Boys, get mean, get tough, play hard."

And they yelled, "Yeah! We will, we will!"

Shaking hands as we left, we hugged and slapped one another on out shoulder pads and rear ends.

So that Saturday came. We gathered in a big side yard of one of these wonderful old brick homes in Gallatin. The grass was still as green as a bell pepper; it was about fifty degrees with a few brown leaves falling, sunny, and a big bunch of students and parents gathered. They had to bring their own chairs.

No time was to be kept. We agreed to play till somebody quit. Alvin and I, meeting in the middle of the yard with their two best players, decided that they would kick off to us first.

Getting back in the huddle, one of our guys said, "We can't beat them. They're too big."

All of us were afraid, but Alvin in his base, mellow and controlled speech, said, "Don't worry. We're gonna beat them."

They kicked off. Jay caught the ball and took off, alluding all but the last two players. Then we knew we could play with them.

Play with them we did. They were bigger; we were faster. They had more experience; we had the guts! I scored two touchdowns on long runs. Alvin ran for one and passed for one. Final score after two hours was, south side, 24; north side, 12.

What I had already learned in life was that a trailer boy could play with anybody. I had learned that a bully would run if stood up to. Better uniforms doesn't make the player, nor does big talk.

After the famous north side and south side game, when we met those guys downtown or at the ball games, they spoke and often said, "Great game."

The Winter Coat

As winter came on, Dad's work slowed down because of so much rain that fall of '56. He managed his money well, but when you don't have enough, you don't have enough. Hard times often follow.

The temperature dipped into the thirties before school as Jeanie and I walked, along with other kids. In the late afternoons, the temperature would be forty to fifty degrees.

I didn't have a coat that fit me. I had outgrown everything but two shirts, one flannel, and one corduroy, as well as a dark green sweater that Little Grandmother had made for me.

Dad worried. Mom felt sorry. I understood. I was cold. Dad talked with me.

But if there was anything I was beginning to know even as a twelve-year-old boy who had been on the road now for five years and a father who did the best he could is that it would be all right. We would be taken care of by a living, loving heavenly Father.

Just as providence would have it, the weather cleared. Dad got about fifty-five hours of work in the week following our talk.

On a cold Saturday morning in November, with sausage and eggs frying in the big black iron skillet, Dad said, "Breakfast being served in the diner."

All four of we children sat down.

Mom brought the sausage, served our plates, and Dad said, "Let's give thanks," so he prayed a sweet prayer of thanksgiving.

Mom brought the eggs, jelly, and toast. The food was good, and the family was happy.

Dad said, "Larry."

"Yes, sir."

"Do you know where we are going this morning?"

"No, sir."

"As soon as we get through, we're going down to Penny's."

My emotions of surprise and happiness flooded my soul. "Why?"

"We're going to get you a coat!"

Dad was happy and proud. Tears flowed down Mom's cheeks, and my three siblings clapped joyfully.

So we got finished with another great Saturday morning family gathering. You see, Dad went to work before we got up, so the five of us were without "superman," Saturdays were always a thankful time.

I was elated. I was emotional. I was thankful.

All of us walked into Penny's right up to the "Boy's Clothing" sign.

Dad said to the clerk, "Measure this young man and show us coats that will fit him."

Over to the coats, I walked with Mom, holding onto my arm. There it was….here it is. The one I would make my own.

Dad said, "The price doesn't matter." I don't remember what it cost, but I remember that coat.

It was dark green to match my sweater. It had a brown collar, brown leather strips on the pockets, and lined with a dark gray lining. I felt it, and it was thick.

"I'll be warm with this, Dad!"

"I know it, son. Put it on."

Mom said, "Take it off the hanger and put it on."

I did. It felt so good. It made me so warm, and I could still grow some, and the jacket would fit. Softly, I whispered, unconsciously, "this will be my coat."

Mom hugged me. The kids hugged me. Dad hugged me and kissed my cheek. I held Dad tight and said, "Thanks, Dad. You're the best!"

Another thing for which to give thanks. Hard times where turned into "good times" by my compassionate parents.

That night in my prayer before falling asleep, I gave thanks to the Lord. I went to sleep, knowing I would be warm and so proud to wear my new Penny's store-bought coat. Hard times had turned into a joyous good time.

Even a trailer boy has no excuses. Hard times make a better man.

Story 10

Fearless and Thankful
A Trailer Boy Can't Fear

Let me assert my firm belief that the only thing to fear is fear itself....

—President Franklin D. Roosevelt,
*The Public Papers and Address of
Franklin D. Roosevelt,* inaugural address,
March 4, 1933, (1936), 11

My mother often said, "Son, you can do it!" She, along with other influences, besides what was in me by birth, basically gave me a sense of "I can do it. I couldn't live in fear. I had to do it."

Fear is the enemy inside of us. Adventures happen, and great deliverances occur because we overcome fear.

No doubt, faith takes us away from fear, but fear takes us from faith.

God says to His children, "God has not given us the spirit of fear but of power and love of a sound mind" (2 Tim. 1:7). So in this spiritual sense, we are not to live in fear.

But being fearless out of ignorance, a rambling spirit, or unwillingness to learn, will get you into all kinds of trouble.

Being filled with fear and no adventurousness in the soul will leave you with very little knowledge, worldly education, or stories to tell.

Young and Fearless

I faintly remember the apartment I lived in with Mom and Dad and then Jeanie. No doubt a piece of plaster from the radio I pitched out the window still remains hidden in the grass. The refrigerator I climbed so fearlessly to get as high as possible and just to see if I could do it surely is still keeping milk cold for somebody. That fearlessness has traveled with me a long time.

Mammy

In late spring 1949, with cotton starting to show its green face, we moved from Memphis to Grenada, Mississippi. Dad carefully pulling our new, to us, gray trailer said, "A good friend of mine has moved here, and he has a son, seven years old. I think you'll like him, Larry."

I smiled and said, "Okay."

This is when our long friendship began.

This is also the place we loved a precious rather large black lady. She readily said, "I'm called Mammy all over Grenada!"

Mammy was full of love and kindness and simple country intelligence. After she would arrive at our "trailer home," immediately she sat down, took her brogans off, and stuck her thick black-and-tan "sockless" feet into her comfort shoes as she called them. They were well worn with tassels sticking out all over the house slippers of dull yellow. As she moved gracefully like an ice-skater through the little trailer, the slippers would pop up and down, viciously slapping her strong wide heel. Music, music to the soul!

So Mammy helped Mom around the trailer. Cleaning the floors, restroom, windows, ironing clothes, mending torn shirts, and a little cooking, she was a wonderful addition to our family. Her singing went deep into my heart. By this time, Mom had gotten pregnant with Walker's third child. So with two very active children, five and three, Dad—being the loving husband he was—asked around and found this wonderful lady suggested by the owner of the trailer park.

Sure enough, she worked hard, did a great job, and walked down the old country road to the trailer park. This long, straight black road swallowed up by thick cotton fields became a lifelong memory, now seventy years for all who saw her strolling down it. Yet even now, it goes to the depths of my being. Such is the life of a trailer boy.

Dad paid her 0.50 cents per day, five days a week. She was worth every penny of it. Mother was having some difficulty in carrying this child. Mammy truly, as she was known in that part of the country, was sweet, kind, and very attentive to Jeanie and I and, of course, Mother.

At 7:30 a.m., Jeanie and I would wait for her to appear, coming down the long straight road with those "puffy" cotton fields on each side. We got up early because I just couldn't stay in bed when there was a world of excitement lying just down the doorstep and beyond the little green yard. The heartbeat of the blues rolled off the "hill country," sweeping with passion over the "swampy delta."

Mammy rocked back and forth, right to left, as she strolled toward us with the sun coming over from Alabama. The grass was always wet in the morning there on the eastern edge of the Mississippi Delta. Mammy would come just a singin', "Jesus, Keep Me Near the

Cross" or "all to Jesus I surrender, all to Him I freely give." It was beautiful, and she was magical.

The sun started peeping over the trees and casting its yellow light on God's green earth. The coolness of those mornings hang in my mind right now as I feel that life event. So good!

I suppose Mammy rocked as she walked because her legs were short, large, and her shoe soles were higher on one side than the other. It's all she had. We loved her, and she loved us.

On the morning of August 1, early, as we waited for the swelter-ing heat and sweat, Mom called from the back of the trailer, "Walker, it's time!"

So Daddy ran to the back to help a bulging Mother.

Just at the right time, holding Mammy's left hand, joined ours with hers, to escort her to Dad. It was about 8:00 a.m., and the trailer held a furious site. Dad hurrying with the clothes and such to the hospital visit, the trailer was a rocking, and Dad exclaimed, "Mammy, you're a lifesaver. Vickie's going to give us a boy."

Now Daddy wanted another boy but wouldn't make anything out of it for Mom's sake. But just as suddenly as the pains appeared they quickly subsided. "Let's wait and see," Mother said and every-thing slowed down. While Dad was home, I rode with him to the store. He turned the engine off when we arrived, and I could wait no longer. Being observant, inquisitive by nature, I asked Dad, "Daddy, why is Mom getting so big in the front?"

Being rather reserved because of my aristocratic Little Grandmother, a little sweat popped up on his head and staggeringly said, "Well, Larry, as you know, your mother is going to have a baby," as I replied, "Yes, sir." He went on, looking for words for a five-year-old, saying, "You see, the baby grows in your mother's stomach. That's what you're seeing." Thankfully, he stopped, and I said, "Okay."

There was a moment of silence, and the thought came to me, *What is it going to be?* So I asked him that question.

He said, "Son, we can't know."

Not letting it go, I inquired, "Well, what do you want?"

Dad responded (now I know it was out of respect), "I only want a healthy child."

"What kind?" I relentlessly asked.

"Oh, well, Larry, I will tell you if you will hold in silence this secret. Will you promise?"

"Yes, sir, and I cross my heart!"

Dad almost fearfully said, "A boy."

Mother never knew mine and Daddy's secret as I proudly winked back at Daddy. He grinned his big smile.

"Jeanie."

"Yes, sir."

"Larry, come over here to the table with me."

Both of us slowly approaching the "meeting place," not knowing the meaning of Dad's request and tone of voice, slowly sat down.

"Kids, how'd you like to go to Grandma and Granddaddy Macs?"

With enthusiasm shooting directly into both of us, we jumped, almost in a low shout, requested, "WHEN?"

"I'll take you to Memphis on Sunday to meet them, and you'll ride in their good ole' car." He made it sound like it was a "party."

Why? Suddenly wondering why, I asked the obvious, "Why?"

"Your mother is going to the hospital in a few days, so we thought you'd love this little trip."

"Okay, okay" came quickly out of my mouth. (It's always good to make and keep things positive!)

Sunday came, and my good daddy delivered us into the hands of Mom's father at Overton Park, close to downtown. We rode in excitement like when we would go to the Memphis Zoo, and chattered all the way, we in the back seat with Alice and Barbara. Well, Jeanie rode in the front between our two grandparents, as we headed across the Mississippi River, the fifty or so miles into Arkansas.

We rarely spoke of the coming of the new Simpson for our excitement with Alice and Barbara.

In a few days after our Arkansas adventure began, we got the good news. Mother was okay, and so was the baby. Oh yeah, Mother never knew mine and Daddy's secret.

David from the beginning was a pleasure and still is today. He took a lot after Daddy. He and I have remained friends all these years.

The winter passed. Dad was making plans to move back to Memphis and attend and graduate from the Diesel Mechanics School of Memphis.

So in late spring, he and Mom bought a newly built home on Hickory Street as we prepared to move.

The last day in Grenada came.

Mammy came for the last time. We could hardly stand to leave her.

At 5:00 p.m., the whole family walked her out to old Highway 51, wiping wet tears from our cheeks. We said "Goodbye" and "We love you" for the last time. She crossed the highway to the "cotton road" and turned to look one "last time."

"Mammy, we love you. We love you... We'll see you again."

She cried as she turned, and we could hear her praying and humming, "Sweet Hour of Prayer" Sweet hour of prayer, sweet hour of prayer....as her warm, soulish voice faded into the forever future.

We stood there watching her walk down that long road until she got lost into "the somewhere" into the west. Our hearts were broken, and it seemed like Golden Boy, our gold cocker spaniel was crying too. Even Daddy had a tear. David had to wait to be told this story till he was old enough to understand.

Thanks, Mammy.

My heart still fills with deep fondness as I remember her, her big smile, happy soul, and her two plaid, colorful dresses. I hope she got some new shoes.

The Sewage Ditch

My last day in Grenada was a world shocker!

Being basically fearless, I thought I could do anything in my little world. So on our last day in Grenada, I had to try something.

The trailer park in Grenada had a sewer drainage ditch that ran eastward, almost to the railroad tracks. At night, I could hear the sound of the trains rumbling on the tracks like a secret message calling me.

The engineer would pull the whistle cord as they approached an upcoming road. In the dark of the night, when I lay awake to listen for the magical sound, I felt that I was hearing a message just for me. Lonesome, powerful, and far away, the railroad called to me to go with it…to Memphis, Little Rock, New Albany, or Ripley. I traveled away. Gallatin would give me my last love affair with the mystic of the train traveling the long, iron tracks.

I believe I got the blues from that railroad. Muddy Waters, Jimmy Reed, Lightning Hopkins, and the singers of the "hill country" sang to me. The first time I heard "the blues" on the radio in Memphis, it called me out from myself to engage in the natural and faraway world in that lonesome train.

Golden Boy was my every-moment companion. He went with me everywhere, and I went with him everywhere. When he wagged his rear end, his tail being gone somewhere, he wagged all the way to his nose. So on a merciless hot day in June, we were swinging in our tire swing, I saw him stir up a rabbit, and he took off after him and jumped the sewer ditch.

I got up while Happy said, "Don't go!"

He was my long time in the future friend but more careful than me.

You see, back in those days, some towns allowed an open sewer ditch. I had never crossed it because I was ordered not to ever go over it. But I couldn't help myself. Knowing I could jump like a jackrabbit, I knew I could jump the ditch. Jumping out of the tire, I lit on the Grenada earth.

Happy yelled out, "Larry, Larry, don't do it! Don't do it!" But I did!

As the years rolled by, I found that Happy, a little more reserved, was usually right!

Running as fast as I could as I was the fastest kid in our gang. I was scorching the earth under my barren feet.

I judged the time, space, and width of the ditch, all the while, watching Golden Boy out of my right blue eye.

"Go, Larry. Jump…run!" the gang yelled.

Toward the ditch, I was flying. I planted my left foot in perfect position, jumped, and began free sailing through midair. I went skyward almost to the sun. I knew I had gloriously made it.

But oh no, the other side was coming too fast. The bank was too close. The thick green sewage was just under me. I seemed suspended in midair.

I was going to be short. Too short! I hit the other side with my right barefoot on the edge, and the ground was too soft—it gave away!

I yelled, "Oh no!" as I *plopped* down into my new swimming hole. Golden Boy made it by two feet.

Into the stinking water, I sank with the thick mess splashed in all directions and all over me.

Sewage came to my chest as I sank too fast to the bottom. I felt the slippery mud. My new swimming hole truly stank, and I knew that I could have this spot, this ditch, all to myself!

Golden Boy barked excitedly as I grabbed the grass and weeds. Pulling with all my might and excitement, I pulled myself out with the gang, yelling, "Come on! Come on!" while they laughed to tears.

I was now a sewer boy. And you can never live that down! The fun was over, and I had to face Mom! Happy was right. "Don't go!"

The kids ran to our trailer as I jumped across a narrower spot, yelling, "Mrs. Simpson! Mrs. Simpson!"

Out the door, here she came, and here I came. All colors covered me. I stank to the high heavens.

Mom just said, "Boy, get over here for me to hose you off."

Hose me she did with teeth gritted and a wicked grin from ear to ear as she seemed to get a whole "lotta" delight spraying me as hard as she could. The water was cold, but the sewage was coming off as my aggravated mother lathered me with soap three times with a brush! She "shooed" everyone away, had Mammy get a towel, and made Jeanie go inside as she wrapped the towel around me. Into the shower I went for a second baptism of sewage cleanup, and I soaped up three more times, head to toenails, ears, between my toes, hair, and private areas while my skin was getting a little raw. "You'll get over it", Mom said, with a 'hideous' grin.'

Having such an experience makes a smart kid like me learn a little of his limitations, as well as properly estimate the challenge,

consider the possible embarrassment, and the spanking coming up...
then go ahead and do it.

Even a little brave little trailer boy must learn his limitations...
and lesson...and listen to his good friend.

> We has met the enemy and he is us. (Walt Kelly,
> *The Best of Pogo*, ed., Comic Stripballoon, Pogo,
> Earth Day, April 22, 1971, Mistress Walt Kelly
> and Bill Crouch Jr. [1982])

Story 11

Blessing on a Trailer Boy

Living on the road brings its own issues, dangers, and experiences with it, and you get to have some more.

We made friends easily with Dad's character, Mom's sweet happiness and personality, and the personalities of the four children.

I had an outgoing nature and grew up pretty fast. Jeanie, David, and Susan had their own enjoyable natures, so people took to us as we took to them.

When we moved to Inyokern, California, in 1957, we joined the Baptist Church. The principal of the school, Mr. Dial, and his family were members also. So I saw him around school, of course, and we all became friends.

There was a member of this intelligent family that I became interested in rather quickly—a daughter. Rather pretty with light brown hair and blue eyes, she was attractive in every way. Being quite intelligent, she was raised in a conservative manner with always proper decorum. I was immediately attracted to her, and she found a liking to me.

But there was a problem. She was in the tenth grade while I was in the eighth grade.

It didn't seem to matter, I, with a grown-up manner, being new and, of course, handsome! The principal's daughter soon let me know she liked me. Talking with each other at church and taking walks together on Sunday, our interest in each other grew.

Living in a town of about 350 people, the distance from the trailer park to her house was only about a half mile. I would walk over there after school, and we grew real close too fast.

On a Sunday in September, this beautiful young lady asked me to go with her and her family to the drive-in theater. Naturally, being a quick-minded boy, I said, "Yes, and I'll ask Mom and Dad."

Both of them agreed.

It seemed like Friday would never come. All my buddies were jealous and "razed" me some. I had held her hand a few times but never kissed her, so I was thinking I might accomplish that at the theater.

The family picked me up. We drove to the movie, it was dark, and I was alone with this wonderful girl in the back seat. We held hands, I closed the gap between us, and after I could stand it no longer, I looked at her, and she looked at me. We lightly kissed. We both, being new at this sort of thing, just smiled. Our hands squeezed tighter.

When the first movie was over, waiting for the next one to be put in place, Mr. Dial said, "I'll go get us some popcorn."

Now Daddy had given me 0.95 cents which seemed like quite a lot to me, so I blurted out, "I'll buy."

Oh boy, what had I done.

My gorgeous date, to which I'd be with the rest of my life, of course, and I went to the food stand to order hot dogs, cokes, and popcorn. When the server came with the food, she was a rather heavyset woman, all but yelled, "That'll be $2.12."

I was shocked. I went down with my shaking hand and pulled out my pitiful 0.95 cents. Looking sadly up at those blue eyes next to me, I had to confess, "I don't have enough money."

So my date went to her daddy and told them of my embarrassing situation. Coming back with the money, she paid the bill, and we went back to the car.

I apologized over and over.

We never held hands again or took walks.

She must have realized that two years difference was just too much besides what her family may have said. I knew two years was too wide a spread, was intimidated, and somewhat humbled.

The families stayed friends, but even though our looks and peeks at each other were sweet and congenial, I had to move on! She had to move on. After we moved, my sister Jeanie stayed in touch with my short-term girlfriend, Oletta, for many years.

Trailer boys might not be so sophisticated as a principal's daughter, but maybe they'll learn.

Now I tell this in humor, but then it was embarrassing and hurt, but I got over it and learned.

So blessed.

A Horseman's Daughter

Being the first student of one school in Kern County, California, to be allowed by the county schools board to play basketball at another school, I still hold that as a significant blessing. When our little school played against the junior high basketball team from Ridgecrest, my coach, knowing that we would not have any other games and that I could play ball, petitioned the school board. Besides, the Ridgecrest coach entered the discussion with the board also.

They allowed me to go to our school in Inyokern but play for the junior high in Ridgecrest. As I say elsewhere, we were undefeated and won two tournaments, one in Bakersfield.

Mom would pick me up at school and drive me to Ridgecrest. When we practiced, the cheerleaders squad would practice in one corner of the gym and then ride together in the bus on the way to the game.

I had instantly noticed one cheerleader. She had dark, almost-black hair, dark brown eyes, a wonderful face, and very happy. In the first two or three weeks, I only saw her about six or seven times and then on the bus. She always sat with another girl, but her eyes and my eyes always met in an adventuresome way.

Bobby asked, "Larry, have you met Betty Jo?"

"No, but I'd like to."

"Betty Jo, I want you to meet Larry."

And she asked, "Where are you from?"

"Inyokern and Tennessee," I said immediately. "Where are you from?" I asked in return.

"My father is in the Navy, so I've lived in a lot of places, but we are gonna be here now."

We sat down on a bleacher and chatted a few minutes and said, "We'll talk some more," and we both went to practice.

It was instantly in eighth-grade love. She was exactly the kind of girl I liked: positive, happy, pretty, smart, wholesome, and confident. We made plans that afternoon when Mom dropped me off that we'd get together right in that spot. And so we did.

Betty Jo and I could talk without effort. I liked her talk, her interests, and she seemed to like mine. She had traveled around the world, and so had I, so we could talk about that universal identity. She was mature for her age, and so was I. Betty Jo had no issue with saying what she thought but in a gently way. I liked that independence and open honesty.

After about two weeks, we held hands as we sat down to chat. Her face was gentle, confident, beautiful, and expressive. She looked at me with affection. We laughed and loved each minute together.

I looked at her with what was in my heart, a sweet affection and couldn't wait to see her.

On the bus to our games, we sat on the second seat, which everyone seemed to accept, and no one would sit there. The darkness of the bus with the roar of the big engine seemed to make us closer, and we sat leaning on each other's shoulder and often just looked at each other. I wanted to see her heart.

I had a strange respect for her that made me not want to offend her in anyway. We really seemed to have known each other a long time.

Her cheerleader's practice was always over before our basketball practice, so she was picked up by her mother before I was finished. Betty Jo was an outstanding cheerleader with super enthusiasm and captain of the team. Of course, in that day, they didn't do dance routines; they just cheered the team on. Her coordination was smooth, could jump high for a girl, and made me want to watch.

Our affection for each other was limited because I was twelve miles away in Inyokern. We wanted to see each other more. We couldn't.

Our basketball team was the best in that part of California, finishing undefeated and winner of the two tournaments we played in. From Bishop to Bakersfield, Tehachapi to Barstow, we beat them all. Although we had a six-foot-four boy, a great six-foot athlete, a five-foot-eight super guard and very fast, but I led the team in rebounds at five feet eight and averaged nine points per game, third best on the team. But the season was over.

No matter how competitive I was, devoted to the team, played hard, and reveled in our success, being with Betty Jo was the best of all.

We both hoped we would always be together.

But in early March, Dad came home from work on a Friday night and reported that we were moving back east to Memphis.

"After we are there, I'll get a job!"

I could no longer hear his words. He spoke decidedly and happily about going back to "our country," but I could not hear him.

Shock, sadness, and a "No, no, not now" kept coming from my mind, overwhelming me and filled my eyes with tears. I could not talk. I could not tell Mom and Dad that my life was over, that I was leaving the girl I was going to have the rest of my life. My world fell in.

I asked Mom to take me to the junior high in Ridgecrest on Monday. I had to tell Betty Jo.

She cried as we embraced each other, clinging to each other. We had never held each other that close. We softly kissed each other for the first time and mixed our tears. From that desperate clinging, she said, "I'm having a little party on Friday. We'll ride horses and can see each other one last...." She couldn't finish.

We said, "See you Friday," and went home to ponder this devastation.

I would have this same experience once again with Sandy in 1959.

As God would have it, an event happened that seemed to say, "See, this is over. It's painful, but you're just a kid."

When Friday came, after a "longing for her" week, I arrived at Betty Jo's small ranch and boarding stables. Her father was an accomplished horseman, and she loved horses and riding. I enjoyed the connection because my people in Mississippi were horseman.

Our meeting was awkward and little bit cool. I know now that's the way we part from pain. As the night went on, we found that sweet closeness, held hands, riding, but were mainly silent, not knowing the words to say.

But this is the exclamation mark of the reality of life. As I was picking the horses' hooves, picking up the front left foot I was standing too close. When the big animal put his hoof down, on my right foot, the pain was piercing. Being too proud to say anything with Betty Jo talking to me, I tried to get the 1,200-pound horse's hoof off me. My foot was no match for his. I tried to gently lean against the beast, but he only twisted around. As he twisted around on my foot, I just knew all my toes were coming off. Grimacing, I pushed his left shoulder with both hands with all my might, and the gelding stepped over.

"Are you hurt?" Betty Jo asked.

And in pride in humility, I said, "No."

I limped the rest of the night, and I could hardly find my communication skills or get away from my pain of moving away. Of course, she had to pay attention to everyone else as the hostess and less to me, which added to the hurt in my breaking heart. I was the last to leave, and although there was a short little separation between us, we wanted to feel each other one last time. With Mother waiting on the street in the car, I pulled Betty Jo up to me, and all I could say was "I love you, and I'll come back and get you...someday." She wept, and so did I. Childhood love is real. So is separation.

Dad had the trailer hooked up to the green '53 Ford dually, so all we had to do was unplug the sewer and water hose, secure the connection of the brake plug, and a pull away in the dark, with sadness, and hurting foot!

From Inyokern, we had to go through Ridgecrest in the dark on Highway 295, then turn eastward to Memphis at Four Corners. As we passed through Ridgecrest, with a little of the much-needed sunlight coming across the desert, I leaned up against the window in the car and wept silently with the tears on my cheeks smearing on the window. I said down in my breaking heart, "I'll be back. I will come get you..." over and over.

As the truck and trailer moved at fifty-five miles per hour, rambling eastward, each night, I would look back to Ridgecrest and think, "I will come back and get that wonderful girl." This was very clear in my mind. Sixty-two years later, I still haven't gone to get that memory-making cheerleader. "Would God bless me with another? That's another story."

The remembrance of the horse on my foot helped me to move on. The foot pain passed. After all, there is the next place. There is the next girlfriend. There is the next...gracious blessedness. But my thoughts of my eight-grade cheerleader hung over me... They hung over me...

There is none so literate as those who understand
the language of the heart.

—Author unknown

Blessed: God Provides

As we came close to the move from Grove City, at the end of December of '59, Dad's work having ended around December 10, Mom and Dad planned a good Christmas. I had no sense of our dire circumstance.

That for sure was one of the attributes of Mother "keep things sweet and secure" even though she was worried.

Being out of work, without a paycheck for seventeen days, and having to do for Christmas, Dad had very little money. He had been contacted by an independent contractor about some work at Bethlehem Steel in Northern Indiana, so we planned to move on the 29, and Dad would start to work January 2, 1960.

Christmas came with Mom and Dad having kept our sinking condition hidden and gave us a nice even if humble Christmas. We had learned to be thankful for what we had and knew our parents would take care of us. The next day, around noontime, in character for me, I went to the kitchen, opened a door or two of the cabinets, and they were bare!

No food! I thought. *We had no food, and we'll starve.* I cried out in my soul, and then I remembered this: "I will never leave you nor forsake you," said Jesus Christ. I knew we'd be okay. But bare cabinets? I doubted. I worried.

I went to Mom and asked a stupid fifteen-year-old question, "Do you know we have no food, only some cereal and a little bit of milk?"

"Sh," Mom whispered and said, "Yes, I know."

Big tears came to both our eyes, and I said, "I'll keep it a secret."

"I have a few dollars left, and we're going to the grocery in a little while. Don't worry. God will take care of us."

As she wiped away her tears, I said, "Mom, we'll be okay. The Lord will take care us." "Yes the Lord will take care of you."

She hugged and kissed me, yet, in honesty, I still worried!

Mom and Dad weren't prepared for what happened next. I had gone to my room to my money box.

"Five dollars!" I said breathlessly in a whisper to myself, "I'm giving it to Daddy."

Proud and thankful, I went to Dad and told him, "I have saved this from my work at the vegetable stand last summer, and it's yours."

"No, son," Daddy said.

"Dad, please, this is yours."

He took it with a wetness in his eyes and hugged me, patting my back.

But more than that, in just a few minutes, a miracle happened. Before Dad could get away to the store. *Knock, knock, knock.* Dad opened the door, and there stood our pastor, some deacons, and a few wives. Dad had asked some of the men in the men's Bible class to "pray for us because there was no work, and we were moving." Each person had their arms full.

Dad's big brown eyes bulged. "Vickie, come here." And Mother's mouth dropped open, and she smiled in thanksgiving.

Asking them in, they had eight or nine bags of food.

The pastor said, "We know you're moving, but we still wanted to make sure you had enough to make it."

Make it! The cupboards got full again. Mom now had food to pack. We were so thankful that it was hard to let those faithful followers of Christ leave. They were very kind to do this and had to know our gratitude. And although this would be the last time to see them, this wonderful story lives on. They left in joy, and so did we.

We saw some really hard days, but we saw more good days. Such is the life of a trailer boy and family, and the Lord has always provided.

We moved to Gary, Indiana, December 30, 1959.

A Loose Car or No Brakes!

After being in Gary at Keck's Trailer Park, we moved to Highland, Indiana, four miles away into our new house, in May 1961, on Grace Street.

After graduating from Calumet High School in May 1962, I went to Memphis State University. A year later, I dropped out of school and moved back home.

149

Immediately, I went to work at the same steel mill that Dad worked at as a diesel mechanic, him having gotten me the job. I bought a barely used 1963 Pontiac Tempest, which was black with red interior. The engine was 326 cubic inches. But as anyone who knows cars know that that particular model ran faster than expected. It was linked to a rear-end transmission with manual shift three speed on the floor with a white shifting nob. The distance between gears with that shifter to transmission was very long. In fact, one magazine said it was so long that anyone would have to be crazy to try to "power shift" it!

A power shift is a shifting of the gears with the driver holding the gas pedal completely down while shifting. This powers the car faster because of the "rev" of the engine.

The high-geared rear-end ratio of this Pontiac made it slower out of the blocks but faster in a rolling start. Shifting out of first at 50 miles per hour and second gear at 90 miles per hour I would shut it down at about 110 to 115 miles per hour. At higher speeds, this hot rod got faster, more quickly than a low gear rear-end.

I loved feeling the power from start to that top speed, but I didn't want to go faster!

In that day, with cars getting hotter and hotter, faster and faster, it was easy to love speed. Besides, boys having something of a wildness about them loved the speed. Being competitive didn't help me nor my best buddy and other friends having fast cars. What else could a fellow do but beat the next guy.

My competitive spirit didn't help. Muscle cars were coming in, so racing was a thing! Harry, my best friend, had an Impala Super Sport in 1963, with 250 horsepower with a 4 speed, then a '64 Super Sport with 300 horsepower. Adding headers, open exhaust pipes, and a 4:11 rear-end, his black Impala was *bad*! My next buddy had a fast Ford but didn't like to race except with another guy driving, he being a little *backward*, or more conservative or smarter! I would hate to admit that he was smarter.

Dave, my number 3 friend, called up in late fall of 1963 and said, "I'd like to come over to see you in about an hour."

I could tell by innate discernment and excitement in his voice that something was up. I waited in the front yard, not being excited myself, you see, just to make him feel good!

Suddenly there began to appear down Grace Street headed north a beast—a beast of a car. Being a pinkish/gray color, I heard the engine rev up. Dave pulled up with one of the first Pontiac GTOs! Dave had waited for this car to arrive in Gary as the very first one in that city. Dave bought it. Dave had the first GTO in the *region* as that corner of Indiana is known!

Black interior, 389 cubic, 325 horsepower, 4-speed on the floor—it was *hot*, fast! He pulled up in front of 8925 Grace Street, revved it up, and shut it down. We looked, examined everything, with the hood up for about forty-five minutes. But I was dying to *ride baby ride*!

Dave was a very conservative guy but liked to be cool. He walked with a swagger, spoke very softly, a little like James Dean. Getting into the car, he pulled off very slow with a poor management of the clutch so that the car *jerked*. He made second gear, then third, then fourth, all with more jerking. Finally, he "got it" but would not "get on it."

I don't blame him, and I accepted the fact that he wanted to baby his world-shaking new GTO!

Harry was the best driver among us, and I was a close second. We loved to drag race. One evening, as I was traveling west on Highway 6, Old Ridge Road, a guy in a red 1963 Ford 390 cubic inch engine with a 4 speed, having racing mufflers, slicks, and at 375 horsepower with a low gear rear-end—he was bad. Slickers are rear tires that are larger with a smooth flat surface. The purpose of those tires is to allow the tires to slip a little to keep the engine revved wide open. "Ford-man" rolled up beside me, looked over at me, and nodded sideways—meaning, "Do you dare race me?" Of course, I did! So I nodded, and he hit it. He jumped me by two cars lengths immediately. The highway was open, so I meant to get him. As I wound out in second gear about ninety miles per hour, I was holding my own. My little black Tempest was rollin'. But Burr Street was coming up fast on the right.

Burr Street was full. The scene before us was fearsome indeed.

Being a three-way intersection, the eastbound lane had both lanes full with two cars. The southbound, one-lane Burr Street had two or three autos in a row. The westbound Highway 6 had two parked cars filling those lanes. ALL LANES WERE BLOCKED! We were coming on 'em too fast, headed west.

We were bearing down on the rear of the two automobiles in front of us. All vehicles were sitting still as the light was making its change. We either were gonna hit the two cars in front of us or swerve around them.

I hit my breaks with all I had. They began to smoke. They were fading! Fading can't stop a car! I was going to ram the cars blocking the lights!

The only thing I could do with my unstoppable Pontiac was swerve right around the car on the right, then back left, making my swerve like a question mark! This would put me in front of the car headed south from Burr Street. All I could think was that the southbound car was going to pull out in front of me with death written all over it. Besides, there was a service station on my right, a curb, and a light pole on the corner. Besides, it was almost dark.

We were still doing forty-five to fifty miles per hour!

My competitor had to do the same on the left of the two cars, calmly parked at the red light. Little could those drivers know that death was rolling down upon them.

The Ford got there first, swerved to his left and then right into the empty intersection back left into the empty lanes westward. I swerved right next to the telephone pole and curb, set down on my horn in front of the southbound Burr Street car, then back into the intersection, almost at the same time as Mr. Ford! Swerving into the two open, yes, the only two open lanes headed west.

We made it!

We had done a great car move but stupid indeed. I can imagine what those people thought and said, "Blah, blah, blah, stupid kids!"

After about 150 feet, we both pulled over and met each other on the side of the highway as two of the helpless drivers passed us by and honked in anger. Shaking hands, we patted each other on the shoulders and gave each other a light hug, exchanged names, and told the truth about ourselves. Stupid!

I said, "You won, but we'd better thank the Lord we are alive and didn't hurt anybody."

"Yes," he said in agreement.

After a couple of minutes, we were ready to go. Thank the Lord, I was going home and not to the graveyard! Yes, I was whipped and ready to go to my family.

We pulled away slowly as if sedated, and we were...by fear, shock, and gratitude.

Grace Street never looked so good.

I am not proud of racing on the streets but enjoyed my cars and very thankful I never hurt anyone.

A trailer boy always needs an all-powerful helping hand. I've got no excuses.

Lost in the Mountains of California

It was the last Sunday in June 1964. I had been interim pastor of a 155 member Baptist Church for almost a year. Now a nineteen-year-old boy really has no business being a pastor. Although, in many ways, I was way beyond my age, I still had a lot of foolishness in me, plus not enough experience.

Having been in church, or should I say churches, because of our many moves, I had been a member of five different groups. Being a good talker, as some said, "He has the gift of gab," I was told, "You should be a preacher," "You may be the next Billy Graham," and such talk.

In Richmond, Indiana, at the age of fourteen, I was asked by the pastor, Brother Roddy, to preach on "youth Sunday," to which I agreed. In thinking about a text from God's Word that I could present, I picked a passage that I thought I knew something about, the Ten Commandments! After all, just three years before I had gone to see the movie after that title, with Uncle Elaine and family at a drive-in movie in New Albany, Mississippi. Besides, I had read it many times, heard it preached, tried to live it (but couldn't), and simply believed I could do this challenge.

That Sunday came, and I was nervous as a cat. My palms were sweaty, my mouth was dry, and my mind was blank. Mom and Dad reassured me. My brother and sister seemed to believe in me as did many in the church. My teenage friends just said, "You will be fine." The pastor prayed with me before the service in his study, but my mouth only got more "sticky." A girl who had a crush on me but was not my type—if you know what I mean—came to me, took my hand, and said very softly and sultry, "I'll be praying for you," in a breathy voice. I didn't need that!

Here we went—the pastor, song leader, and I—out on to the rostrum. I sat by Brother Roddy, but I couldn't see a thing, well, almost. Yeah, sure, the gift of gab, Billy Graham, a natural preacher, and I was near to passing out.

In a little while, after all the normal procedures, singing and such, it was time—the time. The pastor got to the pulpit, said some glorious things about me, which I couldn't hear because of the ringing, or was it buzzing in my head? Besides, I knew a lot on myself. He didn't.

He turned and, with a smile, said, "Brother Larry, the pulpit is yours."

I sat "numbed" and "dumbed" a few seconds.

For heaven's sake, I couldn't even see it. Where was I? He came over, shook my hand, and pointed to the preacher's stand. I staggered over there. I looked out at 150 or so people, and they looked like strangers—people I had never seen before. I asked for help, stood there, looked and found Dad and Mom, and I got better.

I did find my text because my notes were stuck in my Bible, and I asked all to turn to Exodus 20:3–17. Thank the Lord, I had a long passage to read, which I assure you took plenty of time to read dramatically.

Now think of it. Ten glorious truths wherein God commands us to live in obedience to him. I was way in over my head and was done in sixteen minutes. Everyone was kind. I knew I had tried to faithfully declare God's Word, but I was glad it was over.

While in Richmond, I told Sandy I was going to be a preacher or a coach. I have been both and preached somewhere upward of 4,750 plus times till now.

On that fateful day in June of '64, coming home for Sunday dinner after "preaching" that morning, we settled into naps and then for me to finish preparing for the evening message. Around 3:30 p.m., Mom called me to the phone and said, "Your Uncle LT in Carpentaria, California, wants to talk to you." Mom exhibited a bag of mixed emotions, but I was happy to hear from one of my favorite people in the whole world, Mom's brother, just below her in a family of ten.

We chatted for a few minutes, having a great time, when LT said, "Son, I want to talk to you about something."

"Okay," I quietly said, hearing the serious change of tone in his voice. "Larry, our church has lost its pastor a couple of months ago, and we are looking for one. The other night, while praying, the Lord put you on my heart. I know you're young, but I know how you've grown up to what kind of person you are. You've been preaching now for a year and half, and I want you to come to California. I've talked to the church, and they've agreed to pay all your expenses for you to come out here and preach a 'trial' sermon. Would you be willing to do that?"

I couldn't speak. Leave my family? Leave my fiancée? Leave my friends?

So I said, "Yes, I'll think about it, pray about it, and call you in a couple of days."

He said, "That's great. I'll get off so you can talk about it with Vic and Walker."

We said goodbyes and hung up.

I immediately started crying, boo-hooing, wailing, floods of tears, loud crying! The family came into the kitchen, not knowing why I was crying. They were silent but concerned.

When I could gather myself, I said, "I know I'm moving to California."

Somehow I knew. When I told the family, they felt it too. Fear and sorrow about leaving. *How could I go? I'm nineteen. I'm engaged to be married. I have great friends here. I graduated here. I've got to go back to college. And I'm only going for a trial sermon!* After two days of prayer, I committed to going to California.

I called LT on Tuesday night and told him when I could leave. As I thought about moving, I thought about my Uncle Elaine in Mississippi and that he might like to make the trip with me.

His first remark was "Son, when we leavin'?" Elaine was riding with me to California.

Being the first child of ten, with Mom being number 2, he was honored by all and honorable! Being very humorous, I knew we'd have a ball. Elaine's four brothers were already in California, so we'd have a reunion.

Somewhere, I'll finish this trip's story.

Lost in the Mountains (Part 1)

After being in Carpentaria for a few months in the fall of 1964, Doc and I got together to play some ping-pong. After about two games, Doc said, "Son, let's go hunting!" After all, it was deer season, but 8:15 p.m.?

Doc owned McCollum Plumbing, so he could leave anytime he wanted unless a job was too big. Grace, his wife, though pretty feisty, would pretty much go along with him on anything after some discussion!

I said, "Let me run to the house, get my clothes, boots, etc."

Leaving was no problem for me since my wife was in San Bernardino Nursing School, and I was a high-kicking twenty-year-old pastor. I called Carole Lee and told her what I was doing, and she just said, "Be careful." We told each other "love you" and said our goodbyes.

Arriving back at Doc's, whose real name is Doctor Gillespie McCollum, having received that distinguished title because Granddaddy and Grandma Mac could not think of a name for their sixth child. So they named him after the doctor who delivered the black-haired, blue-eyed boy on February 23, 1934.

Still extremely active at eighty-five, thin, and *ready*, he is a real cowboy with a "let's go" attitude. He rides his mare, Sassy, two or three times weekly in the hills of Coastal California in Santa Barbara County even now. His wife, Grace, of sixty-four years is a small Italian lady and very *spiffy*. Doc is attentive to Grace, but she knows he is going to go!

He and I have always had a strong likeness to each other, love for each other, and I wanted to be like him in many ways.

One story that was told numerous times, as you know how families often repeat the same things, was about Doc and James, me, and our bathtub.

James, being two years younger than Doc, took his lead, and they both loved me. Being the firstborn grandchild in a large family, with nine aunts and uncles on Mom's side and eventually thirty-five grandchildren, I had this peculiar grandchild position. And this position has been a blessing down through the years.

While I was yet two or three years old, before we moved to Grenada from Memphis, Doc and James, then nine and eleven, would come to visit us. They would walk me around the block, push me in the swing, play ball with me, carry me on their back, stand me on their shoulders, and any other thing they could think of, and I was always ready. This physical activity just fit me, my personality, and body type. This also bond me with them forever. I have always loved the outdoors and loved to hike, have and ride horses, and be with the men in my family, my dad, uncle Elaine, LT, and Travis each made sure I was all boy, along with Doc and James. For this, I am very grateful until this day.

When we would come home from outdoor knockin' around, and it was bath time, Mom would run water in the tub, full of hot water and soapsuds, as I recall Mom used Ivory "bar" or "soap flakes." I would bath, and then the fun started. I would say, "Come on, boys, put me under," and here came Doc and James. Sometimes Mom and Dad would look on. James would pick me up out of the water just high enough that it was safe. Yes, you know what happened next. He would let me loose, drop me down the slope of the back of the tub, and at about fifty or sixty miles per hour (or was it seventy?), I would strike down through the suds, under the water, till my feet hit the other end. Coming up wiping the suds off my face and blowing through the bubbles to get it off my mouth, grasping for air, I'd say, "Do it again, boys." And laughing wildly, it would be Doc's turn, again and again, down through the water, and like a seal, I'd go until they gave out.

I wouldn't quit. They said, "Oh, son, that's enough." But I knew the truth. It was enough for them!

Special days and special days lay ahead.

California in 1964 and 1965 were very special days for me. Pastoring my first full-time church was very special. I was forced to study, having to preach three times weekly. I was forced to live alone for five days a week because my good wife, Carole Lee, was in San Bernardino finishing her three-year nurses program, so I had to do for myself. I was forced to face the future regarding my return to college because I was determined to go back to Memphis State and get my secular education, earning my bachelor's degree.

Beyond those things, I had to reckon with leaving my uncles whom I loved very deeply. Until that time, though, I meant to live a "lifetime" in that short time I had there.

Arriving back at Doc's with all my gear, ice chest, canteen of water, long johns, heavy coat, rain gear, package of bacon, a couple of potatoes, and butter, I got out as Doc was packing his blue truck. He hollered at normal, "Heyeeeh...! How you doin'?"

"I'm ready," I said. "Do we need anything else?" I continued as I threw my sleeping bag and a pillow in the back of the truck.

Doc kissed Grace goodbye. I had called Carole Lee to tell her what I was doing, and "I'll come get you Friday." Away we went, about 10:30 p.m.

Black as the ace of spades, the night seemed to swallow us up. We turned south on Highway 101 and went two miles to Highway 150 East since we didn't want to drive into the ocean! Driving in black darkness and a slow fifteen miles per hour, we turned north in an hour on rough Highway 33. These are mountainous, rugged roads, especially in 1965. Having to negotiate such roads in the black is a test all its own. Besides, Doc's blue jeep followed us closely, being hooked to the four-wheeled drive truck.

But we laughed, told stories and lies, talked about Granddaddy Mac and others. I silently prayed. At about 12:30 a.m., we came to state Road 207 turning east. Finding a good-enough-looking road, we headed on up into the mountains, turned into a flat spot, and parked by a big cedar tree so the truck would have a little cover.

Doc said, "We'll follow this road on up close to the top, find a good place for the night, and go on up in the 'mornin'."

I said, "Let's go."

So we loaded up the jeep, and from that lonesome spot, our destiny was before us. We headed up. From that three-thousand-foot elevation, we started climbing pretty fast. The "whine" of the engine was ear-shaking since we had to stay in first gear most of the time. "Cracking and crunching" below the tires and debris slung up under the bottom of the jeep kept a constant roar and banging. Rolling rocks from our intrusion into their natural location flipped down the road and off into midair. We could hear limbs cracking somewhere down below or way "down yonder," hear the thunder of a fifty- or a hundred-pound rock smacking the mountainside. It was fearsome.

Sometimes we would just spin a few seconds for the tires to dig down far enough to grip the rock and earth, catch hold, and sling us forward. Would we not be able to go on at some point?

Doc sat stoical, intently controlling the steering wheel, lest it pop out of his hand. Very few words were spoken, but we both said and knew, "We'll make it."

Besides all this, it apparently had rained at this increasingly high elevation a couple of days back, and there were yet slick, muddy spots in the road. Doc's four-wheel drive gripped the road like a caterpillar, but a few times, we hit muddy spots that sent the jeep, sliding backward a foot or two. I wondered if we wouldn't just slip on off into the next world, but I didn't tell Doc.

The wildest, most wicked spots, though, were the ones with all this but in a curve. Several times, the road cut around a curve into the mountainside where sheer rock stuck out over the road and narrowed the road to almost half of its normal span. Eight feet, seven, or nine feet? I don't know but narrow! Sometimes so narrow and tight I unconsciously ducked my head!

Suddenly the road began to flatten out, the road's rocky surface less loose. We were in the midst of what we came to see, in a few hours, as straight, beautiful mixed conifers and chaparrals as the predominant vegetation. There were Douglas firs and Great Basin sagebrush that all blended together to make quite a delight for the eyes of an outdoorsman. The variations, colors, slopes, sizes were awesome.

After two hours of hard driving by Doc for both of us, with our emotions having to "back up," we found a nice flat spot under some Douglas firs. Doc gathered wood, started a fire, put coffee on the grill while I got the bedrolls out, set the bedding up, locked up the jeep, and sat by the little fire. My uncle loved his coffee even at 3:00 a.m. while I had hot chocolate. He built the fire big enough so we'd still have enough coals in a couple of hours to have a big fire as it got colder and colder. We pulled our clothes off down to our socks and underwear and pulled the individual sleeping bags up around our ears and got warm. All I had time to say was "Thank...you...Lord!" I fell asleep.

"I think I hear popping, and crackling... Is it smoke? Do I smell smoke...frying...bacon...skillet noise?" I raised up, and my uncle was up, dressed and humming a George Jones song, holding a cup of coffee in one hand, a spatula in the other.

Not to be outdone, although I already was, I jumped up almost instantly, shook in the thirty-degree cold, and Doc loudly said, to let the deer population know we were here, "Heeeyeeeeee! How you doin'?"

"Man, I'm wondering why we didn't get up an hour ago," to which Doc replied, "I did!"

I just started singing, "Standing on the corner with the low-down blues / gotta big hole in the bottom of my shoes, / honey let me be your salty dog," trying to sing like Lester Flatt and Earl Scruggs from whom I first heard the old songs.

Doc said, "Come on, Larry, and get cha some coffee."

I obliged him, after I finished dressing and drank my coffee while we chatted, and he cooked. I went to get more wood. With some pretty good pine, I returned as the sun started clearing the distant horizon.

Cold white breath was steaming from our mouths, a white frost lay on the ground, and the bacon smelled better than perfume on a good-lookin' woman.

We ate bacon about six slices, three eggs, grilled toast with real butter, and splashes of molasses two cups of coffee, Doc's third or fourth, and a banana. We sat by the warm fire awhile and talked about the trip up the mountain. We both agreed that it was the toughest we'd ever seen. Once we unloaded that experience, we talked about Granddaddy Mac, now gone, Elaine, and James, who couldn't make this trip, and other precious members of the family.

Doc told some army stories as I sat mesmerized, while he glanced over at me with happy reflection. He told me a "private" story that only a very few people know, even to this very hour. I've kept it a secret.

After only two hours sleep, which I was glad to get, eating breakfast, we loaded the jeep, put out the fire, splashing it thoroughly with water, we headed to a spot Doc had been to once before.

In about thirty minutes, we came to a beautiful spot in sight of a big mountain lake off to the north as the road ended. Blue, clear, and peaceful, the lake lay still. The sun was topping the trees, and we were ready. This was a walking hunt.

Here we go.

Doc said, "Larry, take off westward and make a big circle around the lake and meet me back at noon."

The thin forest, views, and smells with tall, tall pines was stimulating after walking and hunting quietly lost in the splendor of God's creation, we met back, having had no luck but in love with the dry, high mountains that are full of 'game.'"

We ate lunch, sat a few minutes, and Doc said, "Larry, you take about an hour trip around the lake, get you a deer, and we'll meet back in an hour." He said, "I think this trail"—pointing westward—"makes a circle southward and comes back around to here. I'll meet you about two o'clock."

Our journey started. We parted ways.

I watched my uncle walk off to the west then fade into the bush and pines, knowing he would turn south in about a half mile slowly, silently looking for game. We knew it was there, but they had "out-gamed" us so far. I enjoyed watching his white cowboy hat disappear into the mystic, the future.

The lake was enchanting as I approached it, realizing it slowly wasn't a pond but really a lake. Slowly, I cruised along wanting to be silent so the deer wouldn't outsmart me anymore. Through the huge pines and the firs, I wiggled my way, both looking high and low for game, listening to the birds and enjoying the breeze, smells, squirrels, wilderness, alone and wild.

My mind would wander off to Doc, Carole, Mom and Dad, my brother and sisters, my whole family, Harry and Happy with thankfulness to my God. After a little while, I resurfaced up to the lake, a beautiful, clear big body of blue mystery. Up and down and all around, I went until it was time to go back to the jeep.

Doc wasn't there; it was 2:00 o'clock, so I just got a chair, sat down to rest, and wait. After an hour, I was worried. No, Doc! I could see him hurt, needing help, or a thousand other things. My mind began to race wildly.

Realizing I needed to slow down, I leaned against the blue jeep to ponder more in control. So I decided that I could follow the trail ahead of the jeep, follow Doc's steps as far as possible, and track him down. The thought that he might be hurt blew my brain up!

I filled my canteen, grabbed a sandwich, and apple, put it into my backpack, then anxiously headed out. The trail narrowed down pretty quickly but continued straight west. Expecting the trail to turn southward, to the left, as Doc had described it after about a half mile, the vegetation thinned very significantly. I could not believe my eyes!

Ahead was open sky, rugged brown low-lying peaks and a canyon off to the right. The sky covered 50 percent of the horizon with the sun a little ahead of me in the west.

The trail quickly narrowed down and extended straight out to the canyon about seventy-five feet ahead with nothing but air on the north and no bottom in sight. Walking out to the mouth of the canyon, I viewed the small trail winding downward with a large gap of hundred yards between the two walls of the deep canyon. I could not yet see what was beyond. I could see Doc's boot prints in the rocky brown dirt and far apart. I knew he was anxious. He was reachin' out, pickin 'em up, and layin'-em down.

I also knew I had to follow on. Doc might be hurt. The trail narrowed from one foot to three or more, and sometimes I had to step as much as a foot over a complete washout of the trail. The bottom was somewhere way down yonder!

Mountain goats, deer, bear, elk, lions, squirrel, and smaller creatures trusted that little mountain trail.

Coming around a left-hand curve, I could see the bottom that seemed a universe below. My legs weakened. I stopped, took some deep breaths, asked for God's help, and hiked on. Carefully proceeding downward, I made sure not to step on a rock. But, in a moment, rounding a bend in the trail, I did it. I stepped on a rock just big enough to make my foot roll northward toward the emptiness down below. With my foot in mid-California air, I grabbed a rare chaparral on that blistered, rocky canyon wall, and it held! Slowly, I drew my right foot back up so as to not disturb the tough wild plant or rocks under my left foot I got my right foot back on the ground! Landing against the wall of the path, I gave thanks—God got me under control—and I walked on. A hawk soared above, riding the airway.

I must find Doc! I could still see his boot marks. Finally, the long trail came out way down from the top into a wide, dry creek bed. Doc's tracks turned left down the rocky, sandy, dry water trail.

Looking back up the canyon, the bottom was roughly fifty yards wide, a thousand feet deep, and a half mile back to the top.

I headed southward, following Doc's wide boot prints, so wide to make one think they were of a man who was anxious to get somewhere quick. I knew he was worried. The jeep seemed far away. We were at least two hours apart, but I was trying to gain ground. The dry creek bed with but a few signs of life seemed endless. A magnificent eagle soared way up above, just moving with the movement of the winds. He seemed relaxed and disinterested. I was neither.

Trying to stretch my stride to its widest, I followed on with Doc's long stride. I got hot, then sweaty in the late afternoon sun, stopped to rest as I sat on a big rock, and tied my long-sleeve shirt over my canteen, around my waist. I was ready to track in about five minutes, having a drink of water, not knowing what was ahead I meant to consume as little water as possible.

I guessed I had walked about two miles in that rocky creek bed, being good at distances from all our traveling days and running in cross-country and track. Being already a little tired, I picked myself back up and trudged on. In another one and a half mile or so, suddenly, I could see the mountain in front of me. What was this? No creek bed!

Approaching what looked like the end of the creek, it opened up to the right. Sure enough, "dry creek," as I now was calling it in my head, turned right, westward, away from the camp! The walls of the mountain were washed out deeply about seven or eight feet high from the waters of "dry creek" when it was "wet creek"!

By this time, 5:00 or 5:30 pm, the sun still high, hot, and glaring, and now, in my face, burning like fried potatoes. My mind began to play anxious tricks on me.

It seemed to me that I knew there was a town just over the high wall of the mountain now on my north and right-hand side. As I walked along more slowly, thinking this through, I knew that if I could get to the top of this ridge that I would see the town. So I turned to climb the hill. It was steeper than I thought, making me have to lean forward close to the rocky mountainside and sometimes using my hands and sometimes walking sideways on the sides of my feet.

Looking across the mountain, there was a large flat rock hanging out over some open space, so with my mind racing to find escape, I headed sideways toward the rock. This large ten-by-fifteen rock stuck out of the mountain. I thought maybe I could see more out there. Negotiating my way carefully out to the edge of the rock, hoping it would hold to the mountainside, I could see a long way northward and southward being about two hundred feet from the east bank of the canyon. Realizing the tremendous space of open air below me, fear possessed me.

Besides, the evening air was starting to cool with the winds picking up just a bit. The air was hitting me and moving me. I froze! Slowly, bending down to my knees and hands, I gently moved from the edge. Talking about scared stiff? I was and had never before nor since known such fear. All I could do at that moment was sit, stiffly hunkered down, talking to myself, telling myself to relax, "It'll be all right." "Relax, it'll be all right. Relax..." "Lord, help me, help me... help Doc...." I got better control of myself.

In a few minutes, I was able to leave the rock and proceed to the top of the mountain ridge to see the town down below. Basically, crawling to the top, my spirit began to sour as I knew I would see my dream. Scrambling with excitement, I made the last few feet, stood and looked...down. No town! I stared, but no town, left and right, but no town! No town. It was an illusion. I turned sadly, bucked up, and got a new resolve to get back down to the creek and find Doc.

Looking down, I realized two things: it was a long way down to the creek bed and very steep. Knowing that I needed to be reserving my strength, if I had measured the mountainside better, I wouldn't have climbed it, but I had. Besides, the slope with rocks was very soft and loose, making the travel very difficult. The weight of my .30-30 Winchester didn't help.

I began to make my descent. Not being able to walk down, I began to slide, keeping my balance with my hands, turning sideways, sliding sideways. Besides, I was in a hurry! Getting to the bottom, sand and brown grit was all over me, my hands, clothes, face, and everywhere. Reaching for my canteen to wash my hands and face, I realized it was unusually light. At the same time, I felt the wetness in my left pant leg. Taking the canteen out of its holster—yes, it had a hole in it—the holster had torn loose and now a hole. I had no water, and no water anywhere.

Blessed: Lost in the Mountains (Part 2)

I had no water.

Having slid down the mountainside, trying to balance myself, sometimes sliding ten to fifteen feet, shifting my .30-30 rifle hand to hand, I was wet with sweat, as the light of day was narrowing into the night.

Reaching the bottom of that mountainside, I realized, "I had no water." I prayed and believed somehow both Doc and I would make it. All I knew was to keep walking.

By 7:00 p.m., the sunlight was fading. I could still see tracks, and I pushed myself. In another thirty to forty minutes, no tracks! I searched for tracks—no tracks. I went back to the last tracks and walked around in a circle to see if Doc had deviated out of the creek bed. Sure enough, he had turned southward up on the bank that had a little opening beyond it. Within fifty to seventy-five feet, the brush opened up into a picnic area! Two or three tables and a rock cook grill were there and a road to the left back up the mountain.

I looked around, and there had been a fire in the fire hole very recently. Looking both ways, east and west, I knew I had to head up the mountain road east. I moved on.

As 8:00 p.m. passed on my watch, I headed up the road, up the mountain. In a little while, the sun disappeared behind the western earth, and it was dark. By now, it was becoming cool, significantly. In those mountains, it can be a hot and dry: eighty degrees in the day and drop to thirty degrees at night. It was cold. As long as I walked, I stayed warm.

By 9:00 p.m., I was becoming more weak, had eaten my last bit of jerky about 5:00 p.m., and had not stopped to rest. I sat down on the side of the road, leaned up against a flat-sided rock, my bed, and dropped off to sleep instantly. In a few moments, I woke up shivering from the cold. Besides, "there are bear and mountain lions." I said out loud to myself, "Keep going." I figured I'd just get eatin' alive. I was thinking of my sweet family—my wife, Carole, my brother, David, sisters, Jeanie and Susan, especially Mom and Dad. Being thankful and getting ready for death, God seemed to say that "it was all okay either way." Confessing my sins, asking forgiveness, turning only to God in Christ, I was by his grace facing up to death.

The night was black as West Virginia coal. I was struggling to move up the mountain, and it was almost 10:45 p.m. Thinking aloud, I got a magnificent plan. I'd go back down, get under a picnic table, keep the frost off me, try to sleep, and maybe keep the bears from eating me. No doubt, by now, I had my own personal bear tracking me, waiting to eat me at just the right time!

I don't know how far I had walked up the road, but it was 11:15 p.m. when I headed back down. Two or three times, I fired my rifle in case somebody could hear me, but I couldn't even shake out a scared deer! This was lonesome territory! Stumbling like a Memphis drunkard, I was approaching the bottom where my picnic table-bed awaited its visitor.

A noise! A whining noise, way off in yesterday! It got a little louder. It faded almost away. It got louder. I turned to look up that big, fat mountain and stared. Was it a hunter come to set up camp for tomorrow? A forest ranger? An illusion? Looking for hope, suddenly, light began to swing from south to west, out in the black sky. I stood in wonder, joy, and thankfulness. I stared wild-eyed. The lights popped over the mountaintop!

The vehicle moved in the dark in crawling speed. I waited.

Here it came! Four hundred yards, two hundred feet, fifty feet, and now ten feet, now beside me, a blue jeep/truck, Doc at the wheel. He threw the door open, leaned across the seat, and I fell inside. We hugged and cried. It was midnight.

We headed up over the mountain then back down, shared our stories, and gave many thanks. He was scared for me as I was for him. He acknowledged that the landscape just wasn't as he thought. We talked about the tremendous canyon trail, and I told him of my illusion of a city over that horizon.

And here is what happened at the campground. Doc encountered a nice Spanish American family there and asked if they would take him out of the mountains back to the road. They said no. Wide-eyed and desperate, Doc asked again, and they said no again. Then in an ice-cold voice and stare, glancing at his much-used yet beautiful .30-06 rifle, he said, "Yes, you'll take me out."

Feeling desperate about me, time, and distance, he meant to clear those rough mountains. The male in that family took him out to the highway, back to where we started up the mountain and to our parking place at the top. Doc gave him some money, and they had become friends, which is the way of the McCollum's, Mom's family.

Doc then came back down the mountain, down the highway, headed back up and over the top to our reunion.

He said, "Son, do you know how far it was from the top of the mountain where the jeep was and around the whole loop back to the vehicle?"

"No, but a long way."

"Thirty-five miles!"

All I could do was shake my head. I had walked fifteen miles. Back to the highway, we slept in someone's front yard in the damp grass. We were thankful to the depths of our souls.

We went home.

How I loved my uncle Doc!

A trailer boy gotta have some help and no excuses. Blessed!

Story 12

A Life of Firsts
Not for My Glory but Your Good

I was blessed with a good feeling about myself—out of that came a strong self-determination. Besides, the life I lived as a trailer boy, moving over twenty-four times, challenged me to become who I was, defend myself, and prove myself. I really believed, "son, you can do it."

New schools, new kids, different teachers, and new people in the trailer parks and churches were the norm in our travels. It was always a reestablishing of who I was and why.

Many people in my family made me have confidence, and by nature, I was adventurous.

It was always natural to me to compete, so please know I do not tell these wins for self-glory but your enjoyment.

> The only competition worthy of wise man is with himself.
>
> —Anna Jameson (1797–1860)

First in a Large Family

Mom was the second child in a family of ten and the first female which gave her a special place. Being the first to marry, she was treated special. A son named after Dad was born in 1943 but never left the hospital. After nineteen days, the pneumonia took his little life. He is buried in a family plot in Memphis with my Dad's name.

I have always felt a strong kinship to my big brother. A year and a half later, I was born to Mom and Dad.

I was the first living grandchild born in this large family. They lavished attention on me, and thankfully, I've had a special place in the lives of my aunts and uncles all these years. Four are still left in this family into which I was born, and I was like a brother to them.

Being the first of Dad's living offspring, his mother, "Little Grandmother," thought I hung the moon. We always had a close kinship and could talk for long periods. She taught me to walk with dignity, speak correctly, think, and be proud of who I was.

She certainly influenced my life. Little Grandmother was a wonderful stitcher and sower doing remarkable work. I have in my study today a work she did for me, an embroidered, "Now I Lay Me Down to Sleep" prayer with mine and her name on it dated 1947. I write this while I sit on a maroon crocheted "throw" my grandma Mac, Mom's mother, made for me in the seventies.

They made me feel good about myself as the first grandchild, giving me a desire to be "first" in all I attempted. How I love my extended family.

Marbles and the Burgundy Purse

The trailer park on North Water Street in Gallatin, Tennessee, was a great spot to live for a ten-year-old and coming eleven in July 1955. Living there for almost two years was a treat to us, a long time for "travelers."

At the center of the park was a very large colonial-style 1800s estate. The trailers were lined up on the south side of the small park. There were six or seven trailers and several children, two or three about my age.

School let out, and summer began. Back in those days, we got out of school at the end of May and didn't go back until the first week of September. My gang of friends were ready to hunt rabbits, climb trees, go to the city pool, and play marbles.

I had never played "marbles" before like my friends had. Betsy, Samantha, whom we called Sammi, Carl, Ricky, and Roy had played during the summer before, so I had to catch up fast.

But I only had two marbles that I had found in the ground, up to about halfway of the marble. One was red with swirls of different colors, and the other was green with swirls. I was so excited to find these two lonesome marbles, thinking they would give me a good start.

In the middle of the yard between the trailers and the grand colonial two-story house was a worn-off spot where we played football, tag, or kick the can. So we had the right place to play. It is still amazing to me that Mrs. Shaw and "Pappy" would allow us to do such a thing, tear up that part of the yard, and keep it bald. Pappy walked with a cane, wore an old black cowboy hat, twisted in different directions and overalls. I think he was sympathetic toward us because he had roamed the hills of Middle Tennessee as a boy.

He said, "Awe, leave 'em alone. Let 'em play." To which Mrs. Shaw said, "Let 'em, play" with a contradicting, very faint smile in her green eyes, but her bottom lip twitched with aggravation.

The problem with Betsy was that she was too cute, and I couldn't keep my eyes off her. We never even held hands, because we were such good friends and too young anyway. She could play marbles. Being from Tupelo, Mississippi, she had a Deep South–sweet Southern drawl.

Carl lived across the street and down a little in a little "bitty" brown house. He was shy but was tall, "gangly," and didn't say much. Him not talking was good for us because we five talked too much, especially Ricky but Carl could shoot marbles!

A true outdoor type, Ricky had hunted rabbits and birds with his uncle who worked at the shoe factory, where Mr. Langford worked. He had even shot a big ole shotgun. So he was tough and "savvy," which put us in some irritation toward each other. I liked him but didn't care for his braggadocios talk. Ricky had been the champ from last summer, so he figured to win again.

The other four just assumed he'd be the winner again. I didn't.

Now Roy was a case. He had failed the third grade, so he was a year older than the rest of us. He'd cuss. He learned it from his dad who would cuss almost every other word until Dad politely, but with those fiery, deep brown eyes with black eyebrows and Indian brown skin, asked him not to "be a cussin' around my boy." Roy's dad, after that, was careful to guard his language, especially if Dad was outdoors. Roy didn't really care about anything, was up for everything, and wore the same two pair of shorts and jeans all summer. By the end of August, they were almost shredded to a "comparison of shredded cheese." I didn't care. I liked him.

On a hot early June day, "the gang" met at the edge of the play circle, me with my only two marbles in the world with these world-class players and their bags of all kinds, full of marbles.

"Where's your shooter?" one of the guys blurted out.

"Shooter?" I asked.

I didn't know about the "shooter."

Ricky blurted out, "Everybody's got a shooter."

I blankly asked, "What's that? A shooter?"

"Yes, a shooter," Betty sympathetically replied. "It's your favorite marble. The best you can shoot with."

"I don't know," I said. "I've never shot anyone before."

They all laughed, making fun of me. Well, I learned to pick out the best one I could "shoot."

"Let's play," someone said, and Carl scrapped off with his heel a big circle in the dirt. The playing field was set, and I was nervous.

"Let's roll," Ricky boastingly decreed.

And I, in my marble ignorance, asked, "What?"

"Look, we have to have a line in the dirt, and each of us rolls a marble at the line. The one who gets the closest shoots first," Roy replied, showing a little compassion for my ignorance.

"You call that 'lagging,'" Sammi softly explained.

Roll we did, and I ended up last. Ricky's "shooter" rolled up slowly to the "lag" line, so he won first shot. Roy took up my case. He explained about everyone putting marbles in a pattern of some sort, and whoever had won the lag shoots first with the rest following in order.

"Let's put in six," someone said, and they began to take out their marbles to be placed in the center of the circle.

"Whoa!" I said. "I only have two, and one of them is my shooter, so I can only put in one."

All agreed to put in one each so that we had six marbles in the big circle.

Ricky shot first. Taking dead aim on one black-and-red marble, he carefully "flicked" his finger and knocked it way outside the circle. I could see now why he was last year's champ.

I looked carefully at how he held the marble to shoot. Holding a marble between my thumb and forefinger was the only way I had ever shot. Ricky held his shooter with forefinger pointing at the shooter, holding it tightly with his middle finger and sent it flying with airplane-like speed with his already-dirty thumb.

Ricky knocked out three marbles before he missed. *Whoa!* I thought. *I can do that...I think.*

All the rest, Carl and Roy and Betsey each taking their turns, and two more were knocked out. Several shoot "arounds" occurred before I found a little range, and I knocked one out. All cheered for me but Ricky.

By day's end, Ricky had the most, and I was last, but I had learned how to at least hold my shooter the best way. I had gained a marble, going home now with three.

The next day, we went at it again, and I learned to call for a "high shot," by asking for it while holding my shooter hand on top of my knuckles. This was done to get a shot off at a faraway marble. I learned how to get the best angle on the marble I wanted in order for it not be blocked by another one.

One of the sweetest memories of that summer and marble shooting came at the middle of July. I was putting my marbles, which were increasing in a paper gag until it tore open in the trailer marbles rolling wildly everywhere.

Mom said, "Son, let me give you something to carry your marbles in."

She brought out a burgundy purse that was plastic and cracking a bit. She had carried it for a long time. I was thankful to get it and used it that day forward. Although the kids teased me about a purse for a boy, I didn't care. I was happy with Mom's purse and nostalgically kept it until I was thirty years old.

The hot '55 summer wore on with Ricky in the lead with the most knockout marbles. But I was getting better. By the end of July, I had passed everyone but Ricky. He got "nastier" as the games continued.

We didn't play every day because of rain and other activities but spent most of them laughing, debating, climbing trees, and having a "ball." My grass cutting business interfered with the most important thing, "marbles," but I worked it out.

August came on, so we had to play in the morning because of the ninety-five- to a hundred-degree temperatures. By the 15th, I had caught Ricky with one marble to spare. I held the lead to the championship on the last day of August.

We had the same number of marbles each. I was next to last in shooting order with Ricky last.

Each shot was made with deep concentration until my turn. It was knockdown time between me and Ricky. I took aim at a bright red marble I had put in and knocked it out. The second shot came up as I was shaking just a little. Focusing seriously, I pulled the trigger, smacking the black-and-white marble that rolled slowly as I had glanced my shooter off it. I stood, jumped up and down, hollering for it to get out of the ring. It did. I was now two marbles ahead. I missed my third shot completely, too excited!

Ricky, very assured, fired away with great force and knocked his first two out well beyond the ring. The winning shot was next. Who would win the summer marble championship shot? The tough outdoor kid shot, very calmly firing his shooter into the last winning marble, and it rolled slowly up to the west side of the ring and slipped over the line! He jumped up, shouting, "I win! I win!"

Yes, he had. We shook hands like grown men, but we all felt sad that the summer "of marbles" was over, school was close at hand, and we'd go our separate ways as marble competitors.

As the summer had moved by, I was putting my marbles in Mom's pretty burgundy plastic purse. After starting with two marbles, the bag was almost too heavy to carry. While the zipper had been stripped out by rugged use, it was now filled with 127 marbles.

I kept those marbles until my early twenties, and they just disappeared. Thanks, Mother. Thanks, gang. I loved the burgundy bag. And although it was cracking, fading, with the bottom ready to tear open, Mother's "bag" held up those three rugged, hot '55 months.

I had won the most marbles that summer, 125; Ricky won the championship. It feels good to win, but the best win is love between a gang of sixth graders and the burgundy marble bag that my mother gave to me. By the way, I cut my last yard the next day.

Undefeated Eighth-Grade Basketball Team (1957–58)

The experience in Inyokern, California, that I've touched on elsewhere was such fun that I want to show you another wonderful part of this story.

These two things, seizing your opportunity and having someone to help you are keys to a healthy self-view, confidence, sheer enjoyment, motivation, and success to some level of greatness—my level and your level. My basketball coach in Inyokern stopped me in the hall and said that the coach of Ridgecrest had worked it out with the school board of Inyo County to allow me to play on the Ridgecrest Junior High team if I wanted to. What! Yes, we had played the large junior high at our very small gym where they whipped us thoroughly.

"Larry, the coach over there liked you're playing. He wants you on their team if you want to."

"What! If I wanted to!" I exclaimed, with the instant excitement of playing on their very good team.

My coach said, "They saw so much potential in you that they have a spot on the team for you."

The Ridgecrest coach had said for me to call him to make the arrangements.

What he didn't realize was that we had no phone because we moved too much. I walked to the nearest pay phone as fast as possible and listened to him tell what they had in mind.

"You have a lot going for yourself and we believe you can be our sixth or seventh man and get a lot playing time."

I thought right then, "No, I'm not thinking of sixth or seventh!"

I explained to him that Mother would have to drive me back and forth each day, so I had to let Mom and Dad make the decision. Dad was a little negative, but Mom was all in.

She said, "If it's okay with Walker, it's okay with me," looking over at the austere man with her left eyebrow raised skyward.

After much discussion, Dad wagging his head and giving all the reasons we couldn't do it, saying, "Okay, son, but I expect you to work hard, keep your grades up, and help the team."

"Yes, sir!"

The first practice, I met all the guys, and was a bit intimidated because of the size, success, and remembering how well they had played to beat us badly.

They received me almost immediately as one of them, and the comradery was fabulous. We gelled.

"Larry, you can get some playing time if you work hard and follow my instruction."

"Thank you, sir." And I went out on the floor and gave it my all!

That is my story. The team made me feel like one of them, were not jealous, and worked with me to show me their plays and tell me what the coach expected. That team spirit contributed to my success, a sense of worth, and acceptance so that I could do what I do. I became the leading rebounder, averaging nine points a game, and stole the most passes.

Once again, I had found a place and was given an opportunity even if just for a little while. Eventful! I worked into the starting lineup, we were unbeatable, winning two big tournaments even in Bakersfield and were the talk of "Inyo County."

To this day, I reflect on this unbeaten season, the friendships, and the work ethic I learned.

I was a champion.

"You're a champion, and once a champion, you're always a champion," a female horse champion once said to me. I believe that's right.

I learned to work with and encourage others, accept success without arrogance, and know that full-out effort is required to be a winner.

The kindness, acceptance, and comradery of those eleven boys warms my heart today. A trailer boy can use that. But here is the bigger story: the sacrifices Mother made.

Yes, my sweet mother loaded the car with me and my three siblings and took me to Ridgecrest twelve miles away. Then what about picking me up each evening and late after games! I think of this now and know I learned you can't achieve without others. Thank you, Mom, for your effort and sacrifices. You are the larger part of this story!

First, once again…in large part because of others.

Richmond, Indiana, and a City Championship (1958–59)

I remember so well that first day traveling up to a new Pleasant View Junior High, located on former farmland that is beautiful.

Getting to the principal's office, I had to pass through several boys my age. The principal asked if I played sports, and I told him "basketball." In a few minutes, the basketball coach came around to meet me and invite me to practice.

Practice I did and became a starter. This was a big win for me since this was after all the "basketball state." Winter passed, spring came, and we were going to compete in the junior high city championship in track and field.

We did not have a track, so we practiced on the big green field behind the school. Never having run track, I didn't know what to try out for.

"Simpson," Coach said, "what are you good at?"

To which I replied, "Running!"

So he put us all together to see who was the fastest on the team. I knew I was fast and only knew one guy who could probably beat me. All lined up on a white chalk line, the whistle sounded, and away we flew. Bill took a two- to three-yard lead, but once I got rolling, I cut the distance to a foot as I was right on his left hip. Bill was to run the one-hundred-yard dash, but what was I to run?

"Have you ever run the hurdles?" Coach asked, and I said no.

"You will be my hurdler."

So I sat out to run the hurdles. Quickly, the coach came to me and said, "You step the hurdles. You do not jump hurdles so that you can keep your speed."

"Oh!" I replied with agreement as if I knew what he meant.

All that night, I tried to see myself running full speed and only stepping the hurdles. The next day, I began to get it! The city championship was coming in two weeks, and we had never had a meet. The championship was going to be our only meet of the year, but the other eight junior highs had several meets.

Dad said, "Son, your big day is here. Do all you can." That has been a motto for me for all these years. So that Saturday morning in May was blue sky with a cloud or two, warm, and a churning stomach. We gathered at Pleasant View and went together to the "meet."

The track was inside the high school football stadium, around the football field, with bleachers all around. Never having seen a track before or a stadium that big left me standing in amazement.

"Simpson! Come on, let's get warmed up."

"Okay, Coach," I said as I stumbled into the gladiators playing field. The other teams were warming up, so I watched and did the same things.

Practicing at the long jump a few times I had hit fifteen to seventeen feet! I was getting ready. Stretching, jogging to warm up—they gave us two warm-up calls—I felt okay, but I had hit the "jump" line, marked with white chalk.

"Simpson of Pleasant View," the announcer cried out, and away I went. I had an eighteen-foot-six-inch jump, but I hit the white line!

"No jump," the speaker blurted out.

Coach talked with me, saying, "You've got a chance to win. Just don't hit the line."

Twice more, I gained full speed down the runway, and twice more the excitement and pressure to win had me too pumped, I hit the "white" again.

"Disqualified!" I heard the loudspeaker shout in my ears. I had not placed or gotten points for the team. Could I do better?

"First call for low hurdles," the aggravating, high-pitched voice said through the speaker. I had about fifteen minutes to stretch, sprint, talk to the coach, and get to the line. Here was my big chance...*place* and get points for my school, and a ribbon. My eyes bulged as I watched the other hurdlers warm-up, run their practice hurdles, and fly like a hawk. *How could I beat any of them?* rolled around in my brain.

I had no practice hurdles and couldn't find the coach.

The starter said, "You can all warm-up for five minutes on the track."

Step the hurdles they did. Smooth, fast and one or two arrogantly. I was condemned! I felt weak, but Dad's words came back to me, "Son, it's your big day. Do all you can," and my mind got right. My determination soared.

"Don't watch them. Just focus on your job," Coach said. "Focus!"

I did get focused as with mule blinders on. "I only had my row to plow!" Granddaddy Mac would say.

The stands were mostly filled with moms, students, and children. Along with Sandy, Mom was up about two rows.

I looked at Sandy as she clenched her fist and said, "You can do it," even as Mom said the same.

"To the starting blocks," the announcer said, giving the names and schools of each competitor. But I had never been in a starting block! I watched the seasoned guys get in their blocks, and I followed suit.

"Larry Simpson, lane 5," the shrill, scratchey voice yelled out. Getting in the blocks, squishing my legs and feet tightly against them, I got in position. My stomach was churning as I thought, *What are you even doing here? These other guys have had several meets,* as I came back to the explosive moment. "Relax, breath deep, focus, blow out air, relax...."

"Ready, get set," and the starter pulled the trigger. *Bang!* The gun blasted, and 180 yards lay ahead of me with hurdles to stop me. I felt strong, I felt fast, and I stepped the first hurdle. Two tall boys to my right were ahead a few feet, but I felt good and totally focused. The tallest boy sprinted ahead a little more, but I meant to catch him. It seemed so natural to me. I found some more speed and confidence, sailing over the hurdles, as I slid past the number 2 racer. With two hurdles to go, I drew even with the leader. Slowly, I pulled him after the last hurdle. Turning on speed and leaning at the finish line. I broke the ribbon with my chest.

"I beat those guys, and I can't believe it," I said to Mother, Sandy, and my brother and sisters, with my team mates running over to me, with hand shakes and strong pats on my back.

City champion! City champ! And never had run the hurdles before! My family in the stands and Coach ran up to me along with a teammate or two as we hugged. A blue ribbon was handed out at the awards ceremony that I kept for years. Now sixty-one years later, I don't know where it is.

But I learned that I was a winner. Even a trailer boy can be a winner.

PS: I thought I would always be a hurdler, which I did for a couple of more years but found out I was a better distance runner. We change with life.

Doing the Bop at Pleasant View

The assistant principal began his daily emphasis by saying, "On Friday night, in two weeks at the school, there will be a dance contest, so get ready to bop!" He continued, "Any couple can compete. You must wear jeans, and dress shirt with tie. The girls can wear skirts and blouses, and be sure to wear your best dancing shoes. More later."

The time was set for the last day in April.

I loved to dance, but Sandy loved it more. She was also better than I was. Mom carried me over to Sandy's house, where in her basement, she put on Little Richard, Elvis, Chuck Berry, Fats Domino, the Del Vikings singing "Whispering Bells," "Kansas City," and Delbert Harrison, and of course, we got a little slow dancing done to the Platters "Sea of Love" and Phil Phillips and many more.

Sandy's record collection was amazing, so we danced and danced, getting our moves down. We shared this love and ability being so much alike. Wow! I could do the *bop*! But she was better.

The bop was a takeoff from "jitterbug" and today's "shag."

We danced in rhythm with one hand, two hands, sometimes pushing off each other. I would twirl her, do the arm slide going sideways, separate hands, and dance a few feet apart, coming back together. One of our favorite moves was to turn sideways to each other with an arm around each other and dance, facing the same way both forward and sideways.

Besides getting ready for the dance and contest, this was love at its best, both pure and simple almost fifteen years old.

All week, there was excitement in the air as couples practiced together. Some were already boyfriend and girlfriend, but some just found a partner and danced.

The dance was all anyone could talk about.

That beautiful Friday night finally came. Sandy, a happy person in herself, was a great dancer with perfect rhythm. She was fabulous, but we exploded together. We practiced hard, and we were ready.

Dad drove me to pick up Sandy, asking, "Son, how do you think you'll do?"

"I don't know, we're gonna win!" He just grinned.

Arriving, I went to the door, and before I could knock, Sandy appeared at the door, hugged her mother, and walked down the two steps.

"My, my" is all I could say, all other words alluding me.

She rocked me, and I got cold chills. Her hair was black as coal and in perfect position. A soft white pullover sweater fit her perfectly and set her greenish hazel eyes off like a dream. The sweater was short sleeved and rested on top of a black tight-enough skirt going to just below her knees. Sandy's happy, reserved, old-fashioned ways always made her more charming.

The black flats matched just right; besides, they were slick and worked perfectly to slip and slide on the dance floor.

A white pearl necklace graced her sweater and perfect neck. It hung right. On her right wrist was a colorful charm bracelet with turquoise she got in New Mexico the year before on their way to Bakersfield.

Sliding in beside Dad, they greeted each other with Dad looking fondly at my dance partner. She made me flow inside. She made me glow outside.

"Are you ready to dance?"

"I think so," she replied in her customary nonarrogant way.

"How 'bout you?"

"Yeah, I'm ready, and you'll do great!"

Cool, pretty, smiling, yet nervous, she looked almost bashfully at me and said, "I just wanna dance with you."

I was momentarily speechless. That's the way she was.

She smiled and looked too good. I was proud to be with her… and ready to dance.

We only said a few words but looked at each other, saying those unspoken words.

"Thanks, Dad. See you at ten o'clock."

"Go in there and tear 'em up!" Daddy said.

And I replied, "We'll be found trying," as he grinned that big sly Walker grin!

The music was playing. Everybody was ready. We wished our friends good luck. We drank some punch and dug out our place among the dozens of dancing partners until we heard, "Boys and girls, take your places and when tapped on the shoulder, move off the floor."

Almost no space was left on the gym floor with over sixty-five couples and only elbow room.

Our hands were wet, as we held them tightly and waited for "Here goes let's dance," and the music started. "Whole Lot of Shaking," got us going. "In the Still of the Night" was next, sweet doo-wop.

All the slick rock and rollers ready to win, bopped with excitement and held each other close.

There were four judges at the four corners standing, each with eagle eyes and a formula of what they were looking for.

The music started with hollers and whistles. Away each one "bopped," giving it their all. The first few to leave were obviously disappointed. Every few minutes, couple after couple was dismissed with most being good sports and cheering the rest. Mine and Sandy's friends, some that she had gone to school with for these nine years, stood on the sideline, watching us gettin' it on.

As we saw couples leaving and friends yelling us on, I told Sandy, "We could win this," and she smiled ear to ear, saying, "I hope so!"

Finally, there were three couples left on the gym floor, and the bleachers packed. Few left. A judge walked past us, but we just did the bop. The shoulders of one of the couples next to us was tapped, and away they went. All I could think of was "Do it sweet," and we kept rockin' and rollin'.

The music stopped and the announcer said, "Two couples left, Larry Simpson and Sandy Berry," but I can't remember the other couples names from so long ago.

"I want you to have a breather of five minutes seeing we've been dancing for two hours." With sweat rolling off us, we two couples encouraged each other.

"Here is Jerry Lee Lewis and 'A Whole Lot of Shaking Goin' On'! Couples, let's dance."

Dance we did. Turning Sandy around, sidestepping, sliding our hands down each other's arm, pushing off each other, now arms around each other, facing the same way, doing all our moves with smiles covering our faces. Having fun, feeling Jerry Lee and lovin' each other, we did all our steps like warm butter. The judges walked past us, I quivered, but no time for that and we didn't get tapped! Over she walked to the next great dancers, reached out her arm, and touched then on their shoulders.

"And the winners are Sandy and Larry! Watch your winners dance."

We had a good time that night. We would cherish this thrilling event all through the years even though…we moved to Ohio three months later.

Even a trailer boy can really dance…with an Indiana country girl who can dance.

Wow, city hurdles champ and dance champ two weeks apart!

Class President

The summer of '59 was going fast. Sandy and I tried to be together as much as possible. With me working at the old Tuggle's Furniture Store and Sandy babysitting, we would be together in the evenings always on Saturday and sometimes in church.

When I would go to her house on their family farm, we played ping-pong until I learned she could beat me, so I shied away from that long green table as much as possible! Often, we talked about our lives, what we wanted to become and do. We thought alike, had the same morals, could talk back and forth, laugh a lot, and felt that young love. I never got over it.

But Dad came home on a Friday and said we were moving to Grove City, Ohio, in two weeks. Moving had become harder and harder the last three or four moves because of deep friendships.

When I told Sandy, she just dropped her head, sad, "oh no," as tears rolled off her sweet brown cheeks. I cried. We held onto each other. Our young in love hearts were breaking. So we started making the best plans to see each other as much as we could for fifteen-year-olds.

The two weeks were passing too fast. We stayed together as much as possible. One of her girlfriends gave me a going-away party.

We danced a lot, especially close together, had a good, sad time. We wanted to hold onto each other forever. Her mom picked us up. Dad met us at Sandy's. We cried, kissed, and promised, "See you soon." I couldn't sleep that night. "Would I see her soon?"

The next morning, we slowly pulled out of Richmond. I was numb with sad red eyes.

Mom felt my anguish and said, "Son, you can see her again. It's only about a hundred miles." Mother understood. I didn't. My tears wet my cheeks as I pictured Sandy looking out their picture window, down Tingler road, waiting for me. I just knew we'd be together, and I had told her, "I will come back and get you." I meant it.

As we traveled down old Highway 40, the national highway, I was filled with Sandy and how we could be together. I looked out the window at the flat fields of corn and beautiful gardens. We got to Grove City in about three hours, dropping off old forty onto Highway 62 just south of our new town. Dad had been to Grove City and found us a new home for our turquoise-and-white Liberty trailer and ourselves.

Being close to August, with school starting in early September, Mom drove me to the high school to see about preregistration. There were kids outside talking, and one of them followed me into the building to the principal's office.

As we waited to see the principal, the light-haired, fair-skinned boy asked, "Are you new?"

Well, of course, I was, and he had never seen me. I said yes.

"I'm Lamar."

And I said, "Well, I'm Larry!"

Question after question followed, as well as a rundown of the high school, it's sports, good friends, and teachers.

The principal called us in his office. We had a good visit, and plans were made for registration. Lamar was waiting.

"Larry, Mrs. Simpson, I want to introduce you to some of our classmates."

Mostly sophomores, like myself, they were nice-looking, calm, and willing to meet a new student.

When we came back for registration, I asked about the football team, and the principal said, "Practice starts this week. Just be here, meet the coaches, and they'll get you set up."

Lamar joined me there again. He was a big talker and seemed like the school "promoter." I liked him. Besides, a few girls joined in as I met my new friends. As we visited, I told him a little about myself.

He said, "We've not had a new student for a long time, and I'm going to put your name on the ballot for class president."

"Class president! What do they do?" So he proceeded in detail what I would do. I said, "Lamar, nobody knows me."

"They will, and the girls will love you!" It was not hard to make friends with the friendly, high-quality tenth graders I met.

This August was hot as I started work at the vegetable stand. The coach had welcomed me, assigned my uniform, and locker. Practice started in the morning at seven thirty and in the evening at six o'clock with my work at the vegetable stand in between.

Football practice was hard with lots of hitting and conditioning. The coach, Mr. Martin, a former Ohio State Lineman, was young, ambitious, and tough. I liked him and the staff. The coaches paid little attention to me as a new kid and not an imposing stature, five feet nine, 152 pounds. I began to get attention though with my quickness and ability to block coming out of the backfield in open field, especially on a "sweep" play.

In our junior varsity first scrimmage against the big school in Columbus, I scored two touchdowns from a seventy-five-yard run after a punt and a sixty-nine-yard run on a pass play to the right.

Coach asked, "Why didn't you tell me you could run?"

I said, "You didn't ask."

And he replied, "I see!"

After that, I was on the varsity as a second team halfback and started two varsity games.

But the vote for sophomore class president was coming up. Lamar was my advocate. He was a politician, a cheerleader, a representative, encouraging every student to vote for me. I was just along for the ride and being myself.

How could a new person win? What qualification do I have? Who knows me, only being in class for a week? I knew nothing about being a class president.

Lamar promised everyone that I would be the best for the job with new ideas and fresh blood.

The vote was one day away! A long sign was made, saying, "Vote Larry Simpson, the New Kid in School." I was shocked and knew I couldn't win. My competitors were old hands and nice people.

The vote came. I voted for the pretty blond-headed girl Liz.

The announcement came over the loudspeaker, and the principal said, "After a fairly close vote, the new sophomore class president is...Larry Simpson."

The classroom erupted in clapping with a few disappointed faces! I thanked everyone and promised to do a good job. I congratulated my competitors, which I didn't want to be competing with, and they were good sports, which I found to be part of the character of that pretty little *Back to the Future* town. It was a joy to be in Grove City with nice, clean, intelligent kids and pretty girls. I still remember sixty years later! I have the 1959 school annual that was mailed to me by a very sweet girl Ruth and look at it every so often still. Grove City was much like Pleasant View.

Sad, but I left them without a class president when we moved to Gary, Indiana, at the end of December '59.

Even a trailer boy can be class president...for a little while.

No excuses.

Cross-Country Champ

I had only been in Grove City for six months but had made some long-lasting relationships. In fact, one family and a gentleman named Jack from Grove City drove the three hundred miles to see us. Jack came to see us several times. A single man and religious, he actually bought me a car and drove it over to our new residence. He rode a bus back home.

A few years later, poor Jack thought he had been reincarnated into Jesus Christ. We never saw him again.

Before we left Grove City, I saw on TV a documentary about the city of Chicago. It was all about gangs, alcohol, and especially drugs, along with crime. I thought we were moving almost to Chicago, and I prepared myself to go into my new school prepared to defend myself besides being horrified of the images of drug users and their addiction. Having seen such degradation, I purposed never to do drugs. Thank God to this day, I have never used drugs of any kind, in any way, or any amount.

When we got to Keck's Trailer Park, I felt better about my concerns as we were not in Chicago. Besides the high school Calumet High School was only a quarter mile down Ridge Road, old Highway 6.

There was a new trailer park close to Kecks, but they were full. Daddy said, "When they get a spot, we will move over there" since that's where both Mom and Dad wanted to be. We lived at Kecks from December 29, 1959, to May of 1961.

In a week or so, we started school, and being the new kid on the block and close to Chicago, I was ready for anything. To my great dismay, the kids dressed in a styl'n' fashion, talked Chicago style but were basically friendly and common folk. It was okay.

I always made it my way to do something "catchy" to gain an entrance into the new community of students. Things came natural to me, and I acted spontaneously. The principal suggested I go around and meet my new teachers. So I did, and when I went to the English teacher and class, I stood at the door until she invited me in and said, "Yes." I introduced myself as her new student, and after a very few words, she said, "I'll see you in a little while."

Seeing it was my time to leave, I hesitated, got my feet in the right place, and skipped toward the door backward to the end desk and turned, went to the door, and headed east. I learned that by watching a highly educational show, "The Three Stooges." Curly of "The Three Stooges" did that special skit perfectly. So did I!

The class exploded with laughter after three or four seconds of amazement. Later, I was told that the guys in particular Harry Warrens said, "Well, he's one of us," and I was "in" from that point on. The teacher never ever said a word about it, neither did I…to her.

My best friend, Harry, and I still laugh about it sixty-one years later.

In about two weeks, the track coach announced over the loud-speaker that all who wanted to run track meet with him in the gym after school in two days. He announced it again the next day. The meeting came with general information about his goals, what he expected from each athlete, and made appointments to meet with him for new members.

On Monday, the next week, I went into his office, and we talked. He asked if I had ever run track, and I told about my Richmond experience.

He said, "We need a hurdler."

I stretched my eyes, grinned, and said, "Thank you."

Practice started January 31 in the halls of the school! The snow and cold was too much for outside training, and the school did not have an indoor track. On this day, Coach wanted to find those with speed, so we ran two by two, side by side, forty yards against two stopwatches.

I was fast enough for the coach to say, "You will be one of the hurdlers."

"Good," I said, and I worked hard, and being only a sopho-more, I felt good.

Track came, and I was the number two hurdler, ran on relays, and loved every minute.

In May, Coach took us into the gym and had us race around the floor for three or four laps. I beat everybody. I was as shocked as the coach was. Beyond this the cross-country coach was there to observe. After the workout, in which we did the laps four times, Coach Traicoff came to me and said, "You need to run cross-country."

I told him, "I didn't even know what that was, besides, I played football, and I can't run across the country."

He just looked at me.

We met again to talk, and I asserted I wanted to play football to get a scholarship to college.

His reply cut me to the bone, "You're not big enough."

His bluntness shocked me. After the sport was explained to me, "You'll race two miles, we practice twice daily, and I think you can get a scholarship in this way!"

189

"I'll think about it," I said, and by the end of May, I had made my decision, taking the issue seriously. Coach Triacoff was stoically excited and said, "Run two miles a day, three days a week, and you'll be ready to start practice in July."

I was determined that I was going to be the best runner on the team by July even though two seniors were returning, and I would be a junior and no experience.

Running the required three-day-a-week runs, I ran them hard. I knew from those self-practices that I could run long distances. Running was an enjoyment to me, but I didn't know how I could do against the experienced runners.

Besides the distance training, I had asked the track coach if I could have some hurdles to put on the track for training.

He said, "Yes," looking at me a little curiously with hesitation but I said, "I'll give you a key to the equipment building. Just put them back every day."

I trained on the hurdles several days a week, so I had conditioning that way also for cross-country.

July 15 seemed to come like a flood. I was to join up with Coach T and the team and start "conditioning running." Coach had laid out a two-mile course from the junior high school down the street next to the school, then left by a few homes on a dirt, dusty lane and right down to a major street through the neighborhood to a stop sign. Then back to the junior high school, running the distance we would run in competition. We gathered at the north end of the junior high, which is now the high school.

After warming up with the two seniors acting almost cocky, with a know-it-all attitude were in incessantly talking to Coach T. We were stretched out, hot and ready.

The run started. I had determined to fall in behind the seniors, which I did. They ran at a comfortable but strong pace. I was feeling competitive and good. When we got to the stop sign and turned around, we had a little more than a half mile left.

The pace quickened, but I stayed on their hips. After a few yards, I knew I had to push the pace and see if I could beat them. I began to pour it on. My seven weeks of preparation paid off. I broke contact with the rest of the team, stretched the lead, and turned on the speed when the junior high came within sight. Coach T stretched his eyes, called out the time, "10:35," and patted me on the back. The seniors came in at 10:59, and the rest around 11:10 and slower.

The seniors were shocked as was the coach, and from that day as a junior to the last training run as a senior, I was never beaten in practice.

That year, I ran a 9:32, which was the best in the state of Indiana, was third in the sectionals, beaten only by the top 2 runners of our main rival in a close race. I finished ninth in the state for all-state recognition. But I never ran my best race on the Indianapolis course which has always haunted me a little.

The year 1961–62 started with great hope and purpose.

The former two seniors were gone, but the rest of the team was better.

We won every meet that year, except the state championship, in which we were fourth but were sectional champs. I was once again all-state, but the state meet is another story! The "two invitationals"" we won were especially rewarding since they were the biggest in the state. Besides, I was the sectional champion.

The Sectional Champ

That senior year, I was determined to win the sectional championship, which is the qualifying meet for state.

The sectional was held on the beautiful Hobart golf course, where we had run four times before. I was ready. I had done extra quarter miles and three quarter miles, pushing myself to the maximum. All the runners from thirty-five schools gathered at the starting line, and what a thrill that is. I was in the middle of the

front row. The gun sounded, and over four hundred plus runners all started with dreams in their eyes. A pack of about twenty to twenty-five racers stayed together in the lead. It was a fast pace on the new experimental course of two and a half miles.

My main competitor, which had beaten me the year before while I had beaten him twice this year, took the lead. I would have none of that. I retook the lead with five or six others bunched closely.

But I began to weary. I didn't feel good. And others took the lead with Bernie in the front. I fell behind a few yards as we could see the finish line and crowd about three hundred yards ahead. I was weak and weary. I felt defeated and thought I was going to lose. My body and emotions sagged. I was sick with defeat. *Lose the sectional which I had trained for all year?*

As we approached the finish line, there was a line of fans behind the rope fifty yards long. I settled in self-pity and into defeat. But Coach T was leaning over the rope fifty or sixty yards ahead. I could hear his strong voice as he held his stopwatch out in front of him, sticking it out over the rope.

A new emotion came on me. New life streamed into me. The clarity of my desire and goal resurged in me. I dug down inside. My dead legs began to quicken then sprint. I knew I was faster than Bernie and began to gain on him. I started passing one by one each of the other five boys ahead of me. Bernie got closer and closer to me. He looked over his shoulder as I could almost touch him. I lifted my knees, drove my bare feet into the grassy golf course, as the only runner in front of me tried to dig down and get it. But I now knew I was going to catch him. I saw Mom, Carole Lee, my brother and sisters, and the mystical, historic crown.

I blistered the course with sprinter speed, arms pumping, and passed my old nemesis twenty-five yards from the finish line. The finish line looked like a miracle as the white tape hit my chest. I was the sectional champion!

Sectional champion: forty-one schools competed each with ten racers. Over four hundred raced that beautiful, cool, blue sky day in October of 1961. All came in behind me. All were winners in a way as they competed, ran, finished, and represented their school. I congratulated as many racers as possible.

Besides me winning, my favorite teammates ran hard as our school team was first as sectional champs. I was blessed to be MVP three times in cross-country and track. How thankful I am.

If a trailer boy can win so can you.

> Moral courage is great and admirable in itself;
> but it must be pointed out that it almost never
> appears except as part of that greater entity called
> character!

—Foreword to
Profiles in Courage, p. xvii

King and Queen

The junior-senior prom would be in late April 1961. Harry and I cooked up that we go together in his car since mine wasn't as nice and cool as his. Our girlfriends were especially excited as they bought new gowns, had their hair done up, and looked gorgeous.

Mom dropped me off at Harry's where we got dressed, carried on with foolishness, which we were very good at, and "slicked on up" the best we could. We approved our preparations and headed out the door. We picked up our girlfriends a little early because Harry is yet today a very prompt soul, laughing at somethings, anything, all the way.

When the girls came out of their homes, we were shocked and bowled over. They looked like models, like grown women, beautiful and smiling. The two girls said we were handsome to which we heartily agreed. Arriving at the banquet hall, we all whooped and hollered then went in, all dignified but nervous.

We were all very excited like silly teenagers can be, and Harry and I were goofin' off as usual.

Harry said, "Can't you girls put on any more makeup?" And they just gritted their teeth at the two of us and went on talking.

Mine and Carole's names were put on the king and queen's list, and the vote had already been taken. No one knew the results, except the teachers and sponsors of the prom.

The ballroom filled with beautiful juniors and seniors. Doo-wop and rock and roll music ran all over us. The night was filled with love, laughter, and dancing. The prom! We were there. We were doin' it. We drank punch, nonalcohol, of course, ate the hors d'oeuvre, and danced some more. The lights were turned down low especially for songs like "Oh What a Night" and other love songs. We held each other tight in teenage romance. We did the "bop" to every rock and roll song played.

Every once and awhile, the girls would go into the "ladies" room and make sure their hair and face still looked pretty, and I said, "Can't you girls do a little more like Marilyn?" (Marilyn Monroe, of course!)

All the "gowns" were bright and sassy. The "tuxes" were of every color from white to yellow to black. Harry and I had agreed that we both wear a blue jacket, white shirt, black pants. We liked it and rolled with it.

As the cool, dramatic night drew to a close, the announcer said, "It's time to crown our king and queen."

All chatter and whispering stopped. Looking around, everyone was excited and ready for the moment while our hands were too hot and "sweaty" to hold.

"Our king and queen for the 1961 prom, as voted by their fellow students, is"—silence—"Larry and Carole."

And in disbelief, we staggered to the front of the ball room to receive our plaques, crowns, tiaras, and say, thanks."

Prom king in 1961 with a beautiful queen! A thankful, exciting but a fading moment in time had come and gone. The feeling of that sweet, happy, winning moment lingers in the movement of time and happiness of a romantic night.

I'm thankful.

A trailer boy, king for a day but not without that perfect queen.

Up sluggard and waste not life; In the grave will
be sleeping enough.

—Benjamin Franklin,
The Wit and Wisdom of Benjamin Franklin
(Barnes and Noble Books, 1995), 75

College Cross-Country

As my senior year was coming to a close, I was determined
to get a scholarship somewhere. Several universities contacted me,
including the 1960 Cross Country National Champion Western
Michigan University. Dad and I made a trip there, and what a beautiful campus!

No scholarships were offered. I was brokenhearted. But I had a
problem. My grades were too low at 1.9 average—yes, under a C! I
had come to a place in school when I could not concentrate, focus,
or sit still. Having been all over America moving, traveling I knew
a lot of different things and simply could not and did not want to
study. My mind was wandering away to places in my heart and in
my world.

A good friend, Phil, and I cut a lot of classes and days. We
would go in one of our cars to a place in the country to talk, laugh,
and laugh some more. The girls who worked in the school office
would sign us in and give us credit for classes! My, my, how stupid
we were. I never wrote but one single paper or report or any written
assignment; the girls did it for me.

I'm telling you this in honesty to reveal the truth of my whole
story. I'm not proud of this, but it's the truth. I was gonna have a
good time no matter what and not do schoolwork if I could get away
with it. Now things have a way of coming back around. There is
always a price to pay no matter what we do.

Finally, the school caught on to what we were doing, and to
beat it all, get others involved in our crimes!

I came home one afternoon, and Mom said, "Larry," (I knew I was in trouble when she started off with "Larry"), "a man came here today from the school. Is it true?"

I stared at her for what seemed like a long time as I sized up the matter. I knew I was caught.

I said, "Yes, ma'am."

"Son, he said you could be expelled from school," and continued with, "what in the world have you been doing and thinking?"

I admitted my guilt.

Phil and I went to school to finish our senior year. Yes, I graduated but with this black mark on my personal résumé. I blew any chance of a decent grade. The school administration was glad I was leaving, except for my cross-country and track accomplishments. Sad, honesty.

So here I was at the end of my senior year, wanting a scholarship, a college to go to, but none were calling. Somewhere I had gained a knowledge of Memphis State University. The Tigers and the dream came to me to call them and see if there was an opportunity for me there. I got the university's phone number, called the front office, and they gave me Coach Johnsons number. So I called.

When he answered, I gave him my story, my times in cross-country and track, and said, "I would like to come to Memphis State!"

Several days later, he called and said he had made some phone calls, knew my grade problems, but that he wanted me. He said, "We will pay your tuition, books, and fees, but you'll have to handle your own living quarters."

This was the best I would get.

In my thinking about going to Memphis State, there laid at the bottom of my heart, the thought and desire of being close to my larger family, Little Grandmother and Uncle Elmer, who lived in Memphis. As my heart pondered these things, the thought of maybe living with Uncle Elmer came to me.

"Dad, what would you think about me living with Uncle Elmer?"

He studied for a moment then said, "We can see."

"Son, your great-uncle would probably love having you there," Mom said.

196

The next evening, I called my uncle's home.

"Hello," Aunt Jettie answered.

So after greetings, I began to speak to my 240-pound uncle! As he was raising the phone up to his six-foot-two frame to his ear, I heard, "It's Larry."

And he laughed and said, "Hey, son, what you up to?"

We passed aminities, and then I told him that I was coming to Memphis State, to which he quickly responded, "Why don't you live with us?"

I was relieved and excited and told him, "That's what I was thinking about."

We set out working through the details.

Moving there in early August of '62 and living there until July of '63, was a wonderful adventure. The thoughts and memories linger yet with the emotions of those long-ago days.

In 1986, I would preach Uncle Elmer's funeral in New Albany, Mississippi, taking my text from Romans 8:28–36.

That dramatic event holds a place of its own in my aging soul.

I went early to Memphis to train, leaving my job at Pittsburgh Plate Glass and my family. The weather is extremely hot and humid in Memphis, so I knew I needed time to adapt.

Daily, I ran a dirt road on the neighbor's property of a half mile, making sure when classes started, I would be ready to compete.

Uncle Elmer's son Roy and I shared a bedroom, and we became fast friends, as well as with his brother Ralph who lived next door with Nancy, his wife. Aunt Jettie was a fabulous cook and sweetheart. She made homemade biscuits, cakes, or pies almost daily. Lots of Southern country food like collard greens, corn bread, chicken and dumplings, and beans of every kind were all made to satisfy the soul—my soul.

The day to report to cross-country practice, as well as school registration and choose classes, came September 3, 1962.

I made friends standing in line to register as we all had a good time, and later, we always brought that day up. I first had to meet Coach Glenn. We sat down, talked about our backgrounds, and cross-country. The old coach, white-headed and from Indiana, had been an Olympic competitor in equestrian. He was serious, down to business, straightforward, and told me about his methods and expectations.

I said, "Yes, sir."

He liked that.

We talked about what he thought I could do having a time of 9:32 for two miles, but he wanted to assure me that I'd have to work hard and could maybe be the third or fourth best runner by season's end.

Again, I said, "Yes, sir."

Practice started with a four-mile run, the distance in college for meets at that time. I was pushing the guys at the top. Our first meet was the middle of September, and we had to get ready.

The first few meets, we split in wins, but I wasn't getting better, and neither was the team. I was second or third in each meet, winning the fourth meet. Our best runner was a junior, and Joel was smart, dedicated, tough, and a good guy. He didn't say much, but I wanted to listen when did.

I went to Coach Glenn and told him I didn't think he was working me hard enough and that we weren't getting better.

He said, "So you don't think I'm hard enough? Besides, I want you to train on your own," which I had never heard him say before. He was mad. The next day was murder as we ran quarter miles and half miles. He pushed us more than ever before.

I was worn out but said, "Thanks, Coach."

He continued the fast pace with more mileage and speed work. We started getting better. In a week, we went to the University of Mississippi to race them, and they were good. The course was beautiful with different terrains and surfaces. Joel and I ran at the top, following an Ole' Miss all-conference racer. As we narrowed the course down to the last half mile, I was hurting but in contention.

Joel dug in hard but then faded a little. I found new life and chased the Ole' Miss senior and Joel. As we came to the finish line, my competitor was too strong and mature and flew away from me and Joel, winning by twelve seconds. I came in at 21:09 for the four-mile course and was second. Coach ran up with his stubby, short legs and, with a seldom-shown grin, asked, "Do you know what you just did?"

Breathing heavily, I said, "No, sir."

"You just broke Joel's school record!"

"What?"

He said, "21:09, a new school record!"

Joel and my kind teammates congratulated me, but I could see "disappointment and anger" in Joel's eyes.

How long would I hold that school record? The question raced in my mind all week.

The next week, Joel broke my one-week reign as school record holder! Rightly so, and I was humbled. With the season ending November 15, we had a sit-down meal and awards ceremony. Joel was most valuable player, but I was low-point man. Low point? Yes. You see, in cross-country, the place you get is your points. A person in fourth place gets four points while the person in second place gets two point. Obviously, the higher you place is better than lower. So the low-point racer is ahead of the high-point racer because he finished higher.

"Larry, you were low-point man," Coach Johnson had said with a gleeful look in his eyes.

Joel had twenty-eight points while I beat him by one point with twenty-seven! I won that contest, my first year in school over a great runner, while being the record holder for a big week! Even a trailer boy can win. There are no excuses. It takes work!

Last word: I was not prepared for college and left school after my first year. However, I got married, pastored a church, and got ready to continue my education once again.

I knew I had to go back to Memphis State where I had failed to "make it right" at the scene of my failure...one day in the future.

"Winners never quit. Quitters never win," according to a American saying.

No excuses.

199

Story 13

Thank God He Gave Me a Dad
Walker Eddins Simpson
On the Way to Destiny

My dad had Granddaddy Eddins as his father from 1921 to 1930 when Granddaddy died. From age four until age thirteen, Granddaddy was Dad's image of a father.

The old Eddins bloodline was still in Jesse Briley's veins. He was very intelligent, stood erect, until he died as he had stood all his life. Being a successful farmer in Walls, Mississipi, he and my dad's grandmother, Molly Lamb, made a life. He was a man of honesty and integrity, who stayed to his convictions about being a father, husband, and man "in" the world.

Born in 1840, I was born in 1944, a mere one hundred years later. Granddaddy Eddins died in 1930. He was a steady rock, loved his family, his grandson, and was their teacher and mentor.

My father took many of those old-time ways with him that made him a man among men, a man out of time.

Full grown, Dad was five feet seven and a half, but he never seemed like a small man. Spiritual, masculine, and determination drove him to do what he said. That is why men would contact him in another state hundreds of miles apart and ask, "Walker, will you come to Gallatin or Buford or wherever it was and help us with this job?"

Dad was a diesel mechanic and expert at the most difficult of motors to work on.

He weighed in his prime 188 pounds of shear muscle. His hands were very thick with a big muscle between the end of his thumb and forefinger. With a nineteen-inch neck, forearm and biceps huge, with his sleeves rolled up, he was distinct from most men. Besides, he stood very erect and even sat that way. Grandmother in the old-fashioned pattern insisted on him standing or sitting straight, and he held to that same belief with us.

Mattie Pearl, also known as Martha Eddins, Dad's mother, would not allow we grandchildren to slouch down in a chair but insisted on us sitting straight hip and walking that way too. Later, I understood what she was teaching: self-discipline, self-pride, and a manifesto of that in the world.

This story is told about the famous founder of J. C. Penny's. Mr. Penny met a young man for dinner to discuss the possibility of the man coming on his staff as a base executive, running a store. As they chatted, their food came, and the great man sat and watched the possible new executive. The man grabbed up the salt and poured it on his food. Mr. Penny saw enough in that impetuousness not to hire the young man. Why? He was impulsive and in a rush! Knowing the ways of successful men, he knew instantly he did not need a man with weak discipline. They parted ways, and the man was never heard from again.

Grandmother had Jeanie, especially, Mom and Dad's second child, walk with a book on her head and the rest of us a few times. Her point is clear to me today. She wanted us to live disciplined, honorable lives, and this was just her way to help us get there. Obviously, I've never forgotten this but have not always accomplished it. But I honor this from those old-timers who set the path for me.

Dad always sat erect and walked that way and lived that way. A handshake or a word of promise was enough.

When Dad was about eighteen years old, he attended a local baseball game. Many of the fans were standing around the field. There was a farmer there, a little on the rough side who had had a run-in with Walker Eddins a couple of times. Dad was standing close to the man when a baseball came flying at a very high speed. Seeing the errant throw that was about to hit the man, Dad, like a .44 magnum bullet, pushed the man out of the way, who fell down but survived the wild throw. As Dad was standing, watching the next play, the man came from behind and began to hit Dad in the head and wrapping his gangly long arms around his head, pounded him in the face. The knobby fists of the six-foot-two older farmer had cut his skin, and blood filled his eyes. Dad turned, wrapped his arms around the man, as he continued to try to disable his young enemy.

"I'm going to squeeze the air out of you until you pass out," Dad said as blood ran down off his chin.

Walker grabbed him and put a bear-hug on him, lifting him off the ground shaking him, and in a few seconds, the man, not being able to get Dad loose, began to weaken as the hard-muscled eighteen-year-old grunted and picked him up and down to get the best squeeze on him. The farmer fell limp in Dad's arms. While he dropped the man, limp to the Mississippi red mud, people stood around in amazement. A woman from the concession stand started walking swiftly toward Dad with some cold water and wiped his face, his cuts, and hot-steaming head.

The medical report said, "The farmer had four broken ribs."

Awakening in a few seconds, the "fighting farmer" quietly left.

Dad said, "I'll never forget you for this." And you see, he didn't because he told the story to me.

Determined

No one accomplishes very much unless they have a clear vision of what they are doing, when, how, and where. Dad was determined.

In March of 1958, Granddaddy Simpson died in his homeland he had lived in most of his life. What a sweet time we had with him, the two times in '55 and '56 when we were able to meet and see him at his longtime home.

Dad flew to his funeral in South Carolina, helped with the final doings for the funeral and personal possessions. It wasn't much.

On the way back, a severe storm blistered the airplane with winds, rain, and hail. As the flight attendant tried to give assurance from the captain that all would be okay, the plane flew into a vacuum "hole" and dropped suddenly hundreds of feet straight down, according to the pilot. It was as if there was nothing under the plane but a deep hole and wide open with a strong suction, sucking the plane down into its fangs, its jaws.

"The noise was deafening," Dad said.

The stewardess, who hadn't been able to get seated, was thrown several feet down the aisle, injuring her forehead on a seat, and then passed out.

"Soon she dashed around again with wonderful helping hands, helping all she could." As suddenly," Dad said, "as the calamity struck the plane, it leveled out, and we rode the winds on in."

We picked him up in Bakersfield. After hugs, kisses and tears, Dad told us the story and said, "I'll never fly on an airplane again."

He didn't. He was a determined man. When he said it, he meant it—he did it.

He Lifted a Car

My brother David, who is a man like Dad, was helping him grease the wheel bearings of his car. The car was jacked up, but somehow the jack released its hold and fell off the blocks they had put under the car as support.

Thank the Lord, he crawled out from the other side under the car safely. Taking a few breathes, with David white-faced and anxious, he, nevertheless, made sure our father was okay.

Dad was determined. He had a pressing commitment to make. The job had to be finished. But he didn't have another jack. So he told David, "Son, get the two leftover blocks," (oil and grease covered), "and put them on top of the blocks under the frame when I lift the car up."

David said, "I stretched my eyes, looked wild-eyed, stuttered, saying, "What? Sir?"

Being a little agitated, Dad told him again to put his gloves on and get ready. David got ready with adrenaline flooding his veins and gritted his jaw sideways to the left. He couldn't believe that this could happen, but he knew like the rest of us that if Dad said it, you better get ready.

Dad squatted down, with gloves on, putting both hands on the right corner of the bumper, shook his body and arms, blew out air, and began to lift. The car shook just a little as Dad wavered, with red face and bulging brown eyes.

David, like lightning, placed the two blocks and hollered, "Okay!"

The mechanic Mississippi farm boy and keeper of his word sat the car back down.

Sweat rolled off both of them. David from fear and excitement and Dad's from this wild-shattering feat.

"Now we can finish." He went about his business without a "word" as David still couldn't believe what he had just seen.

"Larry, Daddy was unbelievable!"

Our dad was a determined man and somewhat humble because he only told the story twice to John Rice and me. David has retold it many times, and he's an honest, determined man like Dad. So have I.

A Reiteration

Let me remind you of Walker Eddins's determination to get back to east Tennessee from California and to meet the legal length of truck and trailer in New Mexico, he rebuilt his 1953 Ford. He cut the truck in two in the bed, cut out a section, and welded it back together. Yes, the bed was short, but his travels wouldn't be.

Thank God, I Had Daddy

Dad's spirit and generosity was real, but not foolish.

When I was nineteen, I worked at a truck stop owned by the father of a boy who had graduated with me from high school. The truck stop was continuously busy. Pumping ten thousand gallons per shift, we had to fly to the pumps, get the fuel started, clean the windows, sweep the floors, at least enough to show a difference, stop the fuel before the tank ran over and get back inside with the amount sold.

Part of this job was washing down the restrooms which took great pains to do it right. The restroom was sparkling when I finished. Certainly, trying to make a difference makes a difference, and the owner noticed. Some of the men complained about this lowly task, but I knew that there was no tasks too insignificant to do it good. I learned this from Dad.

Late in the winter of 1963–1964, we heard on the local radio station, which we always had on, that a winter storm of fierce cold, snow, and winds were in Minnesota and passing through Wisconsin due to arrive in Chicago and Gary, Indiana, by noon the next day.

The older men employees said, "Wear and bring extra underwear, clothes, and gloves."

When I got home that day, Mom was concerned, but I got ready.

Later in the night, I was awakened by some strange noise—bushes rubbing up against our home. Looking outside, it was already snowing lightly with a slight wind blowing the fine-sparkling airborne flakes. Sparkling in what light there was, I knew it was cold.

The afternoon and evening shift was mine and three others. By noon, there was four inches of snow and dropping temperatures. I climbed in my car at 1:45 p.m., letting it warm up about ten minutes. Wanting plenty of time to make the 3:00 p.m. shift, I left early. Midnight was my stopping point. It was fifteen degrees. The wind made it feel like negative fifty degrees. Cold, snowy, and slick roads.

I had sixteen miles to drive, so I drove about thirty miles per hour to get there safely.

Pumping fuel, cleaning windows, and the floors inside was accomplished with freezing hands, nose, and feet. At 8:00 p.m., the temperature was five degrees and falling, with six to seven inches of snow laying, staying, sticking, and blowing in swirls.

Cleaning the restrooms was a nightmare with an old brown heater inside, yet I was thankful. Complaining didn't help but keeping the big picture in mind and praying did. A few jokes, pranks, and laughter helped with the old-timers telling their stories. I was okay with it all.

One solid week! No brake, winds, snow, and negative twenty degrees, staying for one solid week. Negative twenty below, which I worked in for eight hours for one entire week, seven days! Besides two of our employees got pneumonia and had to stay home, one in the hospital. I rejoiced to see five degrees above zero. I hollered when the thermostat read fifteen degrees and grabbed the cute, smart female clerk behind the counter, and we danced. I liked it but she scared me!

My human father taught me that if you make a commitment, you stay with it no matter how difficult.

But negative twenty degrees? Yes, even then.

While the winter passed a little by March, we had moderate temperatures, almost twenty-five to forty degrees in that Lake Michigan bordering country. On a sunny day, I think a Friday, a family came to get fuel, and all six of them were piled tight in their 1950s model car. But they only had two dollars. The man of the family told me how he lost his job, had no place to stay, and asked if I knew someone who could help them through this time so he could get a job.

Being taught to give and seeing Mom and Dad help people, I knew just what to do. "Take them home with me!" Yes, take them home with me—oh my!

So being on the morning shift, we pulled up in front of 3925 Grace Street. I proceeded briskly into our home, told Mom the story, and she said, "I'll fix them some supper, then we will see what your Dad says."

With Mom tilting her head sideways, twisting it upward with raised eyebrows, she let me know of her "real" thoughts. Mother heated up some roast and potatoes left from the night before, and they ate until there was one slice of potato left. They told us thanks, went to the living room, where the man and his wife instantly fell asleep.

I wondered what Dad would say, but I knew he would be proud of me. Dad came home.

Walking into the kitchen, he said, "Whose car is that?" His tone was full of aggravation.

Here's the short version of the long story. Dad had sympathy for them, took out his little sum of savings, rented them a hotel room, and gave them some money. Mother cooked enough food for us to take meals to the family of six.

On Sunday, the family went to church with us, where Bob, the father, promptly asked for baptism and church membership.

We hoped a miracle had occurred, one of grace.

In a few days, Bob told us his car was broken down, and even though Dad was a renowned mechanic, he could not fix it. Bob appealed to Dad's soft Christian side to which Dad spent $1,000 to buy Bob a car.

Bob assured Dad that he would pay him back and told him, "You just seem like my old daddy." In a week or two, it was becoming obvious that this 'beggar' family were 'con' artists.

Dad confronted Bob. We never saw them again.

My dad was a compassionate man. My mother was a compassionate woman.

"Son, Do You Want to Go with Me?"

On a Saturday, when I was sixteen, Dad asked me in the late afternoon, "Son, do you want to go with me?"

I replied, being busy with nothing, "Where you goin'?"

My wise father, probably a little hurt, with an injured expression on his face but teaching me also, said, "What? Does it matter? I asked, do you want to go with *me*!"

I said, "Yes, sir," mostly not to aggravate him. I didn't get it all then. I get it now. Oh, if I could go on a ride anywhere with my father now! He accepted my apology.

Thank you, Dad, for impressing on me the value of a kind, loving relationship and keeping it going…especially with your father.

A Leader for Me

My human father had faults, but I never held any of it against him and chose rather to look at the very good character in him. All dads should have character traits for which to be remembered. Most do, some don't.

"It's much easier to become a father than to be one," Kent Newburn said in *Letters to My Son: Reflections on Becoming a Man*.

I became a father four times, but I'm not sure I ever learned how to be one. Maybe by the time Lizzy, my youngest, had grown up, I was suited to be a father.

I gave much counsel to younger persons but found it very difficult to live it out in real life myself. Seeing ones faults is good, but it needs to be seen while he has the opportunity and desire to change it. There just comes the time when all you can say is, "I tried. I did the best I could," ask for forgiveness, and continue to give counsel!

My father was a leader for me. But the way I learned life taught me not to major on faults, accept one as they are, and also be yourself. Today I absolutely do not begrudge anything in or about Walker Eddins. In fact, I only thank God for him and trust that I'm forgiven for my failures as a son.

My Leader

Every son needs leadership from his father. Dad was in the world not "drugged out" of it, "alcoholed" out of it, arrogant, or "self-centered" out of the world. He was in the world, this battleground of humanity bearing his duties, loving my mother, and caring for his four children.

Dad had made a profession of faith and submitted to water baptism in the Temple Baptist Church in Memphis when he was eighteen years old. Because we moved so much, he had forgotten to be faithful to the Lord. What was in his mind, I don't know, but I think it was duty, responsibility.

He was strong in his convictions though and never ever used a curse word around any of us. Attentive and loving to Mom, he was a good husband and leader to Jeanie, David, Susan, and I.

But he never took us to church until 1953 when I was nine. Two men from the First Baptist Church of Gallatin, Tennessee, knocked on the door, told Dad who they were, talked with him and to us for about thirty minutes. I listened. Dad told them of his church membership and profession of faith and promised to be in church the next Sunday.

Knock, knock, Dad knocked on the wall, saying, "Rise and shine! Breakfast is being served in the diner."

It wasn't until later that I learned where that saying came from, but he had plenty of "sayings." By this time, we were living in our fifty-foot-long turquoise-and-white 1953 Liberty trailer. It had two doors into or out of it.

The trailer was fourteen feet longer than our previous top-of-the-line silver aluminum Spartan. The living room was in front, then the kitchen with Mom loving the extra room since she had to spend so much time in it and prepare meals for a growing active army of four children. I was nine, and the youngest, Susan, was two years old.

After the kitchen was the first bedroom, then the second with the bathroom between them, and then there was Mom and Dad's master bedroom. There were sliding doors between the front two bedrooms—and of course, a door to the bathroom and a sliding door, closing off Mom and Dad's bedroom.

Being blurred by sleep but already up, I asked, "What is it?" as I rubbed both eyes.

Dad responded, "We're going to Sunday school and church this morning."

So Dad, I, Jeanie, and David got up, got ready with the best clothes we had, and ate breakfast. Thankfully I had obtained a wonderful suit for Sunday school at the Methodist Church across South Water Street, so I was ready.

David asked, "Why are you doing this?" He was and is always one to cut through the mire and get at the core of things. Even at age five, he cut to the core.

"We're going to worship God," Dad said, so we got ready.

After eating breakfast, we arrived for Sunday school at 9:45 a.m., were taken to our separate classes with instructions to let the teacher get us back to Dad on the back side of the huge auditorium. Safely delivered by the Bible teachers, we went through the door into the auditorium. With wild eyes, we viewed the huge place, where we were to hear the preaching. With eyeballs almost popping out of our heads, wondering where we were supposed to sit and what was going to happen. "What is to happen?" I asked myself. What I did know was that a whole lot of people were going to do it.

I asked Jeanie, "What's going to happen?"

She didn't know either.

The only time I had ever been in a church auditorium was earlier in the year when we had gone to Grandma Wise's funeral in New Harmony, Mississippi. I recall the emotions of the day and my interest in it all. So here we were, finding a place to sit on the east side of the auditorium about six rows back. Eventually, the building filled up, and we waited. What's next? Oh yeah, Dad knew what's next. Coming up the aisle close to us, as we were squeezed in, five people deep down the pew, I saw a very strange sight. An older woman, a bit wide, came waddling up the aisle with someone at her left arm. She had hairs sticking out of her face, chin, upper lip, and lightly on the cheeks. My eyes bulged, and I leaned out and looked in shock at Daddy. I soon learned that this happens to some women, but no one knows why. It was shocking enough that I remember these sixty-four years later and still feel sorry for her. Yet I was always goggle-eyed on Sunday when I saw her. We learned that she was very kind and helpful to others.

From that day, church became a weekly matter, and I also began to go to "Training Union" on Sunday evening and preaching. I took what I was hearing very seriously, began to read my Bible at night before bed, and trying to remember to pray. You see, in Southern Baptist Churches, they used to, at that time and until I left that denomination, have a ten-point record system slip. On it, there was a place to mark yes or no to such things as daily prayer, daily Bible reading, church attendance, giving, and such. I was not going to lose. My competitive nature compelling me to answer "yes." I confess, sometimes I didn't tell the truth!

By spring, I had come to a pretty good nine-year-old knowledge of Christ, His death and resurrection, and that to believe on Christ, giving Him your heart, and asking Him to forgive you of sin was being "saved." In April of 1954, Dr. Leonard Sanderson was asked by our pastor, Brother James Crane, to come to Gallatin and preach a revival.

Dad had never talked about these things to me and as was his way to leave matters in our hands until we needed his help or direction, so he did on this Sunday morning. The auditorium was packed, about 1,200 souls filled up even in the balcony, where Mom sat with the other three offspring. But I, having caught up with Dad, sat squeezed in about the twelfth row back, two or three people from the aisle. It was tight! Finding Mother up above us but further back, I waved heartily like I was at a fairground.

Dr. Sanderson preached about Jesus and asked all that would be saved to ask Christ to come into their hearts and to come forward to make their confession of faith. The invitation hymn was "Just as I am...without one plea / but that thy blood was shed for me." Many people were emotional, and many went forward to "accept Jesus." I was moved by it all, the tears, the earnestness, the fear of not being saved. With tears rolling down my cheeks, I looked up at Dad, and he looked down to me and just nodded yes with his eyes filled with tears too.

I pushed my way out from the people closest to the aisle and boldly walking down the aisle, neither looking right nor left. What I understood and believed I was doing was deciding to give my life to Christ and follow him forever as I went to the front of the inflamed auditorium. I have that same determination, emotion, and will right now by grace. The counselor who greeted me, among all those people kneeling and praying, asked me, "Do you want to be saved?"

To which I answered, "Yes."

"And will you follow Jesus the rest of your life?"

"Yes," I said, and he led me in a sinners prayer, asking for God's forgiveness, repenting of my sins, and accepting Jesus as my Savior. The man told me I was saved, and I believed I was. Then he asked, "Do you want to be baptized?" To which I replied, "yes."

In my mind, I had made a lifelong intentional decision. I was baptized the next Sunday night and became a church member for which Mom and Dad were very proud. I would never turn back although I obeyed the Lord better sometimes than others. Within nine and a half years, I was a pastor.

Today I understand all these things in a much different way. I realize that the salvation of the soul is by grace alone without anything you can do. Also that Christ's shed blood alone cleanses of sin and brings in the righteousness God demands which is by Christ's obedience to the law. This alone justifies the sinner from sin. Further, Christ died for His sheep and all those chosen in Christ are redeemed. All this...for a little trailer boy. My! My!

I thank God that he led my dad to get us in church and for the things I learned and yet was eventually totally changed from those methods. In 1985, Brother Scott Richardson baptized me even as the pastor of the church, God started through me in 1980. Today my brother David followed in my footsteps and is pastor of Providence Church now for twenty-five years.

A Decision Made is a Decision Kept

Until Dad learned otherwise when he made a decision, he stayed with it.

That is the way it was—worship at church, reading his Bible, and prayer of thanks at the table for the rest of his life. No matter where we moved, the first thing was to find a church home and join that church.

Eventually, Walker Eddins became a Sunday school teacher, a deacon, and weekly visitation in the homes of people to encourage them to either accept Christ or come to worship. This became a weekly commitment for him.

At the end of his short life, he even became a pastor in Michigan City, Indiana, for about two years. He left us with emphysema, pneumonia, and finally a heart attack that last five days of his life, March 25, 1977.

I fell on the floor—with my family standing in the kitchen close together, with Carole's arms around my four children, hugging them uptight—when my six-year-old Elizabeth exclaimed with deep emotion, "Granddad died."

My leader was gone…but not the leadership.

Visit with a Famous Preacher

Often called the prince of preachers, Dr. R. G. Lee was Dad's favorite preacher. His famous sermon, "Pay Day, Same Day," which was first preached by him in 1919 was later preached 1,275 times. I heard Dr. Lee preach it with Dad, and he heard him several other times.

While I was a pastor in Indianola, Mississipi, Dad moved to New Albany, Mississipi, for a year. His lung condition grew much worse. Finding a doctor in Memphis, he made several trips there for treatments and care. During that time, he and Mom decided to move back to Indiana and ended up in a new home in La Porte. He continued to work outside as a mechanic, but his condition worsened. Deciding to make one more visit to Memphis in the fall of 1976, he and Mom made the trip to my aunt Alice's home.

Attending seminary in Memphis, driving 150 miles four times weekly, I talked with Dad and decided to visit with him the most I could. On Tuesday of that week, with Mom and Dad having been there a day, I took off from seminary to be with them.

Knowing how Dad loved Dr. Lee and I having become a bit of a friend of Dr. Lee's, I asked Dad if he would like to go meet and visit the old warrior. Called the prince of preachers, Dr. Lee virtually had no equal. Pastor of the historic Belview Baptist Church in my hometown of Memphis, his unique voice, personality, and messages with great biblical content made him contagious.

From 1927-1960, this son of a sharecropper mesmerized his hearers. With several thousand members, the church and this pastor were unsurpassed.

Knocking reverently, the famous preacher came to the door. Having preached at my church in Hickory Withe, Tennessee, a year before, he greeted us warmly, invited us in, and I introduced the two men among men. Although of different worlds, they struck up a good conversation, and I would step in to fill in the gaps so their meeting would resume. Dr. Lee took us back to his study where, for thirty-three years, he had prepared his soul-shaking messages. I was amazed, and Dad put in shock.

About 2,500 volumes lined his walls, a huge desk covered in burgundy leather, a leather chair, pictures of men from 1920 and beyond. Mystical. We were in the midst of greatness, the mystery of history, and the passage of time. He spoke of great men, his blessed life, and his wife. Dr. Lee was gracious, but it didn't take him long to tire. At ninety plus, it was okay.

I spoke up and told Dr. Lee how much we were thankful to see him, be with him, and that he took the time for such as "we." So gracious, he said, "I was the blessed one. Come back soon." Both he and my good father would move on out of this world soon—Dad in 1977, and Dr. Lee in 1978.

Dad was elated and wrapped in the mystic of human greatness. He didn't speak all the way back to Aunt Alice's.

I went back to Aunt Alice's with Dad, loved on all who were there, especially Mom and Dad. I drove away with a sense of finality. Dad left us on March 25, 1977.

Confrontation at a Drive-In Movie

Living in Gallatin, Dad and John Rice, after a hard day at work came home and asked all of us if we would like to take in a movie at the drive-in theater, and of course, we all yelled and carried on.

My good friend Happy grinned and slapped me on the back.

We got ready, dressed, and made it to Nashville in about thirty minutes before dark. We were hungry. Dad and John went to the concession stand and bought enough hot dogs for everybody to have two, but Happy and I got three. Potato chips and root beer made it just right.

The theater played the best of the new rock and roll, and we sang along with Chuck Berry, the Satins, and Buddy Holly.

The movie was ready to start so, with previews and concession advertisements, the great western *The Searchers* with John Wayne started. In about thirty minutes, we kept hearing loud talking, some filthy and loud laughter. Three cars down to our right was a group of six eighteen to twenty-six-year-old males. They apparently had brought beer and maybe whiskey with them. They were getting more loud and more "loose." John got out and told them to stop but they continued their brash, unruly behavior.

John and Dad had had enough. John was six feet one or six feet two, very wiry and muscular, not especially a handsome man but looked like an ancient warrior. Both men, brown as Indians from working in the sun, looked like leather. John, like Dad, normally rolled his sleeves up above the muscle. His biceps were huge, well-defined, and his forearm and face like "Pop eyes."

Dad at five feet seven and a half was very thick built with black hair and arms like a weight lifter, with a nineteen-inch neck and would stand toe to toe with anyone. Happy and I stood in front of the car to watch. They looked like Randolph Scott and Glen Ford walking down the middle of Dodge City to settle the matter.

Arriving in front of their two cars, with four of them standing out of the cars, Dad said, "We told you to stop. Now we're going to stop you. Get out of the cars, or we'll take you out. We're going to whip you right here and right now."

All six stepped forward while Dad said, "I'll take these three"— pointing to the left—"and you get the rest."

As soon as the two diesel mechanics started moving with absolute seriousness to get hold of their three, the young men began to back up. Happy and I couldn't stand it and slipped along, stooping over almost to the car next to the troublemakers.

Mom and Wilma cried out to we boys to get us to stop, but we couldn't overcome our curiosity and devotion. Could we help?

By this time, another man from down the other way emerged when he saw he wasn't alone. Moving decisively to lay hold of these cocky troublemakers, they crumpled into their cars. Afraid, giving up, and tucking their tails, they said, "Okay, okay. We'll stop."

> That indeed they did! I learned this: "Force and right are governors of this world; force till right is ready.

> —Matthew Arnold, *Essays in Criticism:*
> *First Series* 1, in Quotationary, (1865), 287

Time Together

> The value of a father being with his children and especially his sons cannot be measured.

> —Author unknown

One Friday evening in early December, as the family watched a little bit of TV, Dad said, "Larry."

"Yes, sir."

You know that's one way we honored our parents in those days.

Continuing, he said, "I'm wanting to go rabbit hunting tomorrow on Dr. Giles' farm, would you want to go with me?"

"Yes, sir!"

So he told me we would be leaving early, that it would be cold, and it looks and smells like snow. I normally got up before the family, but Dad beat me up on this Saturday and shaking me, saying, "Son, get up. Mom's got breakfast going."

I jerked the covers off, got sufficiently dressed to be respectful, and I stepped the five feet into the kitchen and got full aroma of ham, eggs, and biscuits cooking of which I had been recognizing in my half-waking sleep.

Eating, dressing in long johns, taking three or four shirts, my winter coat, hat, toboggan, I also found my gloves. Dad took about the same. It was twenty-eight degrees, and it had snowed about an inch overnight, a pretty "clingy" white blanket.

Out in this winter wonderland, we loaded the green '53 Ford. Dad took a very special item; my great-granddad's double-barreled twelve-gauge shotgun. Imprinted, March 26, 1878, now 142 years ago, I have had it since 1977 and will pass it down to one of my sons.

One hammer is broken off, it shows normal wear, but is an aged beauty. A Parker Brothers—it is a family treasure. The "patina" is 142 years rich in warm brown. Granddaddy Eddins, being born in 1844, fought in the Civil War and was an outdoorsman as well as a farmer. His brother, one and a half years older, died in the Battle of Chickamauga on September 21, 1863.

They were together. In a few days, I plan to go to Chickamauga again, only twenty miles from mine and Sandy's home.

There can be no doubt that Granddaddy Eddins used this gun to hunt many times. Dad inherited the gun as a thirteen-year-old and kept it until his death. This treasure has been kept in our collective possessions for ninety years. Through all our travels as a boy and now as an aged possessor of this historical fantasy, we have loved it in the memory of a good man. Well, over forty moves, my father and now I have held this possession tight to the chest.

I had been with Dad on another escapade in Gallatin. He took Mom and we children with him to visit a new acquaintance and to shoot a little. After much firing, noise, and talk, the countryside and our noses were full of gun smoke. It was fall time, so ducks and geese were in migration to warmer lands.

As men will do, Marvin, Dad's new friend, said, "I bet you that you can't hit one of these high-flying geese."

Well, being so bright, I didn't see how he would either. It seemed to me, at any time, a plane might fly into one of the birds because of their great elevation. I feared the birds might make the airplanes crash. Such is the wisdom of an eleven-year-old.

Marvin, with a new store-bought single-barreled shotgun, probably a twelve gauge, fired away. Getting more frustrated as the moments flew by because he wasn't dropping a single thing, he fired his last aggravating shot. No birds.

"No luck. I'm not use to the gun," he said as he turned it over looking at it with curiosity, as if he might find something wrong with it.

Dad winked at me.

The ducks didn't show much intelligence or knowledge of the ways of men. This large family of feathered friends just kept "winging" by. Dad never said a word, calmly raised the old 1878 family classic to his right shoulder, thumbed back the right hammer, closed his right eye, steadied his arm, and squeezed off the right barrel, just like Granddaddy Eddins had taught him thirty-six or thirty-seven years before. Feathers flew, one hundred feet in the air, and a limp duck sailed to the ground about ten feet in front of us. Dad never looked at Marvin, just went over, and picked up the limp duck and studied it.

Finally, Marvin said, "Wow, great shot."

Dad left the bird with Marvin and left him to kill some himself.

The old Parkers Brother duck killer had done it again.

It started to snow a little bit out of the gray winter sky as we got in the green 1953 Ford with the wind coming from the west. Rabbits were the goal.

Dr. Giles farm, beyond the beautiful big Civil War country home, was all the best in that country close to Nashville. Hedgerows, apple trees, cedars, flat rocks of all sizes, as big as ten to fifteen feet by twenty to thirty feet dressed up the old ground. Passing the cattle, the goats, two or three mules, and a big used-up garden, we came to a rock wall, very long until out of sight and beautiful.

"Why is this here, Daddy?"

"Son, this is a wall built during the Civil War, where sometimes farmers, soldiers, and plantation workers could try to fight off the northerner invaders."

I knew about the Civil War. My little grandmother, Mattie Pearl Simpson, had talked with me several times about that war. She said, "The north invaded our homes, burned our homes and farms, killed our soldiers, all in the name of freeing the slaves. They didn't want to be freed because we treated them good, and we loved each other," she continued.

She also was quite a historian, living with a Civil War "warrior" and having much discussion with other old-timers. "Some were alive during the war for freedom from northern oppression she had said." She said held a strong opinion and emotion for her southland. I enjoyed many talks with Grandmother held, who always had an enlightened viewpoint. Those "mystic" rock walls have charmed me for years.

Grandmother believed that the Civil War was fought for economic reasons and that the north resented the wealth of the south and wanted control of exports and shipping.

This rock wall represented that horrible, violent war between Americans. Southerners by birth to this day resent the Northern invasion into the south, the march to the ocean through Atlanta, and the destruction of Southern culture and humanity. Besides this—the memories through the years from generation to generation of the years after the war and the cruel treatment by carpet baggers.

As I looked at the wall, my mind went yonder, back, back to the 1860s and especially to Grandmother and her daddy.

Dad said, "Son, let's go," as I stared into the mystifying past.

Pushing through the briars, the tall dried brown grasses, and leaning against the wind, we looked and waited for a rabbit. Dad showed me how to build a little fire, and to this day, I love fires outdoors, at home, on the trail with Doc or David or James and a great horse. I love it as well all by myself.

Even today, when we have family gathering at our home in colder weather, I build a good fire. I have a crude, L-shaped wall of bricks, where many sweet times have happened, warming our hands and souls.

We moved on. Coming to a clearing, Dad said, "Shhhh." Whispering, he said, "Be still, and we'll wait for a rabbit to appear in this clearing."

Seventy-five or eighty feet from the edge of the thicket, covered in snow was a beautiful little hill, topped with leafless trees, but the hillsides clear. Suddenly, Dad pulled his 1800s double-barreled shotgun to his shoulder!

There it was—a nice, fat gray with white-and-brown fur victim swiftly hopping from the flat opening to the hillside. As he moved up the hill a little faster, with Dad bearing down on him, he squeezed off the trigger. *Boom*, and the pretty rabbit was blown up the hill about two feet limplessly and then began to roll down the hill a few feet. He waited in silence for us to come and get him.

We walked back to the truck in silence. Daddy threw the ole rabbit in the bed. It was snowing a little harder. The winds blew a little more stiffly.

Dad drove to Manny Williams house, the son of a slave, who worked with Dad but was quite aged with curly white hair. Daddy went to the door with me close behind. Manny appeared at the door. White hairs were spread around on his kind face. What kind eyes.

Dad said, "Manny, I've got a big rabbit here, ready to bleed, and I want your family to have him."

Manny said, "Thank you, Mr. Walker. We'll have him with gravy, beans, and biscuits tonight."

We left with thankfulness in our heart. Nothing was said in the green Ford truck. I was in wonder, with melancholy and joy. History, the toughness yet kindness of Daddy and beauty of our world spread all over me and Manny, so kind, warmed my heart.

The old shotgun lay on the floor…behind the front seat.

I have no excuses; I had a genuine father!

On the Way to Destiny

Dad was cool, calm, and collected. He believed that children should be seen and not heard and that we should sit in on normal conversations between he, Mom, and other adults. We, children, actually did sit quietly, not asking for this or that, lying down, and sprawled out. Thank the Lord, we didn't have cell phones and such. We didn't drink "pop," indulge in candy or other sugary treats that overstimulate the body, especially children's bodies. Candy wasn't set out to be eaten until offered.

Actually, I learned a lot from those experiences. I learned the adult view of things, how to converse, and take an interest in the lives of others. We sat and listened.

Think of it. We never thought of standing up in a restaurant booth, ask for other than what was ordered, or get something we might demand; we didn't demand!

I have seen recently children allowed to walk around in a restaurant, disturbing the patrons, in the way if servers, running under hot food and generally obnoxious.

"Aren't they cute!"

No, they aren't, and in almost every restaurant nowadays, there will be one child left to scream out, and their high-pitched voice simply pierces the ear, especially of older folks.

Candy

On one occasion, while in La Porte, Indiana, Mom and Dad were invited over to an older couples trailer for a visit. All four of we, children—I was eleven; Jeanie, 9; David, 6; Susan, 4—went with them. Their home was immaculate, a modern mobile home, and kept spotless. Mom and Dad set on a sofa with Susan while the husband and wife, our hosts, sat on chairs. In this very upscale home, there were two sofas, so David, Jeanie, and I sat on the other from across Mom, Dad, and Susan.

There was a coffee table, oblong by design, sitting between the two sofas. What was sitting on the table? Were the hosts heartless? Did Mom and Dad not know of our lusts? Besides, we hadn't had supper yet. We were hungry. We lusted after what we saw. What?

Candy! Beautiful candy! Mints. Yellow, green, blue, and every other enticing color. They were half the size of peanuts, a little oblong. The bowl was full. Each one of us could have had ten or fifteen whole mints! Our eyes instantly saw them. Jeanie, very discreetly, hit me in the side with her elbow, as if to say, "Do you see that?" We sat like prisoners. Our eyes were searching, staring, mouths watering. I didn't hear Mother call my name, so she raised her sweet Mississippi voice. I did hear it then.

David's eyes were poking out of their sockets. Besides, they were darting back and forth, hoping to be able to steal some, even if just four or five. Theft, it was in our minds. Would we have to kill for it? Mints!

Dad asked to be excused and went outside for something, and Mom was conversing. David slipped further toward the mints! I would not let my little brother commit this crime and especially be caught. Taking hold of the little thief's arm, I pulled him back.

I was certain that if I could sneak some out, I would. We three hoped the adults would move on outside or at least out of sight! They didn't. Couldn't they find some reason to go outside?

Susan, sitting across from us, was staring across to the table. She had become almost pitiful looking.

Mother nodded, leaning to the right, changing her expression of a "smile" to the hosts but "no" to us.

One hour! Or was it a month? One hour! The candy under our nose, purely visible to our eyeballs. The color danced in our vision and "teased" our tongues.

"Children," the lady suddenly said, "do you want some candy before you leave?"

Are you kidding?

"Only get a few," Mom said.

How much? How many are a few? So we each picked out about five, thanked the lady, and filled our mouths with heaven on earth. Jeanie and I spoke of this just the other day. She remembered it just like I did sixty-four years later. We had a good old-fashioned chuckle.

Rope and Rules

Daddy believed in giving us a "rope" with rules. A rope is that which tied us to him and stated how far we could go and not exceed the end of the rope. Besides, the rope was long enough to give childhood freedom. This gave us a freedom to explore, go see other kids, and have them come see us. If we were hungry, we could have an apple or peanut butter, but not too close to the next meal.

If we tore our pants or dress, Mom didn't get mad. We could have all the food at mealtime we wanted, except pie or cake still.

We knew we would get two or three things at Christmas and something for a birthday. We knew nothing of begging for anything. When we were told to be quiet, we were quiet.

I was used to going outside early in the morning, walk around with our dog, Trixie, and then her baby, Tony, climb a tree or go knock on the window of a friend so they would sneak on outside.

When I was a sophomore in high school, playing both the junior varsity and varsity teams as a running back in Grove City, Ohio, the junior varsity played at another school. We had won all our games up to this point. But this school was good. Not only was I to start at running back, but the coach also came to me and said they wanted me to play middle linebacker in this game. I had always been a defensive back.

What they had seen is that I would "hit." At 150 pounds now, I was not big but fast, strong for my size and would lay myself on the line. This is the way my family is. Besides, having won the "challenge" against a junior I had asked for this! The coaches knew I wouldn't quit.

The longest run I had in a varsity game that year was only fifteen yards. There was one defensive back between me and the goal post. If I had "juked" him, I might have scored. But instead of trying to fake him, I ran straight at him to put a hit on him, but he tackled me. That was my nature.

Later, Coach said, "Next time, try your moves."

"Yes, sir!"

We were outsized. They had better uniforms and gorgeous cheerleaders, but we beat them by a point. Being hot on that October late afternoon, we were exhausted, but some of us wanted to stay together. I had told Dad that I would be home around 7:00 p.m., but it was already 6:30 p.m. by the time we got back to Grove City. One guy already had a car, so he and I, along with three other teammates, wanted to go to "Bobbies Ice Cream and Hamburgers" to eat and be together. A common struggle seems to draw people together.

But I knew I had to call home. So putting my dime in the pay phone, I called the neighbor and asked to talk to Dad. We had no phone, but we had an agreement about using their phone.

Grudgingly, he came to the phone. So I told Dad, "I know you said be home by 7:00 p.m. but some of the guys and myself want to go get a hamburger." I told him about our game and how tough we had fought to win a one-point game.

Dad, who really didn't put much stock in games, asked a couple of questions and then said, "Okay, be home by nine o'clock to nine thirty."

I made it home about 9:45 p.m. and went into Mom and Dad's bedroom to tell them I was home and say good night.

"What time is it?" Mom asked.

I replied, "Nine forty-five." I hugged them both, cleaned up, and went to bed.

Rope, rules, and room. That was Dad's way.

"Do what you're told, and there will always be room" was Daddy's motto. He was ready to let me be a kid as he had been an outdoor, rollicking, and rolling boy. I'm still thankful.

Destiny

Oklahoma through Arkansas

We arrived in Memphis on Friday from Gallatin. Having run around after midnight and happily not being caught by the police, Jeanie and I were very tired. We came alive, though, when we got parked in Leahy's Trailer Court then drove to Granddaddy's and Grandma Mac's. I especially wanted to be with Mom's younger sisters, Alice and Barbara.

But we left them on Sunday night with tears and love.

Monday morning came early with our destination—Eastern Oklahoma. It was breaking day when we crossed the old Memphis bridge into West Memphis, Arkansas. I thought we had already gotten in the west. Along the main street of West Memphis, there were numerous Indian statues, artworks, cowboys in trucks, and cool morning air, even in July on that morning. Picking up Highway 64 into the flat Delta Country, we wanted to see the Arkansas River on the edge of Oklahoma. I thought, for sure, we were in the west.

We knew it would be hot. We didn't know how hot. I was already excited sitting in the truck with Dad. Mom and the kids were in the black-and-white Buick; LT and Aunt Bertha following. LT, mom's brother had come back to visit family, so we made up the plans to travel along together. What a time we had. LT was cool and very comical, handsome, witty and favored me. He made me feel grown-up.

Later while living in Inyokern, after staying for two weeks in Bakersfield, still in warm weather in the fall, LT and Bertha came to the desert to visit. LT had a convertible Ford and slick. I was thirteen. So after visiting a while, LT said, "Let's go outside. I'll show you my convertible." We took off. I had never ridden in it, but I loved it and especially with the warm desert air hitting my face. My uncle let me be a "little man."

Slowly stopping on the side of Highway 395, LT said, "Son, do you want to drive?"

I swallowed and gulped and said, stammering, "Yes, yes, sir!"

Dad had taught me to drive his green 4-speed Ford, and besides, I was driving the trailer park owners pickup around the trailer park to clean up; it was a stick shift on the column.

Slowly, a little afraid, because I knew how particular Uncle LT was about his stuff, I slid into the driver's seat, adjusted the seat forward and backward by rocking my bottom forward with LT doing the same, and our heels dug into the floor. I gripped the steering wheel tight, checking the mirrors, like Daddy would.

It was an automatic, 2-speed Ford Victoria so I pulled it into drive, and we started to roll. Seeing no one was behind us, I gave the convertible some gas, and here we went. Thirty, forty, fifty, and LT said, "Stay right there, son."

So we cruised. Okay, at thirteen, I felt big. LT smiled big.

Later that day, we took another ride, and LT told me this story. I guess he was feeling big britches. He was twenty-eight years old, just married to Bertha with a pocket full of "dough." Suddenly a car ran upon us and then around us, and at the wheel was a beautiful blond-headed woman. Slowly, she looked over at us, smiled, and flew away. I think she was saying, "Look." We looked, then looked at each other, and LT whistled like, "Wow! Wow!"

"That reminds me of a story," my uncle said, feeling his oats. Now this is a story that a thirteen-year-old has no business hearing, but away he went.

"A few years ago, I was driving in North Mississippi and passed slowly a gorgeous brown-haired girl in a convertible, and I hollered, 'Pull over so we can talk.' The young woman pulled over even though she turned out to be thirty-five." They talked. LT said, "Son, we stayed together three days, and what a three days it was." He stopped as if to realize whom he was telling this story to. Thinking of the story through the years from '57 to today, I wondered what that would be like. I never knew...I don't care.

We never mentioned it again all through the years although he was my favorite uncle a long time. We'll never talk about it again. He left us in 2006.

Day 1

On the way to Destiny, California

That first two hours in Arkansas, which is flat delta land, the coolness of the morning rushed away. Heat, hot heat, began to fire up. Hot, humid—desperately hot and humid air. It was miserable. Our clothes got soaked. We, of course, drove with the windows down at about fifty fifty-five miles per hour. A nephew once asked, "Why didn't you turn the air conditioner on?"

"Son," I said, "in those days, we didn't have air-conditioning in a 1953 truck!"

He apologized, and I said, "You couldn't know. It's all right. Just be thankful you've got cold air nowadays."

Yes, no air-conditioning, and it got up to 105 degrees by 10:30 a.m. in that flat then hilly country. The only wind we had was the 105-degree air that seemed to get hotter and hotter. *Would we live?* I thought. We did but only with "sweat" rolling off us and especially off Daddy.

"Son," Dad said, "pour some of that cold water into a cup and pour it over my head."

Naturally, I did it and enjoyed it! I poured it on myself, cold and good! Back then, we had a thermos-type water cooler, old, round, and green in "color" that really kept the water cold. It was fat, about thirty inches around, with a plug in the top and a cup that screwed on and served as a drinking cup.

"Again," Dad said with ice-cold water running off his head with a flattop haircut, down his back and neck and chest. With a cold wet T-shirt, Dad just barely smiled, "Thanks, son." What was I doing? Pouring ice water out of the thermos bottle directly on his wide head! And he loved it. Then at 105 degrees in humid wet delta air, the ice water kept him awake. The good man said, "Thanks," and kept the petal pushed to the metal.

Finally, as it began to get very late in the afternoon, we passed through Fort Smith, crossing the Arkansas River, landing in Oklahoma! We were truly in the forth-coming west in the darkness of the night.

Years later, with my own family, we moved to Fort Smith, 1970–72, and I love the western flavor; of course, I relived those days of traveling and rode back over Highway 64 with those sweet memories. I still love Fort Smith and have been able to be back there and into Oklahoma many times.

We found a trailer park, got set up in the dark, had a picnic meal—yes, in the dark—then fell into bed. The next morning in the "black," we slipped away deeper into the west in this mighty California-bound caravan.

Day 2

Destination Amarillo

We moved across Oklahoma with its wood and iron fences. Picking up the now revered first transcontinental highway, Route 66, we traveled on into history, becoming a part of it. Little could I have known that the beautiful lady I love and live with as my wife also traveled old 66 on her families way to see relatives in Bakersfield, California, in the fifties. I think I saw her in their car passing us in Texas, and I glimpsed upon her brown face...or is that my old imagination sailing once again sixty-two years down the connection between dreams and history?

When we got to Bakersfield, surely, she, the one, was there. Was she? I can only hold this fantasy as possible as reality just enhanced by time.

We spent the night, a very short night, in a ragged old mobile home "camp."

Day 3

Goal Tucumcari and No Trouble

This was to be a short day for some rest. Leaving a little later, 8:30 a.m., we traveled the almost one hundred miles in two hours. As we pulled into the old western town, a highway patrolman stopped Dad with red lights flashing.

"Sir, I had to stop you because your rig looks too long." He measured the home on wheels up one side and then down the other. "Sir, your rig is eighteen inches too long. Here's your ticket, but I have to verify that you can move ahead, so stay parked right here!"

The hours passed slow on the fiery hot blacktop parking lot of the truck stop. Dad paced a lot. He said very few words. Uncle LT left him alone. Finally, after much aggravation and uncertainty, the officer appeared grimly. Too late for us to leave. He handed Dad a "too long violation ticket."

"What?" Dad poured forth in unbelief. "What? How much? $500 dollars!"

In 1957, $500! Dad took the ticket, paid the money as the sun was setting on what was supposed to be a day of rest. We made it. We toughed it out as we all with determined resolve made the day the best we could.

Dad was sick. Half his money was now in the hands of the New Mexico state government. He looked weary, beat.

We went to sleep after a family prayer with Uncle LT leading it. But we had lost one half day and $500! Yes, we had trouble.

"Tomorrow's a new day, and Daddy will get all right."

Day 4

Onto Gallup

Still traveling old 66, we left early in the dark coming upon the edge of the mountain above Albuquerque. What a sight spread out below. The old New Mexico city was all lit up with sparkling, dancing, glittery lights by the thousands. My sister Jeanie and I just spoke about that scene this morning. We were thrilled.

By 9:00 a.m., we stopped, ate scrambled eggs, cooked on our propane stove on the side of Route 66. Dad was determined to get to Bakersfield and start looking for a job on Monday. Passing through Gallup, we beheld the beautiful El Rancho Hotel where so many movie stars stayed and their pictures hanging around the second floor.

In 1991, I flew from Memphis to Albuquerque with Uncle Doc, who had come for a visit with our people. I flew to Memphis, had an exciting reunion with Doc, Alice, and Grandma Mac. We flew direct, went to Doc's truck, and rode to his property of one thousand acres above Dolores, Colorado, close to Cortez. Thankfully, Doc had two horses ready, and we set up camp. We rode together for a week, and he took me back to Albuquerque.

Coming upon Gallup, he said, "I want to take you to an old hotel, and we will have the best 'Huevo Rancheros' you've ever eaten."

I said, "I've never had that."

"Well, you will love it."

The hotel was the El Rancho! We ate up every bit of the best huevo rancheros I have had to this day. Sandy and I have eaten there many times since, spent the night there, and sat mystified by the incredible decor of the lobby in its old southwestern style and the fire crackling in the huge rock fireplace.

We left full. My good uncle (Doc) dropped me off at my motel. He turned determined after a sad goodbye and went back to Dolores to our happy, secluded camp. I waited to go to the airport, reliving every moment of our camp and horses and talks. An incredible trip.

So in our three-vehicle caravan, we approached the El Rancho, and Uncle LT in the lead whipped into the parking lot. Dad had to go around the block with a sigh of aggravation and quipped something under his breathe. Mother followed us around the block, and we parked on the vacant street.

LT was waiting, "Walker, I wanted you to see this old hotel. The kids will love it and Vicki." He was trying to make up ground!

We were astonished by the mesmerizing historic authentic hotel. I was and have been ever since a lover of the turquoise jewelry, colorful rugs, and brilliant clothing. Sandy and I have a special made for us Ganado rug at the front door even as I write.

As we gazed at the colorful second story, I knew I had to go up the long, high, wide steps next to the large rock fireplace and see all the pictures of movie stars: Humphrey Bogart, Burt Lancaster, John Wayne, Maureen O'Hara, and a couple of dozen more. It all transcended time.

Sandy and I long to go back, even this very hour.

Day 5

Friday, Rolling to Kingman, Arizona

From Gallup to Kingman, Arizona, was 332 miles, about half the distance to Bakersfield. So Dad changed his scheduled plan to staying in Kingman and on to Bakersfield on Saturday. The trip had taken its toll on everybody. The heat, staying in the vehicles, the slow travel, the "legal" trouble, and loss of sleep changed Dad's mind.

In Amarillo, Dad had bought a "window water cooler" that fit on the window. We had to fill it with ice two times a day. This took time, which was especially hard on Dad since he had to keep this train of humanity rollin'!

By this time, we were all feeling pressure to get to our stopping place, Bakersfield. And desperately important was Walker Eddins getting a job. Bless him, he was under pressure.

"We should make it on Saturday night by 5:00 p.m. But one never knows," Walker said.

Johann Wolfgang von Goethe said, "One always has time enough if one will apply it well." True enough, if you can control all circumstances around yourself. Respectfully quoted and edited by Suzy Platt (p. 340).

As we dipped into Arizona, I was thrilled at the giant rock formations. We passed state Highway 191 on the way to Holbrook. Little did I know that in 2002, fifty-five years later, Sandy, myself, my brother David, and his wife, Connie, would turn down this highway en route to Eager for a horse stay at a wonderful ranch. Great log cabin accommodations and challenging horseback riding awaited us.

Highway 191 is uneventful, except for the sign on tall posts "Slim Pickens Ranch." Pickens was a great western character actor.

An older cowboy, named Sam, who lived on his ranch nearby the guest ranch had been in two John Wayne movies promised to come and take us up to the top of the highest mountain peak close by. He knew the country like the back of his hand. He was to drive to the ranch to get us. When he saw our black-and-white- and bay-and-white Spotted Saddle Horses, he looked cockeyed out of his left eye and said, "Are you sure these horses can do this? They are kind of 'slight' built. This is really tough terrain."

Spotted Saddle Horses are a little "finer" built than the great quarter horse, and his ride was a sixteen hand, bay "gelding." Besides, his horse had ridden these mountains many times. We both said, "yes sir."

Spotted Saddle Horses are great endurance horses, climb like a billy goat, are very athletic, calm, and willing. I had trained up my two geldings to go anywhere in the mountains of Tennessee. They were ready and willing, in great condition. Besides, they have a four-beat, lateral gate like Tennessee Walking Horses that is comfortable and can be fast.

In one ride in Tennessee with about seven or eight riders, we rode in the mountains on steep terrain for six hours and realized we didn't know for sure where we were. We rode a couple of miles until we recognized a dirt road. Taking that country road, we had ridden for hours and still were ten miles from camp. Asking our gaited horse to get up into their saddle gait, we "saddled" down the road at about ten to twelve miles per hour, arriving at our camp in an hour. Twenty-one miles was how far we had ridden in tough mountain terrain and then ten miles back. Spotted Saddle Horses!

The old cowboy was very comical and entertaining to whom we paid $50. And although I had never heard a man speak this way about his own sons, I must repeat it! Asking him about his family, he told us about his sons who worked on their ranch.

Sam said, "My boys can ride like 'bastards,' and the 'little sons of bitches' ride like the wind."

David and I laughed and still repeat this with "respect" today even though we do not speak this way.

Climbing to the top of Baldy Peak, 11,403 feet, when we got there, he said, "Wow, your horses didn't miss a step."

We had walked along for quite a way on sheer rock, very loose going sideways of the mountain. Mack and Dusty ate it up!

We ate lunch, visited, told tales, and lay back to rest with our hats over our eyes and no talking!

We headed back and soon got off the rocky side of the mountain into the woods below the tree line.

I asked, "McCloud," my seven-year-old gelding to gait on out.

David, following on "Dusty," a brilliant five-year-old Tennessee Walking Horse, sailed along at twelve to fifteen miles per hour.

"Come on, Dusty," I heard David say, and the mighty gelding picked up the pace.

All the poor ole quarter horse could do was trot with the old-time cowboy, bouncing up and down, or work into a canter. "Look, what a canter," David observed, and he was spot-on with his as usual keen observation.

After we had gaited on down close to the truck, we stopped and waited for Sam.

"Boy, you've got your horses in shape, and I can't believe how they travel and smooth!"

We thanked him. I was proud of my two rides who were good enough to win the accolades of the old cowboy.

But in 1957, I had no way to know that I would ever ride on McCloud up in those distant mountains. We lost McCloud this year due to injury, seventeen years after these memories.

Before we left the wonderful ranch, we rode up an old 1800s trail that mailmen traveled on horseback. We were told that we "shouldn't take that trail because it was too tough."

On our last day, David and I decided to make that mail-horse ride. We packed the saddle bags with water, lunch, and our cell phones. We always wore leather chaps, gloves, and, of course, our hats. A .357 magnum pistol was packed inside a towel in the saddle bags for preservation of the weapons and us. You never know.

The trail was easy for a mile or two then began to get steep. Sure enough, it was rugged with all size rocks, loose gravel, and dirt. We were used to that in the mountains of East Tennessee.

"This is it!" David said in gladness.

As we approached the top, we saw why the trail was considered not only tough but impassable. The trail rounded a corner, and there before us was a four feet straight up huge rock wall. At that point, the trail went to the far end of the rock wall and stopped. Mountain in front of us, nothing but downhill to the left and the huge rock wall about twenty feet long on our right.

Traveling out to the end of the trail was the only place where the rock could be mounted. I studied the rock, knowing we would have to turn to the right, face the rock, and ask McCloud and Dusty to stand up and mount the rock with nothing but a long, deep drop behind us!

The trail was just wide enough for the two horses to pass each other.

David said, "I'll go first."

I was shocked but knew he and Dusty could do it. We passed each other, touching boots. David stopped in front of the rock. I knew that when he turned to face the rock, Dusty's hind feet would be just a few inches from the edge and a long way down.

"Turn Dusty easy to face the rock, raise the reigns, and ask him to stand up, place his front feet on the rock, give him a little spur, not in a hurry but all in a split second of each move."

David, not riding as much as me, but my horse was a brave, experienced son of a gun. I prayed for him. He did exactly what I asked him to do! My heart jerked and almost jumped out of my body because Dusty's feet were about six to eight inches from the drop-off and open air behind David's back.

With his hind feet so close to the edge, the loose mountain dirt flew off the trail and down, down. David raised Dusty up by raising the reigns, used a little spur, and with a loud "smooching of the lips," the bay and white raised up on his hind hooves, with his front feet pulling himself and David up, clearing the rock and both hind feet, landing safely on the upside. I sighed in deep relief, praising David and Dusty and the Lord God Almighty.

I followed suit although Macs's right hind foot slipped off the rocky trail, but with Spotted Saddle Horse determination, he pulled himself up. Both of us made it! We sighed, blowing sounds of relief from our mouths with our lips pooched outward.

If I had ever had a doubt about my brother, it ended right there. One heck of a rider!

When we arrived back at the ranch, the owner, her foreman, and a couple of other cowboys were standing under a shade tree.

"How did you do?"

"Good," we said.

"What trail did you take?"

"The mail trail."

"You did?"

"How did you make it on the rock?"

"Good," we said in an indifferent style.

When we walked past them, the owner said, "Very few people have ever been able to clear and go over the rock... Your Spotted Saddle Horses are something else."

"Thanks," I said, and we walked back to the cabins!

We just looked at each other nodded and grinned. We had made it one more time.

Slim Pickens

Coming out from the ranch, we passed Slim Pickens Ranch on Highway 191 as we had coming in.

He was one of my favorite character actors, who appeared in 172 movies and TV events. At six feet two with a very distinguished face and voice, he helped make movies, such as *Major Dundee, The Cowboys, Rough Night in Jericho,* and was "T. J. King" in *Dr. Strangelove.* Slim was a rodeo performer many years and made a great comical or serious presence. Being inducted into the Western Performers Hall of Fame, his real name was Louis Burton Lindly, June 29, 1919 to Dec. 8, 1983. The ranch sign hung very high. It simply said, "Slim Pickens Ranch"!

As we passed Highway 191 in July 1957, we had no knowledge of these places and events to happen forty-seven years later. We just knew that we must make the best of life, have the best time, and get on to Bakersfield.

We pushed day five with a happy spirit, knowing we only had 330 miles to go and knew we would sail on through without a hitch. We just knew it!

Passing through the painted desert, we stopped on the side of old 66 and enjoyed fresh ham and tomato sandwiches with plenty of mayonnaise. The sight of the bad lands, all the desert colors of red, orange, pink, tans, and browns sparkled with lavender was thrilling. I walked over the ditch to the edge of the colorful sand and rocks, which was mesmerizing. Besides, I could see forever, and my eyeballs just burst. Yonder on a small hillside road was a very colorful Navajo on a white horse. My adventurism was stimulated to behold the Spanish explorers, the winds, colors, and the Navajo. Later in life, Sandy and I will travel this county, befriend the Navajo, and love these lands. Trixie sat by my right leg starring across that magical land as if she understood.

"Yeah," Jeanie hollered out the back window, "we're here!"

And we were in Kingman. We all rejoiced, took walks, and settled in for a cooler night. Needles, Barstow, and the Tehachapi Mountains lay ahead with a feel of victory in our bones.

Day Six

On to Bakersfield and Destiny

Luther Thomas (LT) and Dad talking over black coffee felt like it was a good thing for us to move a little slower on this Saturday morning, our last day. After five tough days on the road and with Bakersfield only laying two hundred plus miles ahead, we could move a little slower.

So we did. After a hot, fresh-cooked breakfast in our home on wheels, we casually headed up and out from Kingman to Bakersfield. LT rolled out first with Mom close behind. A slight "dew" had fallen, so we cleaned the windshields.

It was a gorgeous sunlit day, about eighty degrees, and nothing but blue western sky ahead. Just a few miles out of Kingman, the newly built Highway 66, built in 1953, went straight ahead, dipping southward then back west to Needles. Dad, a great map reader, saw on the map that going to Oatman was shorter and turned north westerly on the Oatman Highway, old 66.

The map showed a short rise in elevation of 324 feet up to Sitgreaves Pass, and we knew that wouldn't be a test for our green Ford. We were up to the task.

"What'a ya think, son?"

"We can do it!"

We were very content and comfortable, knowing we had Bakersfield in sight. Besides, we were going to stay at one of Mother's brothers when we got there and planned to see them around 4:00 p.m. Mom and LT were especially chipper on this special day, ready to see Travis.

It was always a good feeling to be nearing the end of a long move. Dad was smiling slightly, which was his way, as we turned on to old 66. We, children, were having a good time, knowing California was just a few miles away and seeing Uncle Travis. California was magic in my mind with views of orange groves, mountains, and the ocean.

We all were very thankful that on this glorious day of our already two-thousand-mile trip, we were nearing our new home, our new adventure.

How thankful I am that my life was full of new adventures. I knew some more lay ahead. The old travel way was a gradual climb for a few miles, past homes, and a few businesses. It was only about twenty miles to the "pass," and we were slowly moving up. Being only 3, 550feet in elevation, we knew we wouldn't have much of a climb or descent on the other side.

However, as we got to within about four miles to the top at the "pass," the road got curvy with huge drop-offs on the eastern side where I sat! My stomach turned over as I looked down the mountain-side and the short distance to the edge of the road and down.

Dad had to slow down into second gear because of the mediocre climb but sharp curves, switchback curves.

We were slowly moving up Sitgreaves Pass and then the 4.4 miles down to Oatman. *We would have no trouble or worry.* "Just enjoy the thrill of the *road.*" because I knew the conqueror of the road had it all in hand.

At the top of the pass, we pulled off the side of the road to look at the view. Both behind and before us was a long view of brown rocky desert country. White clouds, soaring birds, and warm breezes were our companions. The view was blurred slightly because of the morning dew and steam from the increasing temperatures. But the view ahead was strangely clear. Oatman lay somewhere "down yonder."

The pullover was a few feet lower than the highway ahead, and it looked straight and gentle. After petting Trixie and sipping a little water, Dad said, "Son, let's go," with excitement in his voice but uncertainty in his brown eyes.

"Sure, Dad, let's go."

We were all "in," both of us.

Rarely did Dad let the radio play, but as we climbed back into the truck, he replied yes to my question. Nothing but static until I hit on the Kingman station with the Del Vikings singing their number 4 hit, on Dot Records, "Come and Go with Me." I got happy. Dad didn't seem to listen. He seemed too intent on the landscape and the unknown.

As we started down the gentle slope off Sitgreaves Pass, the music began to crackle with static. Dad quickly said, "Turn it off." The gentle slope seemed very innocent, shifting into second gear, then third, then fourth, and everything seemed all right after all, it was only an elevation drop of 840 feet in the next two and a half miles. The descent would be easy... But, that changed shockingly quick, suddenly, blisteringly fast.

But the huge rock formations seemed like walls of death as some hung over the old highway built in 1925. It seemed that the rocks were passing by faster with a slight blur. We were going faster. The rocks began to pass by like racehorses. The slope of old 66 got more steep, then there was a sharp curve to the left. Dad grunted. Briefly changing gears to third, the renowned driver was a little more on the front of the seat. He began to have sweat on his wide, manly forehead. I had traveled in the truck enough through the years that I knew the normal sound of the engine. It was racing with a sharp whine. Dad hit the brakes, and he was having to hit them more and more riding them some.

We were increasing in speed. The slopes dropped off like a piece of sinking earth. The highway seemed to fall beneath us. Besides, as we found out later there are one hundred and twenty turns up to and down this dry, barren, rocky pass. No metal barriers were there. One mistake could end it all.

I glanced over at Dad's face, it was white, and I knew he was worried, that we were in trouble. He grimaced, glanced over at me with great pathos in his brown eyes.

About that time as we were hitting one hairpin curve after another. Dad double-clutched the gearbox and transmission down into second with a little grinding of iron. He grimaced again. Metal against metal meant trouble.

By hairpin curves, I mean curves so sharp that it feels like you're going to meet yourself coming back at yourself. Dad was over the centerline. The tires squalled, and then smoke began to come out from under the bottom of the big green Ford! Smoke! Heat!

We were going faster. Dad had to ride the brakes until the brakes were "smoking." The harder he pushed, the more the smoke rolled. The harder he crushed the brakes…the faster we were becoming.

Looking off the curves on my side down the rocky drop-offs, I knew we were fighting for our lives. I darted my eyes over at Dad, and time stood still. His face was twisted with fear and finality. His look at me was fearful, desperation. Then a sadness!

Then the brakes quit working, no brakes, too hot. In second gear, going too fast to get into first gear. No breaks. Couldn't gear down!

The great driver, who had driven every piece of equipment there is, was fighting the deadly curves, with a sixteen-thousand-pound trailer pushing him. The trailer swerved as we entered a sharp, long curve. I was afraid that in the curves the trailer might push the truck sideways, and we would jackknife.

The thought of plunging off the mountain filled my brain. I knew it filled Dad's. Again, Dad looked at me with what seemed like a sever determination and grit. I would learn what he was thinking, the same thing I was…*jump*! Our long look at each other, stopped time, with sobering fear and passionate love.

As I looked out the speeding rig at the jagged, sharp rocks of death and the straight down mountain walls, I thought, *We're going to have to jump*. I knew he was thinking he must push me out!

That moment of monumental fear, I can still feel and see the passing scene.

Faster with each passing foot, it seemed the truck might just blow up as we streamed ahead like creek water over rocks down a mountainside. The '53 shook. The trailer swerved. The whine of the engine pierced our ears. The howling of the transmission pierced our consciousness.

Suddenly in a left-hand turn, the trailer tilted right, and the tires slid. Squalling and smoking, the old warrior held the steering wheel so tight, his hands were both white and red. Sweat dropped like hot, thick oil off his jaws. Dad looked at me again with heart-melting desperation and pathos in his eyes. I felt with impassioned dread, we faced a horrifying decision and act.

As we fought for our very existence, I still see and feel the utter violence and gut-wrenching fear of that suspended moment in history. I still see the rocks, the deep drop-offs of the wicked mountains. I am in that truck with my daddy and the emotions of that crushing moment right now as I see it all over again and again. Like hot blood drowning me, I thought, *At least I'm with my daddy.*

I decided not to jump but ride it out with my father. But I knew with that utter intensity, he had thoughts to make me jump. But destiny, God's destiny, determined we would ride this out together.

We'd just go to heaven with each other. What could be better?

But finally, suddenly, shockingly, and unexpectedly, we began to slow a little as the road straightened out. We were nearing the bottom! Ahead of us was almost flat ground. Pulling over to the side of the road, we fell into each other's arms and mixed our tears.

Dad said, "Thank you, Lord," as he prayed an inspired, impassioned prayer of praise.

He told me he had thought to push me out the door to save my life, but he just couldn't do it.

We had ridden this storm out together. We were safe. We were grateful to God. We were one.

Daddy told the family. No one could imagine it. He and I only spoke of it once or twice the rest of his life. I'm telling it now, for the rest of my life…and yours.

We let the truck cool, petted Trixie who had ridden down the pass as if it were a joyride, and headed on to Needles. Alive. Together.

God takes care of a little trailer boy…and his daddy…and his dog. Still thankful for a mighty destiny. I've got no excuses.

(You can get a firsthand view of Sitgreaves Pass on the internet.)

> For He hath said, "I will never leave thee, nor forsake thee," so that we may boldly say, "the Lord is my Helper, and I will not fear…," the Lord Jesus Christ.
>
> —Hebrews 13:5–6

By the way, we made our journey on to Bakersfield after a picnic lunch in Needles, where we joined up with the family. We made it to Uncle Travis's in Bakersfield at 10:30 p.m., had a warm reunion, and piled up in bed.

Tomorrow would be another day in our travels with life unfolding into another adventure.

Historical Footnote: Passing through Needles in 2000 AD, Sandy and I with Mother, we looked at the spot where we ate lunch on that fateful day and the same concrete table sits stoically in place unfettered by the passage of time and 'time travelers entering their world once again'

No Excuses, just grateful.

Story 14

Harry and Me
"Escapades"

Tough times never last, but tough people do.

—Robert Schuller

A friend is one that you have almost a mystical relationship to that transcends logic. And we love to live in that mystic with one that shares in that transcendence (J. L. S. 2018).

I have had many acquaintances and especially because I moved to so many places both as a boy and a man. It amazes me how in a group of people you take a liking to certain people, and they you. One emotional transference to that special person, and they to you. How does that happen? There lies the transcendence, the mystic, the wonder of having a true friend.

My friend is one…who takes me for what I am.

—Henry David Thoreau 1817-1862,
Journal, 23, October 1852.

Moving to Gary, Indiana, in 1959, late December, I was prepared to defend myself because of what I heard on TV about drugs, gangs, and killings in Chicago. In my fifteen-year-old mind, Gary and Chicago were the same.

Being a person to never be ignored, as well as one to set myself forth, I presented myself in one class in an unusual way, if not, a stupid way.

"I'll never forget the day I met J. Larry Simpson. It was 1960 (my sophomore year) in my third-hour English class at Calumet High School. It was early January in Mrs. Apples class. We were halfway through the class when someone knocked on the classroom door. Mrs. Apple advised the person to enter and in walked "cool-hand Larry." He stated to Mrs. Apple that he was new at the school and would be attending this hour class in the future, starting the next day. Mrs. Apple warmly greeted him and stated she was looking forward to his return tomorrow. It was at that point, Larry thanked the teacher and exited the room, kicking his legs backward and yelling, "Whoop! Whoop! Whoop!" all the way out the door as if he was one (Curly) of the three stooges. The classroom broke out in laughter."

The author of this account is Harry Warrens. An outstanding individual himself, he lived in a mobile home like me. We met the next day.

"Hey, man, glad to have you at Calumet. My name is Harry Warrens."

Although Harry was more reserved than me that worked into a balanced friendship. We liked each other from the beginning, which made it easy to be friends immediately.

"Good to meet you, Harry," I said as he proceeded to introduce me to a group of guys with whom I also became friends.

"That was the beginning of a great relationship and a sports legacy for both of us," Harry said the other day on a visit to see each other and enjoy some German food in Southern Indiana.

Harry was a good student, much better than me, played baseball and football, and was well liked by the entire sophomore class.

By the end of our high school career as seniors, Harry was voted "Mr. Football" by the coaches and student body. Without question, he was the best player on both the baseball and football teams. Playing first base as a left hander, he had the best batting average and was a leader on and off the field. Mr. Football played offensive and defensive "end" and led the team in catches and tackles. He was tough, down, and ready!

This guy became my best friend. We laughed, talked about all things, double dated, and drag raced together. My friend.

"Hey, man," Harry said in an inquisitive tone, "you wanna go to the junior prom together?"

"Sure," I replied with a definite tone. "Sure, what are you thinking?"

Replying with enthusiasm, he said, "Well, let's go in my car and have tuxedoes alike."

I had never worn a tux before, but it sounded big-time.

"Hey, buddy, for sure, I'd rather go in your car since I don't have one! And Dad might 'kick up' if I wanted to use the family car. Besides, man, you've got the best-lookin' car in town."

"Thanks," Harry said.

A red-and-white '55 Chevy in top shape was Harry's ride.

He was the envy of every kid in school! It was beautiful, and I loved to ride in it.

Prom night came. We joined up at his home and dressed in our black pants, white ruffled shirt, and our light-blue jacket.

"Let me fix your tie," I said as Harry had his tie way too big on the left side at a northwestern angle. Finished out like a show horse, we both said, "Dude, you look great!" And I'm just sure we did. We picked up my date, Carole Lee, and his blond date, Pat. Both were shockingly beautiful. I got cold chills!

Pat is Harry's wife! They got separated, but now for thirty years, they have been back together, in love.

After an hour or so of sweet doo-wop music and some rock and roll with the floor full of juniors and seniors boogyin' down and huggin' up tight.

The MC said, "Everybody have a seat."

After the normal recognitions and thanks, the rather rotund MC in a loud, deep voice declared, "And now it's time for what we've been waiting for. Who's king and queen?"

Loudly clapping and some whistles hurt our ears, but we didn't care.

"In the runner up, king and queen court is Marcy and Ray! Come up and get your award."

Marcy stumbled and fell, but Howie sitting next to them caught her just in time, one foot from the slick dance floor. Red-faced, they both held their plaques as high as they could.

Ray, a really shy guy, couldn't help himself grinning from ear to ear, sweat rolling off his chin, let out a loud, "YES!" hugged up Marcy, and danced back to their seats.

"King and queen," his voice fell silent, and so did the whole room, "the 1961 Calumet prom king and queen"—silence again—"chosen by their classmates is"—silence again—"Larry and Carole!" The happy gang of school-mates roared and clapped.

We couldn't believe it, well, almost, but slowly walked to the MC, took our awards, said thanks to the gang of Calumet. We shook hands and hugged necks on the way to the middle of the dance floor and slow danced to "Oh What a Night" with Carole's sweet tears on my cheeks. After about a minute, the MC loudly called everyone to dance. "Dance with your king and queen." What a night with friends, love, and music.

We were blown away, and as a good friend, Harry said, entering into my victory, "You deserved it. I'm happy for you, and I knew you would win!" That's the way we were.

"Larry and I remained best friends the next two years and sup-ported each other." Harry wrote concerning our friendship, and I will add "for life"!

> Escapade: "a wild, often innocent adventure involving a throwing over of restraints."

> —*Webster Dictionary*

Friendships have a way of exciting each other to adventure, especially as fifteen- to seventeen-year-olds.

Escapade 1: Pick Up Girls

Yes, we did pick 'em up but only twice.

"Get in the red and white," Harry said, "and let's see if we can find some girls!"

My, my, did we find some girls, and I ask for your forgiveness as you make this journey with us.

"Let's go to Griffith," which was our closest town with the city limits, meeting each other, Harry suggested, and I said, "Let's roll."

Driving slowly in the very dark night on this Friday in January, with forty-degree weather, we hoped to find some lonesome girls! Cruising up and down the little town square and then moving out street by street, we turned a corner. I looked down the street and pointing, "There they are!"

"Yeah," Harry said with two girls about our age standing under the streetlight.

The deep darkness of the winter night camouflaged the lights casting shadows on their faces. Their winter coats camouflaged them to our glaring, staring, half-blinded eyes.

"I can't tell much about what we're looking at," Harry said, and I joined in, "Yeah, but we got nothin' better right now."

With my partner in crime, adding, "Let's give it a try. They look lonesome."

And we chuckled a little *wickedly*!

Slowly driving and pulling up to the half-lit scene, rolling my widow down, "You wanna ride?" I asked.

"Sure," and they headed gleefully into the red and white.

I got out, slung open the door, and the best-lookin' one slid into the front seat, and the less attractive one tumbled into my seat in the back.

Being immediately jealous, I said with a disgusted, laughing tone, "Looks like you got the best deal." Harry just looked over his shoulder and winked.

"Okay, well, let's do the best with what we've got," I said, not caring if I hurt someone's feelings at that disappointing moment, much to my shame as I write this.

Harry drove. We tried chitchat. We got them close. They were childish and not near as experienced in the world as us! With him driving slowly, he couldn't make time as good as me. But my good time was quickly turning sour. I was both disappointed and becoming ashamed. Besides, the girls weren't as intellectual or pretty enough for such worldlangs as we and our arrogance!

I'm sure my girl was nice. She wasn't pretty. Besides, she was sadly serious and inched almost into my lap! I had enough.

"Harry, stop! I got to get this one out of here!"

He heard my anxious plea and, as a good friend ought to do, went around the block, and we dropped them off at the same corner where this failing escapade with dim light began. I felt sorry for myself and Harry but sorrier for the girls and the way we dealt with them.

Good friends better watch out for each other. Yes, and we went home lonesome, sad, and fractured. Maybe next time! (I have been forgiven by the Lord!)

Escapade 2

After graduation in the hot summer of '62, Harry and I were sitting in my ragged but dependable green '50 Ford, and he said, "Let's go to the beach," (Lake Michigan Shore) "Saturday."

"Let's go!"

Of course, we went in Harry's car.

Lying on the beach, swimming, and girl watching was all we had to do. The day was sunny, hot, and the water was cold enough. The beach was loaded and filled with gorgeous members of the opposite sex. We swam, lay in the hot sunlight, talked to a few girls, and talked about our upcoming college experience and past adventures.

The afternoon was fading away, and Harry said, "You ready to go?"

I just nodded. We loaded into Harry's car after getting the sand off ourselves and tuned the radio on. We were silent, but Jimmy Reed was singing "Baby What You Want Me to Do" as his '55 Chevy was rumbling with those hot open mufflers.

As we turned the first corner to the right, two pretty, nice-looking girls were standing at the corner waiting for a bus. Dressed for the hot day, they had on shorts of the conservative kind with sleeveless tops and just low enough in the front to show their upper brown chests. Harry, leaning out over his red-and-white steering wheel decidedly exclaimed, "They'll do."

I hollered, "Pull over. Let's take these girls home—to their homes."

"Okay, man," Harry said as he pulled quickly to the curb. As traffic whirled around us, we leaned over and said, "You wanna ride?"

Both walked slowly to the car, bent over to look in, without a word, and sized us up with an okay nod. Seeing that we were handsome, clean-cut, all-American boys and in a great '55 Chevy, the shorter one said, "Sure," as the two of us got out to help them in. Both were pretty. A downtown bus loaded with sweaty kids, swerved to miss us as the driver shook his fist and honked three times.

"Where you girls going?"

"Home."

"Where's home?" with Harry carrying on the conversation while I just sat, looking innocent. "Where do you live?"

"Hammond!"

Hammond—being several miles away and both of us with a date with our girlfriends that night knew the drive would press us. So the next question is, Why were we picking up these girls? We weren't sure! It was just a boyish escapade!

The cute shorter little girl slid into the front seat, and the taller one entered the back seat through the door I had gallantly opened and stood by as a *gallant* gentleman.

We asked them what school they went to, what grade, did they have boyfriends, and of course, what their names were. Sherry sat in the front seat and Barbara next to me. Harry had won again! His "traveler" was very pretty and well-spoken with an outgoing personality.

My "back seat girl" was a bit bashful and timid but a sweet pleasant look on her brown sunbathed face.

Then they asked us for our information! I spoke up, being so very quick and said out what I thought would be of interest to them.

"I'm a sophomore at Western Michigan University and there with a track scholarship."

"Wow!" Sherry exclaimed.

Brenda just smiled.

"Harry, tell them about yourself," I said as I wanted the conversation to get away from my lies and onto him.

"I'm a sophomore too and play end on the Indiana University football team." Quick thinking! The girls were impressed. Both of them were coming seniors at Hammond High, and here they were with very cute and handsome intelligent college athletes!

We did have a nice chat with them, and then it turned serious! Harry was the culprit here. He put his arm up and around his little date and snuggled her over to him and was speaking very softly into her left ear. She seemed to like it. *What's he saying?* myself asked myself!

Not to be outdone, I tried to get my left arm up and over my quick date's shoulders without breaking her neck. Somehow they were too high up for me to accomplish that feat. I held her hand instead, told her how much I liked her, and wanted to see her again, and she was just the girl for me.

Sadly, she believed me. Sadly, I was wrong. But this is after all about truth and "escapades" of boys!

We exchanged phone numbers with promises to see each other again.

We got to Sherry's first then to Barbara's. I got out, and then she got out, and when she stood up, I was even with her neck! I had to look straight up to see her face. Six feet two or six feet three, I don't know, but she was way taller than me. I shrunk in ego and confidence. We left quickly. Her tallness shrunk me even more. The sad epitaph in this sordid story is that Barbara called our house, asking for me several times even after I went off to college in Memphis. Eventually, in October, I think it was, she actually found our home and presented herself as a good friend. Mom told her I was engaged. Barbara was a very wholesome, nice, young lady. I hope life has been good for her.

I have felt bad about this young lady, a very nice human being, that I used for my own interest. May the reader have pity on such a one as I for that Saturday escapade. Harry and I have not spoken of this even for all these years but seven or…ten times!

Escapade 3

While juniors, the loudspeaker at the beginning of an early fall day, the principal announced that all boys wanting to compete in intramural basketball must be at a meeting on the next Monday. Basketball! Speaking up, I said to Harry and Kenny at lunch, "Let's get us a team together and win the championship!" They heartily agreed. The team ended up consisting of three first team football players, two first team track runners, and three other outstanding athletes in football and baseball.

We had the meeting and began practice. Kenny had become friends with Willie, the school janitor, and he agreed to let us practice three or four nights a week in the high school gym, so we got ready.

"We did play intramural basketball on the same team for two years and even beat the school's junior varsity squad in a scrimmage game," Harry wrote recently saying, "These days are never forgotten." We were unbeaten and had a blast. Too fast, too quick, could jump too high, played together, getting the ball to each other, and played "pick and roll" constantly. All over the court, one guy would "pick" off the guy, guarding one of our players, and then "roll" to the basket and hopefully get open for a pass from whoever had the ball.

The camaraderie between one another has been a joy to remember and feel. Besides, we beat most of the teams handily.

Harry called and asked, "You know, pictures are going to be taken this next Saturday morning before our game, don't you?"

"Yeah, but I've got to work because a huge shipment of paint is coming in, and I've gotta be there!"

"Oh, man!"

"I'm sick, but my boss said I had to be there."

I was sick, but I liked working for the largest paint company in the world, and I needed the money. I have regretted that decision to this day.

I went to work, and my buddies got their pictures taken!

Escapade 4

While finishing our senior year, our a cappella instructor said, "Class will be short today." Harry and I went to the first classroom next to where we sang which was empty.

"Get that corner."

So we headed to the northeast corner of the room, arranged the chairs, and we sat down. Feeling our all-American red blood, we started singing. "Da, data, da, da, good night, sweetheart, well it's time to go, I hate to leave you, but I really must say, good night, sweetheart, good night...."

"Hey, we were pretty good," Harry said, and I felt it.

"Yeah, really good!" I said.

A friend in a cappella walked in and started humming the doo-wop tune, and we went on with it. Cold chills ran down my spine. Harry went "whuu" in a loud, high pitch voice.

Janet, with her dark hair and pretty face, walked in, "I heard some tunes."

And we sang on with her sweet alto voice, blending in with ours. Being a pianist and having perfect pitch, we said in harmony, "Come on join with us!"

We were just getting it on with "Oh What a Night" when Andrew walked in. He enthusiastically took the lead with his soulish voice, every bit as good as the lead singer of the Platters! Excitement filled the air, and our souls rocked on. Magic was happening.

By this time, I had had enough.

"Okay, you guys we're going to form a group and determine who will be in it."

So we talked about who we wanted in this new and surely to be famous doo-wop group. Suggestions were made, but Harry and I made the final decision.

"What's our name?" someone asked, and we looked at each other, speechless.

"What about the Night Tones...or the Soul Singers, or what about the Pure Tones or the Night Kings?" and on it went for a few more minutes.

Harry stopped us and said, "I've got it. The Crescendos!"

Silence gripped this little musical ensemble as if a mystical knight had ridden into our midst and struck us with a sword.

Andy said, "Sounds good," while I said, "That's it!"

And everybody else agreed. If Harry liked it, I did to.

The Crescendos were created. A great pianist joined us with a drummer, and we had our sound.

A talent contest was coming up at school, so we registered for our first performance. We practiced every night after track and baseball, learned three or four songs, and got ready.

The gymnasium was full. Each act performed from dancing, singing, and acting a scene from a movie.

"The Crescendos," Mr. Ballard echoed over the sound system, "singing 'In the Still of the Night.'"

We stormed the stage. We sang the song as good as it could be sang, at least we thought. Janet's voice was like smooth butter, Harry's bass was pure, Andrew's lead voice like honey, as good as it gets, and my baritone rhythm sound blended with it all. The student body roared.

They roared until the principal walked out and waved his hands downward and said, "I know how you feel, but now we'll have our last act, the Dance Queens!"

They danced good and looked pretty—pretty girls always do.

After a few minutes with the gym buzzing, Mr. Skruggs, the music teacher, came out and announced the winners. Fourth place, then third place, "And now for second place, the Crescendos, and the winner is the Dance Queens!"

The kids didn't agree and showed it with a flood of boos and yelled, "The Crescendos! The Crescendos!" until the principal walked out and quietened the student body, made a few comments, and dismissed us.

Our senior banquet was just a few days away. To be held at the majestic Marquette Park Pavilion at Lake Michigan, the seniors were talking about it as kids will do. Stopping me and Harry in the hall between classes, the senior sponsor, Mrs. Matthews, asked if we'd like to perform at the banquet.

"Sure," we declared.

"Well, we'd like to hear your version of 'In the Still of the Night'."

Harry jumped on it, his left eye twitching since he was left handed, saying, "We'll be ready! Yes, ma'am, we'll be ready," as he looked over at me and said, "We'll be ready!"

"You'll be the evening's entertainment," and we walked away in shock but confirmed, "We'll be ready."

We gathered the rest of the Crescendos together, told them the good news, and made our plans.

"We'll knock 'em dead," Andrew said with his super smooth voice and rhythm and blues personality.

"Ain't he cool?" Janet whispered and then hugged Andrew and the rest of us.

Oh yeah, and I forgot a historical footnote to the contest.

One of the girls in the Dance Queens was Harry's girlfriend, Pat. They've been married now for thirty years, in love, but still in disagreement over who won the talent show! The debate continued, and we love to redo the "heated" discussion when together—of course, the Crescendos won! But the issue is still not settled fifty-eight years later!

"We beat you guys all to pieces," Pat loves to taunt us with to this day.

Escapade 5: The Senior Banquet

What a cool night. Harry and I with our girls drove in my dad's 1956 Buick. When I asked him if I could drive to this great affair in our family car, he did as he always did, "What time do you need it?"

"I'll have to leave at about five thirty."

"Anybody goin' with you?"

"Sure, Harry and the girls."

"Okay, how far is it?"

"Remember the state park over from Gary on the big lake?" (We called Lake Michigan the Big Lake.)

"What time will you be home?"

"Probably about eleven thirty."

"Eleven thirty…?"

"Well, Dad we won't leave until about nine thirty, and we've got to take the girls home, I'll drop Harry off at his home, and after, all we'll probably want to go to Wilson's to have a coke."

"Have you got money and does the Buick need gas?"

"I got paid down at PPG," (Pittsburg Plate Glass) "last Saturday, so I've got about $15."

"We won't spend anywhere near that much. And oh yeah, there's about a half tank of gas."

"Okay, son, since it's your senior party."

"And oh yeah Dad, our band is playing."

"What's the name of the band? I forgot."

"The Crescendos!"

"What kind of music do y'all play?" he asked as he looked over at Mother, raised his eyebrows, and sighed heartily. He knew.

"Doo-wop, this tune." And I began to sing the first two lines.

"Oh, oh, I know, but I don't understand why the boys or men want to sing like a woman…so high pitched!"

"Oh, Dad, it's just what we do," which was a very weak, youthful response.

After Dad's investigation, he patted me on the back and then a soft hug with one arm and slowly went up the stairs with Mom on his heels.

I did the same with my children, and I know why. We have to be in charge and call them to responsibility!

"It's all right, Daddy." How I miss him and Mother.

Saturday night came. We dressed in the best we had, picked up our girls, and went to Jim's house to harmonize one more time. We were ready, and each one spoke up and gave encouragement to the rest. Our Crescendo partners were almost all open and forthright.

Andy spoke up, "See y'all there and let it roll."

We all agreed. Great expectations, excited, filled with both confidence and adrenaline, and a lifetime memory.

The girls were chatty and asked, "How do you feel?"

"Good, ready…," Harry said.

We didn't say much on the way to Lake Michigan, just a soft chatter from our sweet girls who couldn't quite understand our silence.

Finally, I said, "Man, this is it. Our senior banquet. How do you feel?"

Carole Lee said, "Happy."

Pat responded, "A little sad."

Harry spoke up clear and resilient, "A little tight."

"How do you feel?" Pat asked.

And I replied, "Emotional, happy, a little sad, and ready to sing!"

We arrived, greeted our classmates, parents and teachers, ate our meal, and listened to remarks about outstanding students. Then Mr. Harold got up and said, "For our final senior celebration, our homemade rock and roll band, the Crescendos, will perform." He announced each band member and spoke of the four senior members.

The senior class yelled, whistled, and clapped, some standing up.

On the first note of the Satins's "In the Still of the Night" from 1956, everybody stood up and made rock and roll noise for the entire song.

"Encore! Encore! Encore!" a few classmates called out.

We looked at the principal, and he shook his head no.

Our picture of that night performing remains at the end of the school yearbook summer addition. Harry is singing bass, my buddy, standing in the middle.

Escapade 6

At the end of this dramatic night, the Crescendos met by the stage to say goodbye. Our hearts were breaking. I was going to Memphis. Harry was going to Terre Haute. And the other seniors were moving on into work, college, and loafing! The sweet undergraduates would still be at Calumet with this lifelong memory.

"Let's meet and still sing together for the summer," Janet said, and we all agreed.

Twice a week for two or three weeks as summer rolled upon us, we relished our short time together and continued the far-off hopes of fame.

Sure enough, on Thursday night, we were making music, and the phone rang.

"May I speak to a member of the Crescendos?" a clear female voice asked.

"Larry, you take this call. It's somebody calling us!"

"What? Okay. Hello?"

"I'm calling from WWCA radio station, and we would like to hear you sing."

Obviously, someone had called them, and now they're calling us! We never knew the source of this call.

"This is Larry Simpson. WHAT!"

"Yes, sir. We have been called and told we needed to hear you sing. So could you make a time in a few days to come to the radio station and audition for us?"

"Sure, let me talk to the band, and I'll call you right back."

We hung up, and I was delirious. Once I could get the words out of my mouth with stuttering and stammering, I told our guys the deal. "Sure, yes, let's go," different ones said, so we worked out a time, and I called them right back."

We set the date, and I asked, "Do you have a piano?"

"Sure do!"

The evening was set.

All of us changed our plans and met each evening for three nights and then drove in two cars to the radio station on a Friday night. Going in with cold, wet hands, we met Rus "Rufuss" Johnson, the renowned disc jockey and his team.

He chatted with us a few minutes to chill our "hot chills," and we all relaxed, and each one entered into the comments.

"A mister, whose name I cannot remember called me, raved about you, so I was determined to have you here, record you, and see if we can sell the Crescendos!" With a bit of a serious look and nod, with his oily black hair flopping, he asked, "Whatcha think?"

We all looked wide-eyed at one another and at him and almost simultaneously said, "Sure!"

Having decided to sing "In the Still of the Night," we warmed up, stood before three microphones, Janet warmed up the piano, and the music master said, "When the bottom light turns green, let 'er rip." And so we did.

We performed—yes, performed as if veterans—since all of us were competitors at heart. After the first rendition, the music master, ole "No Fuss" said, "That's good for a first effort, but let's do this…," and he gave us some suggestions about tonal quality, loudness of parts, balance of sound, and said, "Let's do it again."

We weren't sure if he liked us or not, but we sang on. Our hearts were overflowing, our intellect was hoping, our bodies stimulated, and our voices were like warm butter and silk.

The evening went on with rehearsal after rehearsal, and eventually, the exuberant high-spirited disc jockey said, "I really like your sound with just a piano and that you create such a sweet-blended harmony. Yeah, I like your sound!" All seven of us stood in wonder, slapping our hands with some high-fives. "Especially Andy's lead voice and the young lady's female voice sort of holding it all together with purity and a feeling, soft sound," the famous radio music master said. We could only stare at him, filled with gratitude, and dismay.

"I want to send this recording to WLS in Chicago and see if we can get some response or backing. I'll be your representative. How 'bout it?"

Harry and I looked at each other then turned to the rest of our speechless members and tuned back in unison and said, "We're ready. Yes. Sure. Let's make a record!"

The enthused music master (i.e., No Fuss) said, "I'll be in touch if anything comes of it."

We left and went to the well-known old-timer restaurant in Gary at the corner of Highway 6, Ridge Road, and Main Street. We sat in silence for a moment at the wonderment of the event and beaming with hope. We wondered about the meaning of this, but how could we do this with Harry and I gone?

By July, we had met five or six times, filled with hopes and enjoyment but some fading enthusiasm. The time had come. We had not heard from the great disc jockey. Commitments in life were separating us.

I was leaving the first of August in my turquoise-and-white '56 Chevy sedan for college in Memphis. It was necessary for me to get there to adapt to the climate and train for cross-country at Memphis State.

Harry was leaving for college at Indiana State in September. Our last time together on a Thursday night was a heartbreaker. We tried to sing but didn't have it in us. I said, as it was my way to get people to talk, even to this day, "Andy, what do you have on your heart?"

He spoke softly but short, "I'll never forget...I'll never forget this."

Janet followed with tears rolling off her chin and wet mascara but couldn't say a word. Each one spoke about our little family, the amazing time of just three months, and hopes to get together again and that we might still hear from the radio station. We never did.

In Harry's strong way, he closed with a remarkable gathering together of our little but significant time together.

He said, "We won!" as everyone sat silent holding hands. Every head nodded.

I tried to speak and said, stammering, "I'll never forget you, and this, I love you all. Thanks."

Harry ended our last medley with "We'll always have this."

We hugged. We said sweet things. We drove away. "We'll have always have this...."

How do we understand or realize such a remarkable time of such remarkable histories?

Two notes: (1) one of the guys that we had considered for the Crescendos but turned down went on until this day to have his own band and perform all over Chicago, Northern, and Middle Indiana. He has several recordings. Yes, we missed a diamond; (2) Harry, Pat, Sandy, and I met just a few weeks ago and talked about that time. Harry asked, "Did I ever tell you that I was driving down Ridge Road one day with the music master on, and they played our song?"

"Yes, a long time ago."

I couldn't believe it! What an amazing reunion of time and memories, happiness, friends, success, and hopes all stacked up together. Such a condensed, lifelong, living experience to this day fifty-eight years down the road. A landmark in time: the Crescendos.

I've not seen even one of those fabulous people to this day.

I still ask where all those amazing singers are, friends, and meditate on the meaning of such personal historic experiences.

I desire happiness and send sweet thoughts for each one of the Crescendos. I'll never see them or sing with them again, except in my fading memory.

Escapade 7: On Ice

"Hey, buddy, this is John Wayne!"

"Not, really!" And Harry said, "I didn't know how you are doing, man?"

"Great, listen, I want to go to Chicago to the speed store to look at some things for my Pontiac, come on and go with me."

"Sure, when we goin'?"

"Let's work out a time and let her fly!"

So we worked out a time. He drove to my house and we got ready to leave in my black '63 Pontiac Le Mans. Harry, always ready to go, got there early, so we had a cup of hot chocolate with Mom and the other kids sitting around the table. Mom, always wanting to include and make others feel good, asked Harry about his family, how he's doing, and other such questions.

"Boys, is this a good time to go?"

"Sure, Mom, we'll drive safe and slow. I've got a full tank of gas, and we'll take an extra coat."

We left on this cold, thirty-degree day. With temperatures falling, some wind and a white mist flying around. We both took our letterman's jackets, a sweater, wore long sleeve shirts, ball caps, and threw in some gloves.

It seemed especially cold on this afternoon with wind blowing the white mist all around in a mad swirl and temps to drop to the teens. That country is cold, cold, cold in winter because of the winds coming off Lake Michigan.

The speed shop was world famous and about sixty miles from Highland. We had talked about going there before. Now here we are in a happy, laughing outburst of life. I wanted to check on headers, a dual racing exhaust system, and blocks to raise my front end, about three to four inches. That's the way we liked it back in those crazy racing days, high in the front, low in the tail end. My best friend was going along to help me, and besides, he wanted a couple of things for his new 1964 Impala Super Sport, 327 cubic-inch engine with 300 horsepower. Eventually, he turned this fabulous car into a true hot rod that would run 11.5 seconds in the quarter mile.

Harry, always a purest and thorough guy, had put in a high-lift cam, headers, a 4.11 rear-end with "slicks" on the back and exhaust pipes that could be opened up just behind the front tires and racing mufflers. And the second four-barreled carb didn't hurt!

Here we are on the way to Chicago with the radio on, talkin' away. We talked about his whippin' the horse and what we wanted to do to our autos. But the mist was turning more white. The temperature dropped. The wind blew a little more swift.

When we got out at the speed shop, we both said, "We can't stay long, so let's do our thang and go!"

The prices were high, the parts aplenty, the interest and love of speed whirling around but also was the weather. We looked, which is always fun, talked to one of the experts, learned somethings but didn't buy a single, solitary thing.

We couldn't keep our eyes off the front door, and the manager said, "Boys, you'd better get home."

Out the door we flew but not as fast as the wind or snow. The roads were already slick. Salt trucks were throwing salt as fast and far as possible.

My tires could hardly grip the road for the frozen snow and ice.

Feeling very happy to reach the Indiana state line, by East Chicago, through Hammond, we relaxed. Topping over a via dock covering old Highway 40, it happened!

The tires couldn't hold us going downward. We went into a whirl, a spin-off, a twirl. In circles, we flew to our left, and it looked like we would hit the highway rail or go off the bank, but the left front tire hit a rough spot in the road, which sent the Pontiac in the opposite direction, turning round and round. The car couldn't be slowed or directed. The speed of the revolving car was just right enough that we could see plainly the spinning world "around" us. I gripped the steering wheel with white knuckles and hands. I knew how to turn the steering wheel in the opposite direction to reverse the slide. It didn't work here, there, or then.

I saw Harry from my right eye. His eyes seemed ready to shoot out of his head. He was fixated on the spinning world around us. My thoughts? "God save us," as Harry braced himself, pushing against the dash but still slipping on the reddish, burgundy, and black seat.

We glanced at each other, bewildered and helpless. At first, it was a desperate glance. It became an "oh well, throw your hands up" look. We were communicating silently.

As quickly as we had gone into this downward swirl, we straightened out when we hit flat ground. The speed? We had gone from thirty to thirty-five miles per hour to sixty!

"You all right, man?"

"Yeah, you all right?" we asked each other. Then we were silent with each of our brains judging what we had just been in and how quick we were saved. We squeezed each other's shoulders tight, as if to say, "I'm glad you're okay."

I don't know how many 360s we made—six, eight, ten, I don't know but a bunch. We got home safe, ate some of Mom's world-class chicken soup, explained it to Dad, who had just made it home from work.

Harry said, "I'll call you."

And I replied, "Don't go on any more spins!"

The ole devil came back with, "I won't. I'll be driving!"

"Get outa here! See ya tomorrow!"

Many years passed before we picked the subject out of our mutual lives since I had moved away from The Region, and we were still in wonderment and thanks.

The temperature dropped to twelve degrees, with thirty-five miles per hour winds and six inches of ice and snow. But we were home safe that night.

Friends survive better when together.

—J. L. S.

Harry finally called and said, "I'm home."

Escapade 8: Drag Racing

Harry and I actually didn't like to compete against each other. I never worked to outdo him, or he me. He was happy with the way I was, and I him.

However, we did drag race a couple of times. Harry beat my '63 Pontiac, but the next time he slightly slid off the road and hit a mailbox. That was it. But we loved to drag race and still made it!

Escapade 9: Harry and the Horse

Calhoun Street in Gary, Indiana, runs south close to Calumet High School. The story I am going to show you happened on that street. A very unusual story.

"Hello, big man, this is Harry."

"You know something. I know your ole voice!" I replied.

"You won't believe what I'm going to tell you."

"Yeah," I replied. "I won't!"

Both laughing, but Harry was dead dog serious.

"You know our chemistry teacher long legged Henderson?"

"Sure."

"Listen, I was at Maria's a little while ago, had a polish sausage dog, and coke. Dave was there, and so was Kenny. Well, a little guy was bragging about the speed of his horse, Mr. Henderson's boy, Richard."

"You know I don't know him," I replied.

Harry said, "He's a junior, and the little dude had his horse there, showing her off and braggin' that nobody had ever beat him."

"You mean horse against horse?"

"No, nobody in a car had ever beaten him on his horse!"

"What?"

"Yeah, you heard me!"

"When you gonna race him?" I asked because I saw where this was going.

Richard had proudly boasted, "I'll whip any car here," and walked by Harry, leaned over, and said, "Even you," looking with a stern glare into my buddies flashing probing blue eyes.

"Man, what are you talkin' about?"

"I will beat anybody in an eighty-yard run," to which my good friend quickly replied, "Where and when!"

"All right!"

"We'll meet here, go just past the corner of the gym, a 'starter' will start us, with a 'judge' at the finish line."

Fifteen or twenty people gathered around.

Harry, not one to mince words, asked emphatically, "What time?

I love Harry's direct ways.

Harry picked me up and we got out, met Richard, still on his horse, and Harry said, "Get down. I don't like lookin' at you uphill."

The poor braggard got off as Harry and I towered over him.

"You'll be in the street with the centerline under the center of your car. I'll be on the curb, so my horse is not on pavement. And I see you have 'open exhaust pipes,' and I'll ask you not to open them for fear of spooking my mare."

"Okay," Harry said.

We rolled out to the starting line to check it out with a guy we didn't know, wearing a white T-shirt and cap with "Calumet" on it, standing by and observing.

Harry pumped the engine up in short bursts. His four-wheel ride was ready. What the inexperienced horse racer didn't know is what the '64 was packin'. The white T-shirt Calumet guy was checking Harry's rod out.

Later, we found out this was the trainer of the big racing horse, who had won several world championships in the horse world.

Three hundred horsepower from his .327 stock engine with a Hurst 4-speed transmission was fast. The "shifter" stood up almost a foot was curved and topped with a white ball that had "Hurst" in black letters on it.

Harry had put solid lifters in it with a fuel injection carburetor and headers to release engine backup, also with ten-inch Mickey Thompson street slicks to control low-end power and torque from a .411 rear-end. My buddies ride was running about .426 horsepower and furious out of the blocks with that low gear rear-end.

Richard, all 110 pounds of him, said, "Eight o'clock tomorrow night."

"I want you to be with me, so I'll pick you up at 7:00 p.m. Can you go?"

"I wouldn't miss this for nothin'!"

"Great, I'm goin' to take his $20, and then we'll go somewhere," my good pal said.

We talked a little more with Harry telling me how "aggravating this little kid is, showing disrespect for we older Calumet guys and bragging right in our faces that he'd never been beaten."

"You'll beat him, and then we'll buy him a coke and a towel to cry on," I said, as Harry retorted, "I'm gonna run the best I've ever run. See you at seven o'clock."

Seven o'clock arrived on Friday as Harry pulled up in his blue, almost-new '64 Impala Super Sport.

When we got to Maria's Burger Joint, the horse kid was there, prancing around and talking big.

His mare was beautiful. At 16.2 hands high the sorrel, with flaxen mane, and tail was beautiful and very imposing. Her four white feet made her look like a rocket ship, just taking flight. People gathered around Richard's mare, rubbing and admiring her. We knew she could fly.

Mind you, this sorrel mare had beat all comers, and he was still bragging, but he had also heard of Harry's hot Chevy. He looked a little tight and tense.

We rolled into the drive-in very slow. Kids and adults looked at us then back at Richard, sitting tall on "Rocket." Harry leaned out the window, glaring at Richard and said, "Let's get it on." The kid turned pale.

After going over the rules, we rolled up to the starting line, revving the Super Sport .327, got set, as I whispered, "You're gonna have a world-class run," and patted his right shoulder while he broke the racing stare and said, "We'll push this blue baby to a win.

I got silent.

With his hand gripping the shift knob, his fingers white, the blood vessels popping, full and large, a slight gritting of his teeth and a tight fixed jaw, my ole buddy racer was ready.

The starter had both arms straight up, looking to one, and then the other with the blaze faced mare, prancing, her front end popping up with her feet, clearing the ground.

Richard was trying to hold her in "ready" while the heavyset starter with the flag as high as he could stretch, shook it, then violently dropped both arms suddenly and swiftly.

The Standard Bred launched into the air, the flaxen mane and tail flying backward, she was magnificent, beautiful, and in full speed in four or five steps! With Rich looking like a jockey, the mare jumped to one and half body lengths in front of the Impala. The "slickers" were squalling. The smoke flying.

"Come on, man," I said in a low, deep, hoarse voice as Harry began to close the lead.

Hitting second gear with a perfect power shift, the blue Chevy literally jumped into the front in about three seconds. The engine was screaming, the exhaust blowing burning air. The tires still squalling, Harry hit third, popping the tires one last squall as the mare was fading in the rearview mirrors.

In eight or nine seconds, at a speed of seventy-five miles per hour, the street racer, maybe the best, crossed the finish line. With a perfect performance, Harry had put a young sprout in his place, humbling him.

Slowly driving back to Maria's, with Rich walking his incredible mare slowly back to join us, said, "I didn't think there was any way you could beat me! But you did."

He handed a crisp $20 bill to Harry. "Your horse and you are amazing," my friend said in good sportsmanship.

I shook his hand and agreed, "What a horse, and, man, can you ride."

The young man continued to race his horse and very seldom, two or three times, was beaten. More importantly, Rich's attitude became more humbled and quit bragging.

He told Harry on another day, "I'm sorry for my arrogance."

"Let's get a milkshake. I'm buyin'," Harry said to which I quickly agreed. Dave and Kenny got in the back seat, and we revisited all the highlights of that incredible race.

Almost everyone there and others who came later came to our windows and we "chewed the fat."

"That's the best driving I've ever seen," I told Harry and continued, "Someday I'm going to tell the world."

"Thanks, man… I love you, brother."

"Yeah, I love you too," Harry said. Best friends.

A good time. No excuses just live life…like it's a drag strip.

Escapade 10: A Funeral, Two Girls, and a Whiteout

It's the functions of parents to see that their children habitually experience the true consequences of their conduct.

—Herbert Spencer, *Education: Intellectual, Moral and Physical,* 1860

My experience with my parents is that they were mostly right, and I was wrong when I didn't obey them. This lies at the heart of the adventure that follows.

"Hey, man, did you hear about Johnny's sister?" Kenny asked.

We were standing by Mr. Strickland's office door as he lectured Malcom about wearing his shirt open down the front too low. Malcom had an unusual amount of chest hair for a sixteen-year-old. He thought it made him a man, and he showed it off. Nobody liked it.

"No," I said.

And Harry replied, "What?"

"What happened?"

Kenny told us the sad story of her death. Immediately, we went to find Johnny. We were his friends, and the news hit us hard for him. He was standing alone in an empty classroom, looking out the front window down Ridge Road. Several other of our friends stood outside the door mostly quiet or talking softly so that you couldn't hear them even five feet away. I liked that respect, consideration, and behavior.

Willard, more of a loudmouth, strolled up "cocky-like," and blurted out some nonsense like kids do, and we shushed him with our forefinger over our lips. He stopped.

I say it that way because of our standing in the "ranking of power" among schoolmates. Being seniors and athletes, we stood at the top...or so we thought.

The girls were in tears. All of us were moved, looking at that sad, lonesome, picture of our buddy, looking out the window with a lost, confused, sad expression with tears.

Suggesting, I said, "Harry, let's me, you, and Kenny go in."

We quietly walked past the teacher's desk to the side of our classmate. We put out hands on his big shoulder, didn't say a word, and he just looked at us with a wet face.

We stood there until the bell rang.

"We're with you," Harry said, and Kenny, and I said, "Yeah, man."

The next day, Kenny, who seemed somehow to always know the inner workings of things, said, "If we get permission, we can be out of classes on the day of the funeral to go to the funeral as a show of support for Johnny."

"Let's go," I said, as Harry responded, "What's stopping us?"

I was determined to take my green '50 Ford sedan with turquoise accents on the inside. We met at the set time about 10:00 a.m. at the Calumet parking lot. Harry, Kenny, and George piled in with me. Now the old car, this was 1962, twelve years old, was a rough, slow ride. Something was wrong with the front-end steering "sector," so at forty-eight miles per hour, the car shook like a train off the tracks.

Besides that, the car had rusted out very badly because of the heavy amount of salt put on the roads through the front passenger floorboard!

David, my younger brother, went with me to the store for Mom about two weeks before the funeral trip, and as he got in on the passenger side, his left foot went plumb through the floor! The rotten metal was ragged with a bunch of rusty metal sticking downward. David couldn't get his foot out because the ragged, jagged brown thin metal clung to his shoes. In David's cool, confident way, he just looked over at me as if to say, "Okay, what now?"

"I'll be right there."

Getting the lug wrench from the old truck, I pushed the metal downward to release the caught lonesome foot of the calm twelve-year-old. The last piece was the hardest, caught in David's jeans, but I got it free, and we felt better.

From that time on, I put a large old quilt folded up into four layers over the hole. Of course, the quilt had some light turquoise sticking around the edges with a solid green center with white circling here and there. I thought it dressed the interior up a little bit.

"Yeah, yeah, it was humbling, but it is mine."

Away we went, Harry, Kenny, George, and the driver.

I was proud of my old car because the summer before, working at Pittsburgh Plate Glass, I had saved up enough money to try to buy a car. Dad went with me to a small auto sales place, and I paid cash, ninety-five dollars for it, and drove away a happy first-time car buyer. It was rough, but I was proud.

Very carefully, I watched the speedometer so as to go no faster than forty-seven miles per hour. Naturally, every once in a while, I'd slip over the forty-eight-mile-per-hour mark, and we'd all shake like Jell-O since the car was shaking. Cars passed me on a regular basis. After all, the speed limit was sixty miles per hour. I won't say what the guys said, but we made it to Knox and the funeral home, just a little shaky. In fact, I sang Elvis's song "All Shook Up" several times on the way. The boys joined in.

We met Johnny's family as they, with a conquering spirit, greeted guests at the door. They said to all who came in that they were "sad but rejoicing that their girl had gone on to heaven." I liked that.

Their family and friends seemed to appreciate us for coming so far. The welcoming line of friends and loved ones was halfway to the front of the burgundy and white, with brown pews, auditorium. The pulpit stood in front, where many a message had been preached to help broken hearts.

Several feet from the end of the welcoming line of people were quite a number of girls and boys who were friends of Louiza Mae's. We nodded at them, hoping they'd pay attention to our red-and-white leather-armed letterman jackets with "Calumet" in big letters. My, my, such pride at a funeral!

When we sat down, Harry leaned over to me and said, "Did you see those two girls at the front of those kids?"

"Do you think I can't see? Sure! Let's meet 'em after the service."

He shook his head up and down slowly in agreement like "oh yeah!" Besides, we just knew they had paid a little extra attention to us.

After everyone had gone through the long "viewing line," I questioned, "Where are those girls?"

Harry shrugged his shoulders in an "I don't know" gesture as he twisted his head around as if it sat on a merry-go-round. We went out the front door, and there they were. Both had blue eyes, one with gorgeous blond hair, the other with auburn shining hair as if on a full moonlit night. They were waiting for us, I'm sure, since they had their heads raised as high as they could at the top of their necks looking our way, holding each other's hands.

We looked assuredly at each other and headed for the very cute, confident girls. They didn't leave. They stayed put.

With a little bit of arrogance, although I'd rather call it natural self-confidence, we walked over to them, thinking that since we came from the metropolis of the big city, we'd have an edge on them. No! They had the edge. They were on home turf. They knew they looked good. They were cheerleaders. They were confident. But they liked us, some anyway.

We introduced ourselves, got their names, Sherry and Lou, and I simply said after a glance at my partner, "We wanted to meet you."

They looked at us with a look of "really?" with stretched, wide eyes, all four of them, charming blue!

Being humbled a little, we asked them about Louiza Mae, their school, their activities at school, and then they turned the questions back on us. As we exaggerated on our life's goings-on, they softened to us as we had already done to them—softened, I mean. These country girls knew where they stood! We knew it…about them too.

The conversation went on with humor, our common ideas, and activities. We liked them. They liked us. Harry looked over at me, and we both, knowing each other so well, nodded at each other, meaning, "Let's go on with this."

Being motivated with my partner's confidence, I said, "Well, ladies, we'd like to come back to see you and get to know you better."

Sherry, in her spirited way, after looking a Lou, said, "When?"

Wow! We could hardly speak from this exciting prospect of coming back to Knox. We fumbled around from nervousness, excitement, and the meaning of this commitment. We made a date for the next Saturday to meet them on Main Street at a really neat grill with a jukebox, hamburgers, and a pool table. The kids in that little county town filled it up on Saturdays and after ball games. We set 5:00 p.m. as the time to meet, shook their hands in awkwardness, and said, "We'll see you Saturday."

We walked away in unbelief but all four in broad smiles.

Traveling back in the car, Kenny said, "Looks like you boys hit a gold mine!"

In defense of the girls, I said, "They're really nice, down-home, smart, *pretty!*"

"Well, good luck," George spoke sarcastically.

But I made a mistake. I asked Mom and Dad if it was all right for me to go to Knox.

"No," Dad said. But I was going to go! Whatever it meant—I was going! Dad used to say, "Son, don't set a trap for yourself."

Well, here goes.

The weekend came with Harry and I leaving on Saturday at 3:30 p.m. We sure didn't want to be late. We laughed, talked, and played the radio. Talking about and visualizing Sherry and Lou, we both liked those girls.

We arrived at 4:50 p.m., went into the hip grill, and there they sat, on their home turf, very secure. We weren't. We were more nervous than they. But that didn't last long. In a few minutes, all four of us were engaged in common conversation. We talked about our families, school, sports, our futures, and any other thing we could think of. All four of us were articulate, and the girls were smart. They had common sense. Sherry came from a farming family while Lou was a pastor's daughter. We were lovin' it.

We four liked each other. We two did also.

But there's always a but! In our excitement, we had forgotten to take our jackets off, and from the beginning of our visit with Sherry and Lou, some of the guys had come by the table and spoke kindly to their friends and classmates. But with an eye of jealousy and suspicion, they looked at us and nodded in aggravated recognition.

We ordered hamburgers and fries, drank a coke, and settled into this romantic venture.

But there's always a "but" and a "butt." Over to our little foursome comes strolling two guys with the biggest and boldest in front. They and others had looked at us with disdain and dislike. We paid no attention to it until these two stood over us with chests out.

"I see you're a letterman," the big one said to Harry. "What sport?"

"Football."

"Oh yeah, what ya doin' here with 'our' girls?" Before we could speak, he said, "Let's take it outside!"

Harry was quiet and cool as I said, "Just leave it alone. We want to visit."

"No, get up, and let's take it outside."

Harry spoke up, "No, let's settle this some other way. We just like your girls. We got nothin' against you."

"Okay, okay, I'll beat *you*"—pointing to Harry—"in arm wrestling!"

Harry, in silence, got up, pulled his jacket off, rolled up his left sleeve, and said, "There's an empty table."

It was the only one with four or five coke bottles standing upright like soldiers with a fight comin'.

The big mouth yelled out, "Come and watch me break this city boy's arm."

Seeing Harry had rolled up his left sleeve, the arrogant bully said, "No, I'm right-handed, but I'll beat you your way."

They sat down to battle as the larger group of kids huddled up tight to watch around me and the two sweethearts.

"Beat him, Harry," I said as I glared at the smart aleck, ready to "get it on" myself!

Getting their elbows in position, each jockeying for their best angle, an older guy holding their shaking hands in place said, "Go! Go!"

Their arms shook in deep pressure for a few seconds, then Harry's arm began to give. At that time, Sherry shouted, "Beat him, Harry!" and a new fire got in his bones.

Later, he said, "I was moved by Sherry!"

Harry grunted and, steadily with quivering hands, pushed the big mouth's knuckles down then back up then down. Grunting a violent grunt, Harry powered the big boy's wide wet hand down with a grinding sound of bone and flesh on the table. Both gladiators slumped in their chairs. Sherry jumped and clapped then hugged Lou.

As Harry stood up, she threw her arms around him for about five seconds, and he said, gasping for breath, "It was worth it just for that."

My hand had slipped over to Lou's soft left hand, almost uncon-sciously squeezing it too tight.

We danced, played pool, ate some chips, talked, and opened up our new foursome world. Lou suited me to-a-tee. Oh yeah...the guys left us alone.

After making a time to see the two country girls in two weeks, we hugged them with a little kiss as we left looking at them in the mirrors. Time and space faded away. All seemed so natural and real.

We sat in silence for a few miles then it flooded out of our souls.

"What a time," I said, and the emotional feelings of this night bolting out of our seventeen-year-old hearts.

How could this be? So far apart. Magic had happened. Love so quick. Physical attraction and mental agreement. It was all so sweet...and perfect. All so quick, too quick.

I thought of Lou constantly as Harry did Sherry. We didn't talk about it much because love hurts so bad and feels so good. We made our plans to return to Knox.

However, whatever, parents always find out! How? I don't know. Mom had found me out before! She found me out now.

Harry's mother overheard Harry taking about the little trip to Kenny. She called Mom, and they both agreed with our fathers that we shouldn't ever go back.

"Don't ever go back down there, and there's no talking about it," Dad and Mom said. Harry's parents said the same.

But we were going! We would cover it up some way, and it will be all right. Harry and I agreed. We were going no matter what!

The Saturday came. We met and left in Harry's '55 Chevy. We felt so brave, adult, and defiant. We were going to see these fabulous girls. However, there was another storm a-brewing. A snowstorm. A bad snowstorm, yes, a bad one, but we were determined—no matter what. We left the Calumet region to drive the fifty or so miles, even with the temperature at thirty-three degrees and light snow flurries. The drive was a ball with us, not ceasing to talk and excitement to see these fabulous girls with rock and roll playing from WLAC radio station.

The movie house was in the dead center of the main street through town. As we entered the theater, we didn't see the girls, but here they came out of the restrooms and greeted us with a happy excitement and so sweet. Perfect! We made it. They were here with us. We talked like teenagers do until we heard the announcer proclaim, "FIVE MINUTES!"

Finding seats, the movie, *Ride the High Country*, with Joel McCrea and Randolph Scott was showing, and we ate popcorn, drank cokes, held hands, and whispered to each other. Lou and I were fascinated with each other and talked some serious seventeen-year-old talk. All four of us settled in, kissed softly, and got consumed with this great film. Both actors were fabulous with a very good cast! The color was great, but Lou's hand was better. Harry and I joked as the girls caught on to our humor. (Each weekday now, I watch *The Virginian*, which stars James Drury, who was one of the bad brothers in *Ride the High Country*. This was also Randolph Scotts last movie.)

Suddenly, the movie shut off! A male voice came flashing out across the lush movie house, "We are closing the theater. A serious snowstorm is close, and a whiteout is predicted...again...," as he repeated the fearful message several times. We scurried up to help the girls get their coats on and grabbed ours quickly.

Going to the foyer, snow was falling furiously almost sideways, with an inch or more already on the ground. There was nothing we could do as parents began to arrive and get their children. We had to get home. We saw the girls to their ride with our faces wet with snow and lips so cold. Sherry's old white pickup was double white with blizzard, sticking snow, kissed them, saying, "See you soon. We'll call." We meant it. We and they meant it.

We left Knox. We left the good, sweet country girls. We left some history behind us. They began fading away as we looked in our rearview snow-covered mirrors. Now everything being covered with more and more snow, we could see them no more as their farm truck faded in the opposite direction to white on white on white.

Yeah, the air was white in back and in front! The snow was falling so fast that the '55 windshield wipers weren't fast enough to keep up with the loads of snow spit out of the sky in speed and volume.

Within eight miles, we would be coming to Highway 30. By this time, we were just hoping to see the four-lane black road. The falling temperature managed to make every flake stick and blind Harry's hardworking eyes.

Wondrously, we did see the red light, and the great driver made the turn by getting under and past the light, rightly judging the distance, and we made the left turn headed west and homeward. By this short time, another two or three inches had smothered the Indiana farmland.

Now we were a little closer but forty miles lay ahead. The earth and everything else was white. With snow piling up by the inches, "It looks like a flat blanket," Harry said, "and no sight of anything else." The trees, the few houses, the ditch, the bank on the side of the road beside the drainage ditch, the hood of the freezing red car, everything was visually flat, all mashed flat by the fast-flying white frozen water, every flake sticking to the next one.

We knew that if we stopped on purpose or a wreck or running into a stopped car, we could freeze. The radio didn't work. We had no forecasts. It got colder.

Thankfully, the moon, hidden behind the clouds and flying volumes of snow, gave us a little light. We could see maybe forty feet, but all was a white blanket of ever-increasing snow. The white stuff seemed flat from the middle of the road out across the cornfields as far as we could see. The ditches were filled with snow. We were in a white world.

We talked only a few minutes about the girls, then no talking at all, except about our drowning condition in the ocean of frozen water. Besides, I wanted Harry to be devoted only to driving, and he wanted the same. Silence and intense starring with a little fear gripped us.

Turning on the radio again, we got static with the only words "get home" audible.

"Larry, our parents must be mad and worried," Harry stuttered out of his mouth, to which I replied, "Yeah, and we can't get in touch with them. We're in trouble, but we're gonna be all right."

We had to sneak along with some crunching sounds coming from beneath the car as the snow turned to ice on the frozen pavement. I prayed silently then echoed, "The Lord is my shepherd. I shall not fear," saying God's Word over and again.

We were averaging ten to thirteen miles per hour and studiously figured our time of arrival at 12:00 to 12:15 a.m. We knew our parents were up, and besides, the gas tank was getting low.

"Wonder if the girls made it home?"

"I hope so," Harry replied.

"When we goin' back?" I asked with a sneaky chuckle.

"We ain't," my good friend said. "Right now, we've just got to get home."

We inched along. He jerked me back to the issue at hand as the policeman to be went about his duty with single determination.

Harry's car was great, except the heater didn't work very well, so we had to keep our coats on, but the toes got really cold. Not being used to staying up late since I always had to get ready for cross-country or track, I got sleepy. Trying to stay awake, I pinched my cheeks, no doubt apple red, shook my head, patted my legs, sucked in cold air, tried to talk, but my words ran together and faded off. Dozing, I jumped and jerked, suddenly thinking I ought to be a help to Harry. But he had to do it all. I was going to miss the second half of this icy event, asleep!

At one point, a deer ran out in front of *my* driver, so he naturally hit the brakes as the "red and white" turned sideways going down what seemed to be Highway 30. Since everything was white, only white snow was in sight, no ditch, no signs, no farmhouses; there was only deep and slick white snow. The Chevy got straight as I jumped and saw the good ole car get it right with Harry's help!

My eyelids weighed ten pounds or more. I tried to hold 'em up, but they were winning the battle. My head would drop, and I'd jerk it back up.

"Hey, man, you're goin' to break your neck."

"Yeah, I ...I...I...," and I was gone again.

To this day, I am ashamed I couldn't hang in there and assist the weary driver more. Harry just makes fun out of it and assures me it's okay.

I worried in my waking moments about Mom and Dad's worry and the trouble I faced. I had plainly disobeyed them, and now this.

Everything was closed, no phone, only snow at twenty degrees.

The car jerked me sideways as Harry turned north on Grace Street from Old Highway 6, Ridge Road. The rear-end of the car was about to pass the front end, but my world-class driver turned the front wheels in the opposite direction as the rear-end came back behind the front end.

"Hey, man, you and the Lord, of course, got us here! You da man!"

We talked excitedly now. "Let's go back... Hahaha...." And I said, "Let's get home and face the music."

We drove in deep thought and the "music" ahead of us, the last few blocks to where we thought I lived! The snow was still falling, and the twelve-inch mass of white stuff covered and flattened out (like a blanket) everything. The gas tank was down to the bottom, but we had made it. Now Harry had to drive through the mountain of snow back down Ridge Road to his home in Johnson's Trailer Park.

"Man, make it back home. You'll have enough gas," but under my breath, I said, "I hope so."

I stumbled out of the '55, looked back in at Harry, and we shook hands with a long hold. "I love you, brother."

"I love you, man," and I closed the frozen door.

I stood there until my lifelong buddy turned around and headed south. The lights faded away quickly, and I turned to slide through the snow into our home. "Pay the price" time.

"What's this?"

Mind you, snow was twelve inches deep by now plus wind sweeping it smooth and making it crisp.

"What?"

There was a piece of white notebook paper flopping in the wind sticking up in the snow, anchored with two pencils holding it in place. Snow was packed down around the bottom of the paper, helping to hold it in place.

I grabbed it with expectant excitement and dread.

"What could it be? What's the meaning?" I asked myself as my mind raced out of a fear for self-preservation. Were Mom and Dad awake? How mad are they? I jerked the frozen paper out of the snow and opened it up as the wind tried to snatch it out of my shaking hands.

Larry,

Mom and Dad know you went to Knox. Don't lie!

Jeanie

Well, now at least I knew that murder awaited around the corner, behind that door, and justly so!

It was unlocked, and I thought for sure that it was a trap. My great life is over. I won't be able to go anywhere ever again. No Knox girl, Lou.

Sticking my head around the edge of the door, bent down way low, I twisted my head on the top of my neck like a giraffe and what! Nobody was up!

I looked at the clock, 12:25 a.m., way late for my curfew. Tiptoeing up the stairs, there was a faint light in Jeanie and Susan's room. Like a thief, I barely opened the door, and Jeanie raised up slightly off her pillow. With sock-covered feet and almost-frozen red toes, I crept over to her and whispered, "Thanks. I'll make it up to you."

"It's okay, but they know and are mad and *worried!*"

We hugged as normal, and I slipped on into my bed next to David. Susan never moved.

Finally, I got warm, tried to pray, and the next thing I knew I was waking up, and the clock read 7:37 a.m. The smell of bacon, coffee, and the furnace circled into my nose. I lay there and decided I'd tell the truth, take my punishment, and give thanks to them (Mom and Dad). My warm clothes felt good. My toes weren't really frozen; they had just felt like it.

Is Harry okay? Is he alive or frozen on Ridge Road? I worriedly pondered.

Walking out of my room, Jeanie emerged out at the same time, and I whispered, "Let's go."

We slid down the stairs and walked into the kitchen and dining room. Mom was standing at the stove. Dad was reading his Bible, and Mother said in a suspenseful, interested voice, "Where'd you go last night?"

Dad looked up over his glasses with an 'I gotcha' look and a half frown with a grin.

"Harry and I went to Knox to see the girls, but we'll never go again."

Not saying another word, I went to the chair across from Dad. He kept on reading, and Mom stirred the gravy.

Then he said, "Son, you worried us, and you know how dangerous that trip was."

"Yes, sir."

Silence seeped around the kitchen, and not another word was spoken! But Mom had tears and a look of sadness, gladness, anger, and relief.

That was an incredible Sunday morning. Harry had gotten home safe and sound. Jeanie had saved her brother. Truth had prevailed. I kept my word; I never went back...except in sweet wonder. But you see, I still tell this memory fifty-eight years later.

Lou became one of those glorious memories of youth passed in time but locked in the heart forever. I never saw her again. I thanked the Lord for having mercy on me and Harry.

PS: Harry did go back to see Sherry two or three times; "nothing came of it," my pal said a couple of years ago. We reminisced a couple of minutes, then the subject faded away into history, all swallowed up.

Don't make excuses, live life fully, but always make it right.

Escapade 9: A Fair and a Fight

If you want to make good use of your time, you've got to know what is most important then give it all you've got.

—Lee Iacocca

In June of 1962, Harry and I had graduated from Calumet High School. We were singing with the Crescendos and working. Preparing for cross-country at Memphis State, running several times a week, I was busy.

Besides, my aunt Carol, who is two years younger than me and Jeanie's age, stayed with us after a visit with Aunt Alice, Uncle Lloyd, Grandma Mac, and herself. She is a sweet, kind, and funny person. We always had a good time together.

"Larry, the phone is for you," Mom said.

It was Harry.

"Hey, dude, the last day of the Lake County Fair is tomorrow night. Let's go."

"Oh yeah, you don't have to ask me twice. Let's take Jeanie and my aunt Carol."

He agreed. We set a time, and he arrived at about 5:30 p.m. on Saturday evening. After introducing Harry and Carol, we piled into his '55 Chevy and arrived at the fairgrounds by 6:20 p.m.

Now as young people do, we think wrong!

"Man, let's wear our letterman's jackets!"

"Okay, but it's gonna be in the eighties," Harry said. "It'll be hot."

"Yeah, but we need to show those Crown Point dudes a real letterman's jacket," I foolishly retorted.

Pulling up in his cool ride and after picture taking, we lit out, with doo-wop and rock and roll playing out of the great Gary radio station. We chattered away like kids and crows do or chipmunks. We were relaxed, happy, and glad to be out on our own. No doubt a fun time was a comin'.

We didn't know what the night held. We didn't know what our history on the night would reveal.

Relaxed, flip, and laughing at everything, we were carefree and singing with Chuck Berry.

Besides, Harry and I were feeling a *little* arrogant about our red-and-white letterman jacket. After all, we had to go in among our Crown Point rivals and show them a real "jacket." All of us just wanted some carefree fun.

"I've never seen a crowd like this at a fair down home," Carol said.

The entrance and ticket station were filled with happy-go-lucky fun seekers. Twenty-five minutes later, having started with a line of these excited 'seekers,' all laughing, chattering, but some pushy. People were lined up for over 100 150 feet of the Ferris wheel. They couldn't wait to get in, so they tried to push the line to make it all happen more quickly. It didn't work.

The line of *rudeness* pushed up against Harry's back, and he turned to an older gentleman and said, "Please stay off my back."

"Sure, okay...I didn't mean nothin'."

The noise of the trains, Ferris wheel, and music were aggravating. The crowd seemed untamable. But we worked our way to the money taker, bought our tickets, and smiling like a Cheshire cat, we joined the mass of unmanageable, untamed body of flesh with jeans and shorts on.

"This cotton candy is the best I've had," Jeanie said, and we slowly walked around to see what all was there.

Kids were hollering uncontrollably, running between our legs, and bewildered mothers chasing after them. Men were in groups of five all trying to out loud the other. Bellowing laughter was particularly aggravating. Apparently, the liquor had already flowed. An old couple creeped along in front of us, both with man-made canes, and we wouldn't pass them for fear of bumping into them. Harry stuck his arms out, without a word, but meaning, "Let's slow down!" That was okay with us as our tender eyes tried to absorb this mad scramble of humanity.

"Watch out! Watch it!" Harry, the policeman to be, loudly said as some foolish teens (unlike us) jogged past us. And it happened.

The long-legged blond-headed guy hit the good wife of the caned-up man. She hit her crippled husband ferociously. Their canes flew into the air as both of them hit the ground hard. The unmanneredly, loud boys ran faster to not be caught. We stayed with them, trying to help.

The cute couple lay there as the swelling mass of sorry flesh pushed and gouged past them. A few looked down on the fallen victims, and I heard one say, "Damned old people." The parade of inconsiderate humanity kept going.

Finally, the medics came, washed their skinned-up elbows and knees, gave them cold water, and got them up.

"Let's go home. This is no place for us," the nice red-cheeked gentleman said to his handsome, aggregable wife.

After thanking us and assuring us they could make it out, they pressed on and faded into the fearsome flood of inconsiderate human offspring.

After scoping out the joint, Harry asked, "Ya wanna ride the Ferris wheel?"

He knew I'd be ready, but we wanted Jeanie and Carol to be also. They did.

Finally getting to the end of the line, we slowly inched along to get our ride. We were having a pretty good time by now after adapting to this loud, swirling warfare. We crept along. But loud, rude, vulgar talk was coming from the front of us.

I pressed up close to a five-foot-ten or five-foot-eleven male, about 220 pounds. He had an older motorcycle T-shirt on, sweating like a stuck hog and smelling on alcohol. And though this group of five or six twenty-year-olds were loud, we tried to mind our own business. These motorcyclist seemed to know nothing but bike riding with very little manners.

But their business became our business as they got louder, using foul language. One man looked at me from behind and just shook his head. Everybody was watching them, most with disgust. They didn't care.

The nasty language got nastier, and I could see that the girls were irritated and flushed with embarrassment. Neither they nor we heard vulgar language in our homes and no alcohol.

Gently, I leaned forward and said, "Hey, man, could you guys cut the language down a little? The girls are bothered by it."

I should have known. The rough-shaved black-headed leader of the group, sweating profusely, with liquor breath said, "Mind your own d—business! They call me the Chunk, so I'll just whip you!"

Not wanting trouble, I said, "Man, I don't mean anything. I just want you to respect my sister and aunt."

He turned to me with dark, dangerous eyes, almost snorting from his big nose, gritting his teeth, "I'll whip your a—right here and right now!"

"No," I said. "No trouble."

Harry was backing me up, and suddenly it happened!

A big right hand, brown from riding without gloves on, flew past me with a shush and caught Harry right in the chin! The sneaky, cheating punch sent Harry backward, and he tripped over a lady's cowboy boot.

I turned back to Chunky and said with disgust, "I didn't want this. I'm here only for a good time."

Ferociously, he let a fist fly, but I dodged it. A big fist, but I made him miss. I caught him with a right punch on his big nose with my fist coming from the hip past my rib cage. He fell back then skimmed a right off my forehead. I'm just glad I'm hardheaded and was wet from running sweat.

We grabbed each other, went to the ground, wrestling. He was stronger, but I was faster. We tried to punch each other while rolling around as the two girls screamed and got out of the way of the Ferris wheel—yes, the Ferris qheel! Sure enough, we were under the flying, circling cars filled with frightened, screaming riders. We could hear the breaks squeaking as the driver put the brakes on. Feet, metal, wood, and death was flying close enough that I could feel the wind. We rolled out from under the flying cars.

All we could do was get blows on each other's shoulders and backs until I made a twisting move, came free of him, and over him. I had a clear shot at his head. I had him. My right-hand fist raised, all crumbled up, I reared back to put a lick on him, but I couldn't pull the trigger! I didn't want to be fighting. I came to enjoy my sister, aunt, and friend.

Suddenly, loudly, a whistle blew as a county policeman and fair attendant pushed through the crowd, hollering at us, "STOP! Stop now!"

Chunk was on his knees. I stood up as the thick biker yelled, "Let's go now!" to his motorcycle gang. He got up, circled behind the Ferris wheel, and ran as fast as he could. The raunchy bikers followed him with bellows of unrepeatable vulgarity. Then they disappeared in the Saturday last-night crowd.

The officers started in on me but eased up when they heard the story. "Do you know who those guys are?"

"No," Harry said as I was still out of breath.

"The guy you were fighting with just got out of the local county jail, and his gang is notorious here and Gary! They are just roust-about thugs. We'll get 'em!"

By this time, I was mad, gathered up about four of our friends, scattered around the fairgrounds, and started looking all over for the bandits. In a few minutes, we could hear their bikes blistering the pavement with pipes blasting as the red lights sailed around the first curve, and they disappeared. They were gone from what we wanted, a good night at the Lake County, Crown Point Fair. Thankfully, we got over it, settled down, had a ball, and went home happy.

Harry stood by me and did himself proud. The girls were nervous but happy it was over. We went back to Grace Street, settled down, played rook, drank some lemonade Mom had made, rehearsed the night, and were glad it was over.

"Do you realize how close to being hit you were? We were scared to death!"

"So was I, but the Lord took care of me again."

I went outside and sat in the dark.

Harry's red chin cleared up in that life changing summer of '62. We parted ways in a few days on our way to college. I couldn't see any signs of that night on his strong chin.

Escapade 12: Mississippi and Memphis

> Every tub has to sit on its own bottom, blame no
> one else.
>
> —J. Larry Simpson.

New Albany

"You don't spend enough time with me, and you don't seem very happy…or I love you more than you do me," so my fiancée said to me for a whole week and other such accusations. I fought through these as best I could until on a Thursday night. I was at my wits' end, frustrated, and aggravated.

Leaving her home at about 7:30 p.m. to 8:00 p.m. after dropping her off, I wanted to go to Memphis. It was early March of '64.

Having talked to Uncle Elaine a few weeks before on the phone, he made the mistake of saying, "Larry, I would like to see you. Come see me."

I had been thinking of that since I loved him, wanted to see him and some other loved ones, as well as be down in Mississippi and Memphis.

By the time I got home, I told Mom and Dad, "I was going to Mississippi, I have to have a break, and I'm going to call Harry."

Both parents looked shocked, but I was nineteen. "Hey, man, you wanna go to Memphis with me? I've got to have a break from life's aggravations."

"What time are we leaving?"

Both of us had to call our work bosses. Harry made plans with his employer, but I couldn't get hold of mine. So in my nineteen-year-old mind, I threw caution to the wind and said, "I don't care. I'm gone!"

Both Mom and Dad were concerned, but Dad said, "Son, every tub got to set on its own bottom."

Harry called back and said, "I'm clear."

"We'll go in my car and let's meet at your home. I'll pick you up in thirty minutes."

I filled the black '63 Pontiac Tempest with premium, chunked the trunk full of my bags, and made room for Harry's stuff. Getting to his trailer home, we loaded his suitcase.

"I know I'm going to lose my job, Harry," I spoke with strong definition. "Mr. Ruggles can't put up with such behavior, but I don't care. Besides, Dad has been telling me I can get hired at Bethlehem Steel as an oiler on a crane."

"Man, it sounds like you got it. You'll make more money, so let's get it."

"Dad said, '$3.25 an hour!'"

An oiler keeps the crane clean, changes oil weekly, and oils all joints daily. Besides, this would be a "truck" crane, meaning, it could be moved from place to place on its own power. I had done that once before, and I loved it. I had an ace in the hole and couldn't wait to drive the crane even if just five feet!

"I don't want to do my boss wrong, but I've got to travel!"

"Me too," Harry said. And we lit out!

It was 9:30 p.m. and we had 570 or so miles to drive heading down Old Highway 41. We would go through Kentucky to Highway 45E out of Fulton, Tennessee, to Jackson then Highway 18 and 125 to Bolivar and ride Mississippi 15 to New Albany.

We knew if we could average sixty miles per hour, it would take nine and a half hours to New Albany. Driving about five to ten miles per hour over the speed limit, we began to eat the miles up.

"We should get there around 7:30 a.m., and they'll fix some breakfast for us."

"Watch it! A car stopped!" Harry exclaimed, and an older car was sitting still on the road. We swerved around them, saw they had a flashlight and a cop comin' down the other side with siren blaring.

Harry talked excitedly, "Man, do you think this rattletrap will make it?" He grinned with tongue in cheek and said, "Yeah, it'll make it. It's not a Ford!"

We were GM guys for sure but loved any hot rod...as long as we could beat it!

We talked about our dogs, our parents, our families, his football and baseball career, my running days, the girls in Knox, and the snowstorm we drove through, our cars, jobs, ole schoolmates, the Crescendos, lost dreams and new ones. Then our women, our sweethearts, and the aggravations we were in. Finally, we agreed this trip was necessary and tried to find some music, but none was to be found until we got close to Evansville.

"A blues station!" I shouted.

And Harry said, "Just like 'Livin' with Vivian' in Gary." Muddy Waters, John Lee Hooker, Sonny Boy Williamson, and all those old guys still making you feel your soul, your loves, losses, and life. We loved the blues and still do.

By 12:45 a.m., we stopped in Evansville at Eds Hamburger Place, got fully-dressed burgers, lettuce, onions, pickles, mayo, mustard, tomatoes, french fries, and cokes. Away we flew with the dark night on our heels.

"From here, buddy, we won't see much. It'll be black, a few cars, and *no girls!*"

We slopped the chow down, drank our cokes, with Harry driving.

"Hey, man, I got to give it up. I'm too sleepy."

"It's all right, partner, find a spot, pull over, and I'll give it a try."

Taking over the wheel, with a full stomach, in five minutes, my codriver was snoring. Harry snored so loud I thought, *Surely...it'll keep me going or deafen me.*

But I was getting miserably sleepy. Pinching myself, stretching my eyes, slapping my legs, twisting and turning, trying to find a radio station on these country highways, nothing was helping me. After all, I had worked all day at the truck stop, keeping the diesel tanks full, and cleaned the restroom after getting up at 6:00 a.m. Now it's thirteen hours later, and I was an early, about 9:30 p.m. to 10:00 p.m., "go to bed" sleeper.

I pulled over at a closed service station and walked in the cooler air, stretched, and said out loud, "Now I'll be all right. I must do this! I must do this!"

Climbing back in the car, Harry was sawing 'em off, but I felt refreshed.

Within twenty-five to thirty minutes, about 1:30 a.m. I was miserably trying to whip my sleepiness. My eyelids weighed about twenty pounds. My mouth dropping open, with water creeping out of the corner between my cheek and edge of my mouth down to the jaw. My head falling down, I jerk it back up. I thought I was winning this victory. After all, it was only four hours to light. I tried to sing, but my head was about to break off my neck, and I was mostly slurring my words, and strange thoughts would break in on my sleep work. I lost the battle.

Honk, honkkk, a horn was honking! I looked up out from under my eyelids, jerked my head up, and I was in the northbound lane. A car swerved off the road onto the berm of the road to miss me. Jerking the wheel to the right, I found my proper place and realized it was 4:00 a.m. and breaking day! Breaking day? Through sleeping hours, after losing my fight with sleep, I looked up and saw, "Welcome to Tennessee," "Tennessee Highway 45," "Jackson 79 miles!"

"Jackson 79 miles?"

Harry came alive, "What! What?" he asked, jerking himself up out of his slumped body.

It dawned on me that I had mostly been asleep and didn't remember anything from that last head jerk.

"Harry, I don't remember driving through Kentucky. I woke up when I saw 'Welcome to Tennessee.'"

"What? WHAT?" he said again.

"I'm telling you the truth. I guess, I've been asleep for three hours!"

"What?" he said, leaving off the second "what?" this time.

"We'd better thank God for his miraculous power."

"For sure," my soul brother declared.

To this very day, I do not remember passing through most of Kentucky or getting to Tennessee. How could that be? I still don't know.

We chatted about it and then looked down at the gas gauge, and the tank was empty! But there it was, a standard oil station just into Tennessee. We whipped in, filled up, went to the potty, and drank some black, black coffee the best I ever drank to this day.

When I think of all the things that could have happened, I knew it was the hand of a gracious God that kept us safe.

"About two hours, and we'll be at Uncle Elaine's!"

"All right!"

Passing through Jackson, we picked up Highway 18, then Highway 125 in Bolivar down to Highway 15 through Ripley then New Albany, close to the origins of my family on Mother's side, the Wise's and the McCollum's.

At 7:30 a.m., we pulled into Elaine's driveway on the west side of Highway 15. As a nineteen-year-old might do, I hadn't called ahead since we suddenly left just late last night, but I knew it wouldn't matter. It didn't. A surprise is always good—tight hugs and cheek kisses, a whoop and holler. We rejoiced to see each other. Uncle Elaine and I had a special relationship.

It was a sweet reunion with my uncle, aunt Christine, cousins Diane, Steve, Ricky, and Randy.

"Fix up some breakfast darlin'. I'll call the shop."

Sausage, eggs, gravy, molasses, biscuits, and real butter! Wow, what a time. They all loved Harry, and he enjoyed them. We visited, caught up on the family, and left at noon.

"Where'd you get a family like this?" he asked as we hugged and kissed everybody so long.

Then we headed back north to Ripley and my aunt Alice's, twenty-five miles away.

Six weeks later, Elaine and I would travel to California together. I called him and told him I was going out there to preach to Uncle LT's Baptist Church in lieu of becoming their pastor. He jumped all over it, so I drove from Indiana to New Albany and picked him up. We drove all day and all night, stopped in Flagstaff, Arizona, to sleep, then another five hundred forty-two miles to Carpinteria.

I drove and rode when Elaine was driving over those three and a half days about 2,850 miles. We rejoiced to see our family in California and played rook the first night.

In a difficult footnote, I preached Uncle Elaine McCollum's funeral in 2010 in New Albany. Rejoicing? Yes, a child of God with a good hope by grace gone to heaven. The funeral home was packed full of friends and family. My good uncle had spent his whole adult life, after fighting in WWII, in New Albany, and everyone knew him. He was called "the friend to all."

As I stood on this warm May day beside his grave, my poor mind raced back in time to the morning with Harry at Elaine's, the California trip, and other times in his home, his trip to see us in 1959 in Grove City, Ohio, with his great family, and all the trips he and I made to see our people in New Harmony. We loved to play cards together with Uncle Doc, Uncle James, and others, laughing the whole game! He was a comic, giving himself to others, a horseman, a faithful churchman, leading the singing in his Primitive Baptist Church, honest, and a faithful, good husband, father, and larger family man. Besides, he was a teller of jokes and a good story with the best of 'em.

I love and miss him. We headed to Ripley.

*****

Ripley

At noon, we made the square in Ripley and drove around it, looking for Aunt Alice's new beauty salon. Throwing the door open, she ran to me, leaving a wet head of the complainer. We hugged, kissed cheeks, and she threw up her hands, saying, "Oh my goodness!"

Then she ran hard back to the woman's drying head. The grumpy dyed black-haired lady looked disgusted, and Alice said, "Oh, let's get your head rinsed and dried."

Then she looked closely, intently at me, and winked twice. She plunged the woman's head under the hot water, gritting her teeth with a little bit of aggravation, then pulled her back upright and said, "Now then!"

We chatted with Alice a very few minutes because the Southern women were gathered together, every chair full to get their weekend hairdos. We hugged, and back to work she went, looking over her shoulder, saying, "Carolyn is at the house with the twins."

I knew the twins. Two years younger, same age as Carol, basketball all-stars and tomboyish, smart, outgoing, and pretty, "I said pretty!" One of them and I had become special friends, but this would be the last time I would ever see her.

Carol was looking out the door when we arrived. Having been with her two years before at the fair "affair," she and Harry lightly hugged each other. I hugged Carol but tightly hugged my favorite twin and then her sister. We all chattered away, laughing with me, refreshing old relationships and Harry getting, or should I say, wanting, to get to know the twins.

Lunch was ready—bacon, lettuce, and tomato sandwiches and tea. Carol put the music on. Harry leaned over and whispered, "Man, where'd you find these girls?"

We all danced the bop or the twist and just had a short ball. My slow dance with my special twin was too close and warm. We liked each other much. Harry and the second twin got attached quick! It would be the only time he would see her.

After a short game of basketball in the backyard where the twins were too much for us in more ways than one, Harry said, "Man, can't we stay longer?" as he chuckled with his sly grin, knowing we had to go.

"Yeah, I want to, but Uncle Elmer knows we're coming. Let's crank it up."

As I hugged my favorite twin, too warm "too warm," "too close," so I kissed her goodbye, hugged my aunt Carol and Harry's twin.

We said, "Thanks for the good time."

We drove away in the black Pontiac. The car was silent.

Memories can be sweet but oh so hard.

Later, Harry and I talked about that wonderful three-hour magical time of music, dancing, love, and the inability to describe it. He…and I were lost in "magic" time, never to quite understand.

We drove the sixteen miles to Highway 72 at Walnut, the historic highway to Memphis. Sandy and I take 72 sometimes when headed west. Turning west, nobody was in front of us, so I dropped the '63 into wide open power, shifted into second at fifty-five miles per hour, then the same at ninety into third. We were free, young, and on fire. Excited, happy, and already filled with wonder… headed to Memphis. Uncle Elmer and Aunt Jettie would have supper ready.

A Patrolman and a Judge

"Boy, we've got a free open road, but I want to see those girls again," and my reply to Harry was "yeah" as I nodded slightly.

After a minute or two, he asked, "We don't have time to go back, do we?"

I, in a bit of melancholy, said, "I wish we did."

But the highway was open. No one in front of us and nobody catching us. So was our life. We rolled about seventy-five miles per hour on an open road and aware that the speed limit was sixty miles per hour.

We topped a hill, as was our lives, headed down a little grade, and hit eighty-one miles per hour. Suddenly, in my state of euphoria, I saw it. A red light, flashing and whirling around, seeming angry and vicious. It sat on top of a yellow-and-brown Ford that was gaining on us.

In a state of unbelief and aggravation, I asked, "Man, do you see what's behind us?"

And Harry looked in the rearview mirror and let out an expletive, "Hey, dude, do we think we can outrun him? Let's try!"

"No, man," and I agreed.

Our euphoria of the twins, Alice and Elaine, was slipping away. We need excuses. "The small highway was dry and open. We passed no cars. We were just havin' a good time. We had no alcohol. We had to get to Memphis. We're broke. We're sorry, but we knew all those frantic ideas would be a failure. No excuse would work.

Pulling over very slowly, I said, "Buddy, why don't we just whip him?" as we exited the Pontiac.

The officer was on the ditch side of his aggravating car, lights still flashing and laughing slightly and slyly at us. We stared at him, looked back at each other, and just shook our hands back and forth no. The man was six feet five, 255 pounds, and now frowning. We got humbled really quick.

His right hand was on the police special .44 with white pearl handles. He looked mad, mean, and nasty. We got ready real quick, ready to say, "Yes, sir."

"Why so fast? You runnin' from the law?" As I groped for words, gagging on each one, I replied, "No, sir," and tried to give him one excuse after another. "We got to be in Memphis by five o'clock. The road was open. No one was in danger. We forgot the speed limit. We lost our mind. No cars in front of us. We're from Indiana. We've been down to see relatives. We've—!"

And he'd had enough. "Stop! Follow me down this road," he said, pointing to curvy Highway 5, a small short road that looked dangerous. "Don't try to run. I'll catch you, and you'll go to jail!"

"Yes, sir," we harmoniously said.

Arriving at the county judge's home, just a half mile away, and free-standing office, we turned in behind the officer, behind the judges country home, with a long country porch with five or six red and some white rockers. The judge's office had two flags hung on the front wall, a Confederate, Sons of the South and the Mississippi Ole Glory!

He ushered us in, and there set Judge Seemour. I'll never forget the name. He had his head down, writing, and the patrolman kept quiet with his hands folded in front of him. His desk was in a storm of a mess, paper everywhere, a picture of an ugly woman on his left, and a .38 Smith and Wesson on his right, lying naked. Three coffee cups sat on the north side of the desk with a little bit of coffee laying on the bottom.

"Be quiet, and I'll see you in a minute or two."

It was obvious this man was the boss and acted like it. His white shirt was tattered around the collar and cuffs, but his cuff links were big, square, and black. His hair was a little long, like Benjamin Franklins, and he was sucking a red-hot cigar. The office was full of austerity and smoke. A lamp hung from the ceiling, white and green and deeply rusty. The bulldogs chained out front continued to bark. The hogs in the hogpen next to the office were stinking like hogs will do, and the lusty, repulsive odor circled the office inside as well as out. His cigar smoke rising like train's smoke made the air thick with brown and gray, eye-watering irritation.

Harry coughed. The air was full of gray smoke. We kept silent, looking mostly straight ahead, but behind his desk was a picture of George Wallace and Jefferson Davis, the president of the Confederacy. Robert E. Lee was there and the confederate flag. Martin Luther King's image was not there. Stone Wall Jackson's was.

Finally, he looked up, picked his front teeth with his little fingers long, very long fingernail, and said with a low growling voice, cutting each word off short, "Whatcha boys done gone and done?" He looked at Harry and smiled wickedly and then turned to me and said, "Boy, what's your name and whatcha doin' here in Mississippi? Are ya down here stirrin' up trouble with some of the local population?"

"No, sir, no, sir."

I breathlessly tried to tell him, very softly, and he started his lecture. With a fireplace poker, burnt with fire, he slapped it down on the desk. As papers flew, he said, "Now you see what you've done? Made me mess up my desk, and I won't put up with smarty-pants Yankee boys!" I knew we'd never see our people again.

Actually, I thought, the desk looked better after some of the ticket copies and other papers hit the dirty, oily oak plank floor.

"That'll be $45!"

I lost my fear.

"What! I can't afford that. We're nineteen years old and traveling to see family. Besides, we've got to get home!"

"Now its $55!" As he slapped the desk again, shaking the dingy, old lamp, he added, "Do you want some more?"

"No, sir," I said.

Harry then said, "I'll put in some."

"No, buddy, this is my doings and my trip. I'll pay," I said as I opened my poor wallet. Even I saw the writing on the wall and knew my sterling personality and powerful talking were vast underdogs here. "I'd lost."

Sadly, I handed the county judge two $50's, which only left me $70 ($45 change with $25 my pocket).

He looked at them and growled, "Don't you have anything smaller?"

"No, sir."

"Now, you've aggravated me some more. Does your hand fit a shovel? I bet cha have no calluses, do ya?" he said, with his voice getting louder with each phrase.

He jerked open the bottom drawer with much money laying there, shuffling the money around to see if he could find $45 in bills. Nothing was small enough there. Opening the second drawer, the ominous judge ran his hands through a two-inch layer of bills, but no help there.

"Too big," he snorted under his breath, cocked his head to the right, and looked up at me with glaring green eyes. "You little b——ds cause me a lot of trouble."

Harry rolled his eyes and head at me.

Finally, he opened the top drawer and said, "Uh-huh…I found a five," as he buried his right hand down under the money but located no twenties, too many hundreds.

He pulled a roll of bills from his pocket with a rubber band around it, took out two twenties, joined them to the five, and said, "Now get the h—out of here and don't come back! Stay off Highway 72!" The six-foot-five patrolman watched us leave.

Three drawers full of money and nothing small enough for $45 in change!

We drove carefully out of his private money machine. Turning left on 72, we got to sixty miles per hour and tried to explain and understand what had just happened. We had been robbed. Our humiliation and anger didn't fix the matter!

Several times, I have traveled that grand ole concrete highway and looked down the judge's road. His house is crumbling down, the office's roof is caved in, a yellow ribbon was over the doors, and huge blankets of kudzu smothering the whole place. The entrance is blocked.

We rolled in soft speech, then anger, on to Memphis, sixty miles per hour.

*****

Memphis

All this in one day after driving all night! Elaine's, Alice's, Carol, and the gorgeous twins, the highway robbery, we were tired. It was four thirty in the bright afternoon, and we were only sixty miles from Uncle Elmer's.

Looking at my watch, it was 5:30 p.m. as we turned north on Whitten Road and pulled into my great-uncle's short warm country driveway, covered with large maples and oaks. My big, good uncle, brother to Mom's mother, came to the door with Aunt Jettie close behind. Grinning from ear to ear, "Get in this house," he said, with Aunt Jettie holding his shirt from behind to steady herself.

"Boys, what have you got to say for yourselves?" the six-foot-two mass of a man asked.

"We've come to see you!" I retorted, and Harry just half-grinned.

After squeezing me too tight, he shook hands with Harry with the black hair on his hands standing upward.

"I've got a pot of Lima's on, so we'll eat in a little while, and, Larry, you'll both stay in Roy's bedroom."

Roy, two years older than me, with whom I'd stayed with in his room during '62–'63, was away with his new job.

I took Harry out to show him where my car, the '56 Chevy had fallen on me, and Roy two years before. One of the big blocks was still laying there all oily and black. For a moment, I could only stand and stare, lost in time and clear vision.

We had a great meal, some good talk, but our eyelids were cheating on us. We went to bed about 9:15 p.m.

"Larry, Larry," in a hushed tone, Uncle Elmer said, "son, y'all ease on up. Breakfast will be ready in twenty-five minutes."

There was no lying in bed at Uncle Elmer's; after all, it was 7:15 a.m.! Family time, food, and fond memories.

I had kept the phone numbers of some of my friends from my first year in college and as minister of music at Aunt Jetties Baptist Church. Johnnie, a good, pretty Southern girl, and her brother Martin, James, tall and skinny, along with Danny who became a Memphis fireman gathered together.

What a reunion we had in the church parking lot. After almost two years, we were back together...for this day. Four great people and friends piled in the car with Johnnie, bunched in between me and Harry in the front seat.

I and my four old partners couldn't get enough of each other's chattering with some new stuff but mostly our old memories.

Harry looked around Johnnie at me and stretched both eyes. She must have seen him because she smiled, like, "I caught cha."

We drove around Memphis all afternoon, stopped, and ate the best country food in America, greens, pintos, real mashed potatoes, fried chicken, homemade biscuits, and real iced tea at Ferguson's, a great Southern restaurant. In those days, a Memphis radio station played blues all day. We got the blues and me, and Harry have had 'em for a lifetime. We rocked on...drivin' all over my hometown.

The talking, the laughing, the remembering was unending. Besides, the Memphis Fair Grounds had a "spring fling" open all day, and we walked, looked, rode, and no fights! With our arms around each other, it was sweet!

I had been looking for a drag race all day, but I guess all the racers had raced out on Friday night. Memphis was and is known for drag racing. In fact, my cousin Roy and his two sons built hot rods and drag raced up until recently. As night began to fall, Harry and my sweet friend Johnnie had hit it together…just walkin' and talkin'. But they never saw each other but that one time. Well.

As the sun set, we were sitting at a red light on Summer Avenue when a new 4×4×2 Oldsmobile pulled beside me. Four-by-four stood for a 4-speed and four barrels. The Elvis-looking guy, with two more in the car, revved his motor, and it did sound bad, jumping his hot Old's forward three or four times. The three Oldsmobile boys looked at us and yelled, "Let's get it."

Being a guy who seldom turned down a challenge, I revved my black Pontiac back at him. We rolled down our windows, so Harry blasted out, "Let's do it!"

"You bet," I shot out of my mouth.

"I'll whip you're a—all over the place," the arrogant Memphian declared.

And I just said, "Let's find out."

Danny spoke up from the back and said, "Remember Larry, the runway at the Penal Farm?"

"Yeah."

So I told the racer how to get there, and away we went. When we could, because Summer Avenue is really busy especially on Saturday nights, we showed off how bad our cars were by romping the gas pedal and laying a little rubber.

Getting to the dark, lonesome runway, not a mile from Uncle Elmer's, we two drivers with Harry got out and agreed on the rules. We'd rev up, count to three, and be gone. I didn't like this guy, his arrogance, smugness, braggadocios way. Besides, his car was tough.

In theory, I should not be on a raceway with this guy. He had a four-barreled carburetor, and I had a two-barrel; he had a 4-speed; he had a lower gear rear-end that got you off the line quicker, and his 4-speed had a short shift. My 3-speed had a long shift; I had 250 horsepower; he had 325. I had six people in my rod; he had three, but his car weighed more. But I knew I was a better driver. Surely, I was!

My long-shift 3-speed means that when you shift, it is a long distance between transmission engagement. It was said in a car magazine that a person would have to be crazy to try to power shift the new Pontiac Tempest. My competitors Old's with a low gear rear-end means the engine stayed revved up more than mine and quicker.

Power shift means you keep your foot on the gas pedal and pushed all the way down while you shift. I could do it. It took quick hands and feet. I could do it.

Getting back in my Tempest, Harry asked, "Do you want some or us to get out?"

I knew what he meant because the more weight in the car, the less speed. I had six people; he had three! Harry was right.

"Thanks, man, but no. I'm stickin' with them that 'brung' me!"

Lining up, I was too tense with wet palms. I jumped on two. I backed up. Again, Harry started the call, "One, two...," and my companion jumped. We lined up again with motors revved up.

Harry yelled, "One, two, three!"

With tires squalling and smoke puffing up from spinning rear tires, we fired off.

"Yeah, Larry. Go, get it!"

He pulled me by two car lengths right off the line with his new Old's, a bright red and hot.

He shifted into second at about forty miles per hour, his tires burned, but I was winding out of first at fifty-five miles per hour and came back a half car. Now in second gear, I thought that if I can stay close, my higher geared rear-end might get him.

It didn't. When he shifted to third, he jumped another car length in front. The black Tempest made up another half car length when I hit third gear at ninety-two miles per hour, but he crossed the finish line one and a half car lengths ahead. He won fair and square.

We stopped, the cars still running, and everybody piled out and had a nice conversation with the Old's 4×4×2 owner. He wasn't arrogant. After all the combat, he was an okay guy.

"If you only had two guys in your car, it would have been a little different."

"Yeah, but no, I'm stickin' with those that 'brung' me. You won fair and square."

After a congenial little talk, we went homeward. We all hugged, kissed the sweet girl on the cheek, and promised to see each other at church the next day.

After a good service in which we were reminded of "the good forgiveness of sin by God in Christ," we loved on all my family and the four Memphis "cats" and promised to return. We never did. I return…in these sweet memories.

When I would see Uncle Elmer, Ralph, or Roy, we would speak of that short visit they'd ask about Harry, and I'd say, "Haven't seen him in a while, but we were then and are now best buddies."

We drove all the rest of that day to get home by midnight. Harry had to get to his job, I had to find one!

Pulling up to Harry's home to let him out, we shook hands, patting each other on the back, feeling that there might never be a time like this again. There hasn't been.

I saw Harry in 1974, played some basketball, but not again until 1989.

Another eighteen years passed until I'd had enough!

I called my boyhood, racing buddy. We made plans for us to come from Tennessee to Indiana. Kenny O'Dean was there, and we had a beautiful reunion. Thank God, since 2007, we have gotten together once or twice a year. Not enough, but I'll take it. So will he. I'm proud of Harry for his hard work as a husband, father, friend, and policeman.

We're boys again each time. The same magical stories are never old.

It was Harry and me—it still is.

Thanks, Harry, for the good times.

No excuses. I'm thankful I was a trailer boy, and there is more to come.

Realization

I have come to understand that in a life of so many memorable people and events that we cannot see, in the flesh, all those who so preciously make up life-altering experiences. We cannot repeat these events, except in the playhouse of the mind. Living in the past is not positive, but not having a memorable, good past is not positive either. I am blessed to get the good out of my experiences in my life!

It was God's purpose for me to be in many places, with many people, and be blessed by it all in one way or another. I have lived in forty-five different places, across ten states. The people, my children and their sweet mother, the events, the good, the bad, the losses, the wins, the gains, the laughter, the tears and family—yes, the family—all make up who I am, what I am.

It's all by the sovereign grace of God.

I'm a trailer boy. I'm grateful for it all. I have *no excuses*. I hope you don't either.

Reunited: A Cherished Friendship by Harry Warrens

"We were reunited thirty years later at my home in Indiana. Larry was a resident of Tennessee at that time but was able to get my phone number from a mutual friend and contacted me. We have been close friends since and see each other as often as possible. Our affection for each other never diminished through the years, and we look forward to many more years of a cherished friendship."

"Thank you, my friend, my true friend."

This has been my life...up to age nineteen. The wins, the good times, and the hard times...the same story has lived till my old age. That's another story!

And I've got no excuses.
The adventures of a little trailer boy.

*****

The fire simmered on down with the setting sun as the air turned sharply cooler, and there was no more coffee in the bottom of my favorite thirty-year-old chipped Tennessee Vols cup.

"Thanks, Dad, I'll never get tired of hearing it and tell it next year." I muttered as I musingly said to myself softly, "Will there be a next year?"

We left the fire to burn out and the adventures of the little trailer boy. I gave thanks to the good Lord for the fire, the family, friends, the love, and the stories of life, but the little trailer boy was still mystically far away, sailing down old 66 with Walker, Janice, Jeanie, David and Susan and our dogs, Trixie and Tony waiting for the next adventure. I've really got no excuses, just a heart of gratitude. Praise You My Lord.

About the Author

The author lived these stories. He is the only one to tell them.

Born in Memphis, Tennessee. The family hit the road in 1951 and did not stop until ten years passed.

He is a graduate of Memphis State University with a bachelor's in political science and secondary education. With a master's degree in theology, a three-year program from Mid-America Baptist Theological Seminary the author has pastored and ministered since age nineteen.

Having worked in the hearing aid business for forty years, he is experienced in the business world, also.

An avid horseman, winning championships, Larry lives with his beloved wife, Sandy on their horse ranch. Together they share a 'blended' family of seven children and soon to be seventeen grandchildren.

"I want the world to have a joyous ride with me and make 'no excuses' in their own lives."